D1583088

The History of Motorcycles

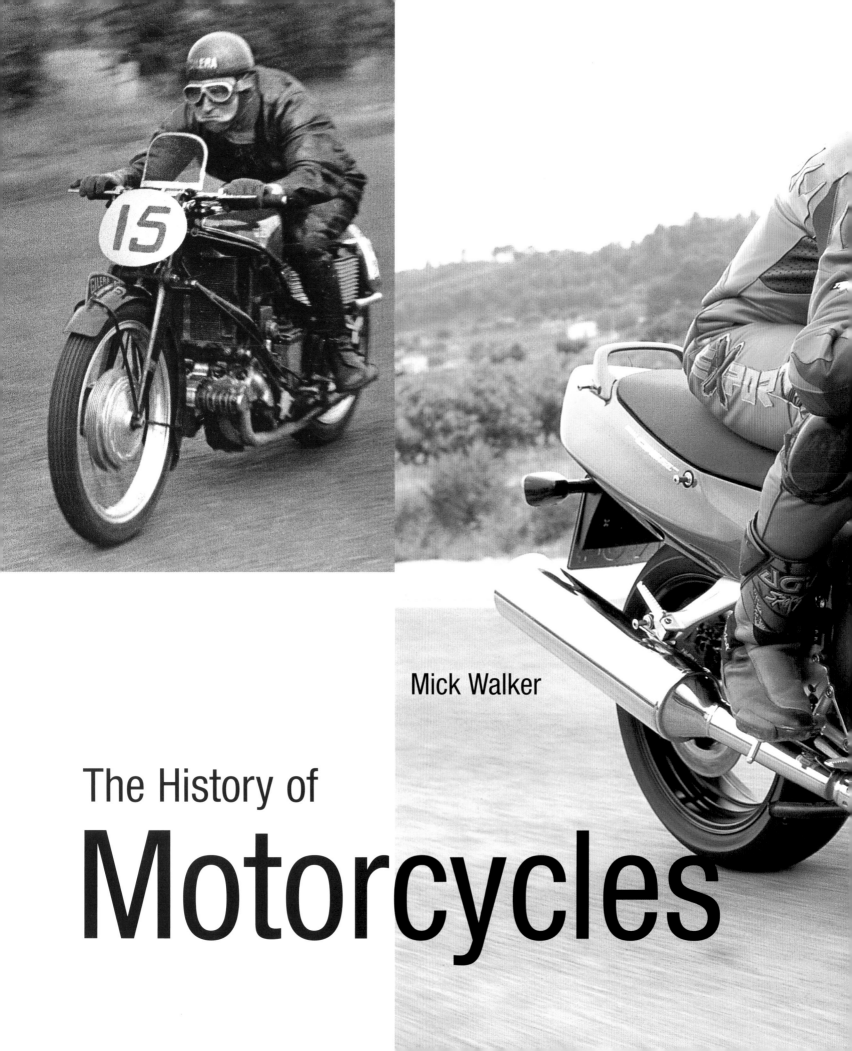

Mick Walker

The History of
Motorcycles

Publishing Director Laura Bamford
Executive Editor Julian Brown
Assistant Editor Karen O'Grady
Art Director Keith Martin
Executive Art Editor Mark Winwood
Designer Darren Kirk
Picture Researcher Charlotte Dean
Production Controller Josephine Allum

First published in Great Britain in 1997
by Hamlyn a division of Octopus Publishing Group Ltd

This 2002 edition published by Chancellor Press, an imprint of
Bounty Books, a division of Octopus Publishing Group Ltd,
2–4 Heron Quays, London E14 4JP

Reprinted 2004, 2005

Copyright © 1997 Octopus Publishing Group Ltd

ISBN 0 7537 0632 6
ISBN 13 9 780753 706329

A catalogue record for this book is available from the British Library

Printed in China

CONTENTS

Chapter 1 – Early Days: Pioneers   6

Chapter 2 – The Twenties and Thirties   20

Chapter 3 – The Second World War   36

Chapter 4 – The Post-War Era   42

Chapter 5 – The Rising Sun   62

Chapter 6 – The Swinging Sixties   70

Chapter 7 – Road Racing   90

Chapter 8 – Dirt Bikes   118

Chapter 9 – Classics and Retros   136

Chapter 10 – The Customising Cult   152

Chapter 11 – The Super Bikes   164

Index   188

Acknowledgments   192

Early Days:
Pioneers

GOTTLIEB DAIMLER

Although there were several prototype steam-powered motorcycles constructed during the latter half of the 19th century, it is the German engineer Gottlieb Daimler and his associate Wilhelm Maybach who today are credited with producing the first powered two-wheeler to feature an internal combustion engine.

Built in 1885, this was an extremely crude affair and was only ever intended as a mobile test bed for Daimler's 264cc 4-stroke single cylinder power unit. The little engine had two flywheels, one each side of the crankshaft, all enclosed in a cast aluminium crankcase.

The machine had wooden wheels and a wooden frame with an auxiliary wheel on either side, but it did have some features of later motorcycles. The rear wheel was belt driven, whilst the fan-cooled engine was mounted in the frame on rubber blocks. Starting was by crank handle, and featured a freewheel. With a weight of 90 kg (198lb) the machine produced 0.5 bhp at 750 rpm, and the two gear ratios gave the Daimler speeds of 3.5 and 7 mph respectively. Other notable features included an evaporating carburettor, heated tube ignition and almost conventional handlebars.

Daimler patented his design on 29 August 1885, following a successful short test session in the garden of his house and the streets of Canstatt; the longest journey being some 3 kilometres. But he soon realised that not only was the engine not really powerful enough, but his 'Petroleum Reitwagen', as he named it, was not easy to use. It was not only difficult to balance but was a real bone shaker, thanks in no small part to the dire state of the roads at that time. So instead he concentrated his efforts upon the development of motorized carriages, which in essence were the forerunners of today's cars. But even so history has, however, ascribed to Daimler the title of 'Father of the motorcycle'. His original 1885 machine can still be viewed in the museum of the Daimler-Benz Company in Stuttgart-Untertufürkheim.

But even though Daimler is the acknowledged originator there was an earlier petrol-engined device – if 3-wheelers are included – in the shape of the work carried out by the Englishman Edward Butler of Erith, Kent, whose drawings and detailed description were shown a full year prior to Daimler's machine at the 1884 Stanley Cycle Show in London. But Butler's Petrol-Cycle was not completed until 1887. This featured twin steering wheels in front, actuated by twin hand levers, at a twin cylinder engine driving the rear wheel direct. Ignition, originally provided by a Wimshurst machine was by Ruhmkorff coil and battery, while the design also boasted the first float-feed carburettor ever fitted to a motor vehicle. The cylinders were water-cooled, the water tank forming the rear mudguard. Instead of a clutch, the Butler Petrol-Cycle employed a pedal operating two small idler wheels which pressed down on the ground and raised the rear wheel so that the machine could be started.

Though it was patented as 'The Petrol-Cycle' and worked quite well, the British design never got into production. Unfortunately for Edward Butler the company formed to develop the machine, the Petrol-Cycle Syndicate Limited, who had advanced the finances needed for its development withdrew its support and the whole project was doomed. But even so it is worthwhile noting that Butler used a 2-stroke engine for his 3-wheel vehicle to avoid contravening existing patents taken out earlier by Dr. Nicholaus Otto who, along with Eugen Langen, had already patented the 4-stroke cycle for the internal combustion engine; thereafter always referred to as the 'Otto Cycle'.

Another crucial development was to be the advent of the pneumatic tyre. This had been invented by Robert William Thomsen back in 1845, but soon forgotten, only to be retrieved (and patented!) by John Boyd Dunlop in 1888 after successfully winning several bicycle races.

Above: Gottlieb Daimler, with his associate Wilhelm Maybach, produced the first powered two-wheeler to feature an internal combustion engine in 1885.

Opposite: Daimler's 'motorcycle' was an extremely crude device and was only ever intended as a mobile test bed for his 264cc four-stroke engine.

Another early pioneer was the Englishman Edward Butler who designed a three-wheeler before Daimler, but was unable to complete it until 1887.

HILDEBRAND & WOLFMÜLLER

The honour of the world's first series production motorcycle goes to the German marque, Hildebrand & Wolfmüller. The company Motorfahrrad-Fabrik Hildebrand & Wolfmüller was set up in Munich, Bavaria, in 1894 to manufacture a new machine employing a horizontal engine in a twin-tube open duplex frame.

Not only was this the first design to be given the title *motorrad* (German for motorcycle), but it also featured the largest engine fitted to a series production motorcycle for the first 90 years of history, the bore and stroke being 90 x 117 mm for each of the two cylinders, giving 1489cc.

The pistons were linked by long connecting rods in a similar way to a steam locomotive. There was no flywheel, the solid disc rear wheel serv-

ing this purpose. Ignition was by a platinum hot tube, as pioneered by Daimler, whilst petrol was supplied by a surface carburettor. Automatic inlet valves were fitted, while the pair of exhaust valves were operated by long rods and a cam on the rear wheel.

The huge twin cylinder engine only turned out 2.5 bhp, giving a maximum speed of almost 30 mph (48 kmh) – this might not seem much now, but in 1894 it was sensational, ensuring orders totalling over two million deutschmarks in only a few weeks. This prompted the company to start work on a massive new factory in the Colosseum Strasse, able to house 1,200 employees.

A Paris-based Englishman, H.O. Duncan, who was a partner with Louis Suberbie in a large cycle business, was impressed enough by a

Hildebrand & Wolfmüller of Munich manufactured the world's first series production motorcycle in 1894. It used a massive 1489cc twin cylinder engine and could achieve 30mph (48kmh).

Frenchman Felix Theodore Millet constructed a unique five cylinder rotary-engined motorcycle in 1892.

THE MILLET ROTARY

On 11 June 1895, the first official long distance auto races took place over a course totalling 1,200 kilometres (745 miles). Twenty-one vehicles were entered, including names such as Panhard, Peugeot and de Dion-Bouton, over roads from Paris to Bordeaux and back. Only three motorcycles took part, one of which was the five cylinder, rotary-engined Millet in its latest variation.

By 1892 Millet had begun attracting much attention throughout French engineering circles, with the result that backing for his work came from no less than Alexandre Darracq, a senior partner in his massive Gladiator cycle concern.

The original Millet design was a front drive Velo-á-petrole, but by the 1895 race he had produced a far more practical version with the rotary engine transferred to the rear wheel. The rigidity of its cylinders acted as a reinforcement of the wheel, which was subjected to strong vibrations from the engine. The rear mudguard doubled as a reservoir for the fuel, the front wheel was supported with both horizontal and vertical stays in place of the more usual cycle-type forks. Pneumatic tyres were specified, while a hand-operated central stand was the first of its type.

Millet claimed a maximum speed of 55 kph (34 mph) and said the endurance was 12-hours. But in typical pioneering fashion it is highly unlikely this latter figure was ever put to the test.

demonstration ride to convince Suberbie to secure a licence to build the Hildebrand & Wolfmüller *motorrad* in France, where they were sold under the Petrolette name.

But elsewhere problems were beginning to show up, particularly with the hot tube ignition, which was both unreliable and difficult to operate. And although the company's publicity stated that 'the ignition ensured prompt and regular explosions' the truth was somewhat different: the tubes had to be pre-heated with a plumber's blowlamp before the machine could be started! Another minus was the poor flywheel effect of the rear wheel which made for erratic progress, not helped by the awkward handlebar mounted thumbscrew, which was the only means of regulating the engine's speed.

Both the German and French factories also soon realised that the selling price was actually *less* than the cost of manufacture. The situation became even more acute when the first customers began to receive their vehicles and soon complained of poor starting and of how difficult their machines were to ride.

Things came to a head when a dissatisfied customer won his court case in France, and there followed a rush of others demanding their money back. Similar problems were also being experienced by Hildebrand & Wolfmüller in Munich.

Early in 1897 both the French and German ventures collapsed, but whilst the French concern went back to pedal cycle production, the German firm went into liquidation, with all its dreams turned to dust.

Henry Martin (left) and
F. Dayrell on Martin-JAPs
built by Daymar. This
picture was taken in
July 1909.

THE BRITISH INFLUENCE

Victorian England was still a society dominated by horse-power. There were a host of regulations impeding the development of self-propelled vehicles, including a speed limit of 4 mph. It was only in 1896, with the passing of the Emancipation Act, that some of these restrictions were lifted and the new transport industries began to flourish. Despite this, it was an Englishman, Major (later Colonel) Henry Capel Lofft Holden who built the world's first 4-cylinder motorcycle in 1897.

On the Holden, the four cylinders were in two horizontal pairs; with bore and stroke measurements of 54 x 114 mm, the engine capacity was 1047cc. Originally air-cooled, it was converted to water cooling in 1899, when it finally entered limited production. Unfortunately, this move did not help sales, which were limited because of the Holden's high cost.

By the turn of the century several famous British cycle makers had decided to enter the motorcycle field. These included Eadie (forerunners of Royal Enfield), Excelsior (not to be confused with the American marque of the same name), Matchless and Raleigh.

A major problem for the British was engines, so many early British bikes used imported power units. A notable exception was JAP (John Alfred Prestwich), an innovator and pioneer in the very best senses of the words. He originally made his name in the world of cinematography but turned his efforts to building proprietary engines for the emerging motorcycle industry.

The first JAP engine had the time-honoured ioe (inlet over exhaust) valve layout, inherited from de Dion-Bouton, but in 1904 JAP took a quantum leap with their own ohv (overhead valve) layout.

Major names such as Norton and Triumph now appeared. The product associated with James Landsdowne Norton was the Energette. Built in 1902, this had a French-designed, British-built 143cc four-stroke Clement-Garrard motor clipped to the front down-tube of the frame.

James Landsdowne
Norton wearing his
Salvation Army uniform
circa 1889.

Meanwhile Triumph had been formed in Coventry by two German immigrants, Siegfried Bettmann and Mauritz Schulte (the latter having worked previously as an engineer for Hildebrand & Wolfmüller). Originally Triumph built only bicycles, but in 1902 they fitted a Minerva engine into one of their frames. This experiment worked well and also sold well – some 300 units in 1903 leaving the Coventry plant. They then launched an all-British 3 hp Triumph single with the new 293cc JAP engine for 1904 and its success set them on their way to greatness over the following decades.

AMERICA JOINS THE RACE

America's first motor race, the Chicago to Wankegan held in November 1895, attracted about 100 entries of motorcycles, as all vehicles were called irrespective of the number of wheels they had. Although very few actually were able to take part, the non-runners were propelled by an amazing array of different types of fuel, including kerosene, compressed air, naphtha, electro-turbine, ether, acetylene, hot air, city gas and even carbonic acid!

But as for the newfangled petrol engine, the American reaction was largely sceptical. One of the earliest Americans to try the new technology was Hiram Maxim, an engineer working for Colonel Albert Pope, one of the country's leading cycle manufacturers. Maxim built a petrol tricycle in 1897 – but didn't manage to convince Colonel Pope to start production. Yet, ironically, it was Pope's own Columbia motorcycle, built at Hartford, Connecticut in 1900, which was to be the first American production model, using a single cylinder ioe engine in a standard Columbia bicycle frame.

Another early American design was the Holley, the work of a 19-year-old from Bradford, Pennsylvania. George M. Holley built his own ioe single in late 1900, even making his own patterns and castings in true pioneering fashion.

Holley built his bike with the intention of taking part in America's first ever pure motorcycle race. Staged from Boston to New York in the summer of 1901, Holley not only took part but won the race.

Thereafter came a veritable flood of new Stateside manufacturers: Indian, Royal, Marsh, Mitchell and Wagner in 1901; Merkel and Yale in 1902; followed in 1903 by Harley-Davidson, Curtiss, Tribune, Rambler, Thiern and Thor.

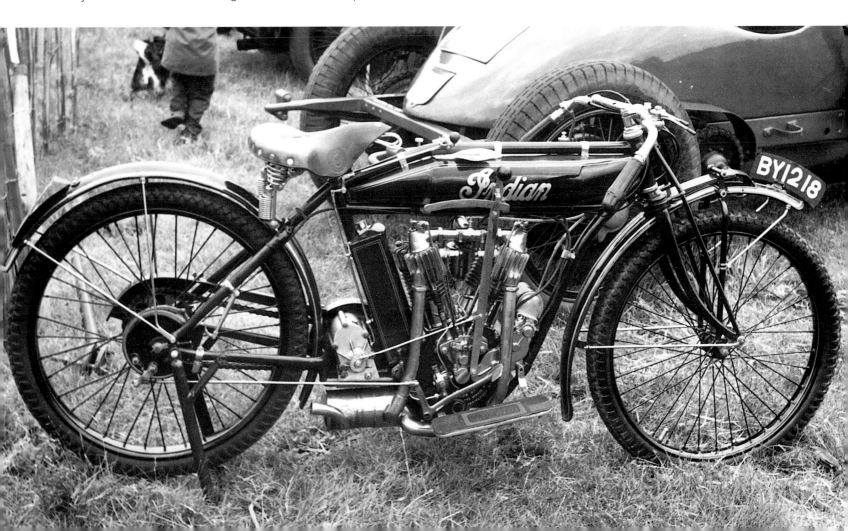

EDOARDO BIANCHI MASTER OF ITALY

One man alone stood head and shoulders above the pioneering days of the embryonic Italian motorcycle at the turn of the century; Edoardo Bianchi. Born on 17 July 1865, Bianchi was brought up in a Milanese orphanage, but from an early age showed a remarkable aptitude for engineering matters.

In 1885, at the age of 20, he set up a small machine shop for bicycle manufacture. Bianchi moved to larger premises in 1888, when he produced the first Italian vehicle (a bicycle) with pneumatic tyres. The business expanded at a great pace throughout the 1890s when cycling became as fashionable in Italy as elsewhere in Europe.

In 1897, Edoardo Bianchi carried out tests with a de Dion single cylinder engine mounted in a tricycle. Although the prototype caught fire there was still the great satisfaction of having been the first Italian to propel a vehicle without resorting to muscle power.

In 1901 the first prototype motorcycle appeared, going on sale the following year. The production version was the first Bianchi vehicle to be constructed entirely out of components manufactured within its Milanese factory; including a 2hp engine built under licence from de Dion. In 1905, by which time it was also producing automobiles, the company was incorporated as Edoardo Bianchi & Co. and turnover increased dramatically year on year.

The developments had been greatly assisted with the opening of a vast new plant in 1902 in Via Nino Bixio, Milan, not only allowing expansion but the development of improved models, including a much improved single with such luxuries as magneto ignition, leading link front forks and belt drive. In 1905 a new design of Truffault fork appeared and by 1910 a brand new 500 made Bianchi the envy of every other motorcycle manufacturer in Italy.

During the First World War Bianchi concentrated on building aero engines, but also supplied a 649cc v-twin engine and a purpose-built C75 military model. These were manufactured in considerable numbers. At the end of the hostilities the v-twin was increased in size to 741cc.

Below: One of the top selling Italian motorcycles of the period up to the end of the First World War, the Bianchi 498cc ioe (inlet over exhaust) single was built from 1914 to 1919.

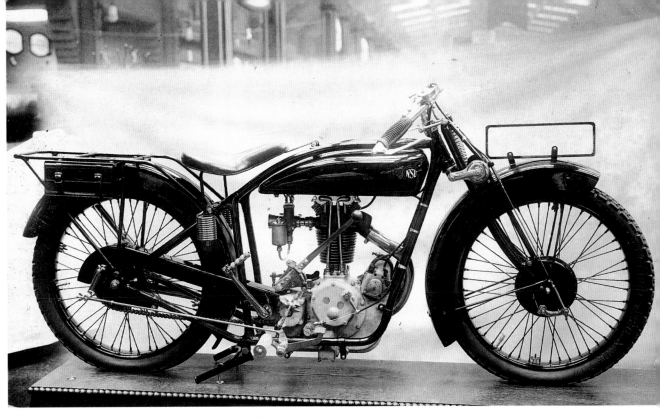

Right: A 1914 NSU 1.5 bhp single cylinder motorcycle. The Neckarsulm company had earlier made its British debut way back in 1901 at London's Crystal Palace.

Below: Born in July 1865, Edoardo Bianchi was brought up in an orphanage; but his engineering genius saw him build up one of Italy's largest industrial empires.

GERMAN DEVELOPMENTS

With the work carried out in the latter part of the 19th century by men such as Langen, Daimler, Maybach, Hildebrand, Wolfmüller and Otto, Germany was well poised to enter the new century.

New entrants into the 2-wheel motorized revolution came onto the scene in the shape of NSU (1901), Wanderer (1902), Adler (1902), Victoria (1900), Express (1903), Diamont (1903), Opel (1901), Mars (1903) and Dürkopp (1901). But, with the exception of NSU, the really big names in German motorcycling – DKW, BMW and Zündapp – didn't arrive until the true pioneering days were over.

Together with the Belgian FN and Austro-Hungarian Laurin-Klement marques, Dürkopp brought out a four cylinder model of its Bielefeld factory. Rated at 4.5 hp, its inline cylinders were equipped with individual finning whilst there was shaft final drive. The engine was of the T-head variety, with the Bosch magneto enclosed and driven off the crankshaft. Dürkopp's 1905 catalogue listed not only its air-cooled inline four, but also singles and v-twins, making for a comprehensive line-up.

Victoria was one of those German manufacturers who originally used proprietary engines bought in from the likes of Minerva, Zedel, FN and Fafnair. It built its first prototype motorcycle at the turn of the century.

Opel, the famous car builder which is now part of General Motors, was a major name in the early days of the German motorcycle industry. The company had been founded by Adam Opel in 1862 to produce sewing machines (like NSU). Its first bicycle appeared in 1866. The five sons of the founder, Carl, Fritz, Heinrich, Ludwig and Wilhelm, contributed to the success of his new venture by their victories in bicycle races. After Adam Opel died in 1895 the five sons decided it was important to become involved with the so-called *Motorwagen* – motorized vehicles. Although their first motorized carriage was not a commercial success they were undeterred and in 1901 produced their first motorcycle.

One of the most popular Opels was an air-cooled 4-stroke single of 204cc. Lubrication was by hand pump; there was belt final drive and braking on the front wheel only. Although Opel were to become more and more heavily involved in automobiles, they still produced auxiliary engines for bicycles and a small 148cc motorcycle in the immediate post-war period during the early 1920s.

BELGIUM

Two marques stand tall in the history of Belgium's early motorcycling industry, FN and Saroléa. Both companies, like the British BSA, came from a background of weapons manufacture. Of the two Saroléa was the oldest, started by Maison Sarolen in Liége during 1850. To start with, the sole purpose of the factory was the production of precision arms, then switched to bicycles, before entering the world of motorcycles in 1898. A third company, Minerva, also entered production a few years later.

Of the three, FN, or to give its full title *La Fabrique Nationale d'Armes de Guerre*, was to be the most successful. But FN was not started until 1889, when the Herstal company set out to rival Saroléa in arms manufacture. And like their rivals they then turned to pedal cycles, before in 1901 turning their attention to a first motorized bicycle.

The standard FN bicycle was equipped with a narrow petrol tank beneath its crossbar and a 133cc engine, belt final drive and large flywheel dominated its specification. Over the next three years FN continued to develop the original design, but in 1904 the company's chief designer Paul Kelecom built a all-new 363cc (45 x 57 mm) four cylinder model which was air-cooled and featured the luxury of shaft drive. To achieve recognition for the new design FN despatched one of the fours on a much publicised tour of Europe. It finally arrived in Paris at the end of 1904, in time for a major sales drive for the 1905 season. The four cylinder engine was enlarged over the next few years and also for 1908 given a clutch, gearbox, internal enclosed brakes and new spring forks.

The Englishman R.O. Clark (later a well-known Norwich dealership) took 3rd place on an FN four in the 1908 multi-cylinder class at the Isle of Man TT. He covered 158.5 miles (255 km) in 4 hours 11 mins, at an average speed of just over 36 mph (57 kmh). Also of interest is that his FN was the most economical machine in the race, with a 90 mpg figure.

R.O. Clark was a real all-rounder and also used his FN four in long distance trials such as the MCC (Motor Cycling Club) London-Edinburgh-London run, winning a gold medal in 1908, as well as racing successfully at the Brooklands circuit in Surrey.

Then in 1909 a new lightweight 285cc single made its bow, both this and the four continuing in production until the outbreak of the First World War. After the war, the single and four re-entered production in 1919. By then, the multi-cylinder machine's capacity had crept up to 780cc before it was finally axed in 1923. Although a revised four (750cc and chain-drive) then took over, the days of the FN four cylinder model were numbered and no more were made after 1926.

Above: The 1914 Belgian FN four-cylinder. This is the 500cc model with shaft drive and two speed gearbox.

Right: FN made their first four cylinder engine in 1904 and together with Saroléa were Belgium's leading marques. Shown is a 1913 750cc model.

(Britain 1909-1969)

Today the lightweight, water-cooled, two-stroke, twin cylinder is the accepted formula for success in the 250cc Grand Prix racing category. Yet when Yorkshireman Alfred Angus Scott pioneered this design at the turn of the century it was branded an elaborate freak.

Alfred Scott had begun by developing a small 130cc two-stroke engine as an auxiliary power unit for bicycles in 1902, but it was not until 1908 that he made a prototype of his twin cylinder two-stroke. This original prototype and the early production models which came the following year featured air-cooled cylinders and water-cooled heads. But soon water-cooling was used for both cylinders and heads.

The unusual cooling principle was not the only original feature of Scott's models. The engine featured a novel crankshaft – both cranks having overhead connecting rods, with the flywheel located between the cylinders. The two-speed gearbox had chain drive and the rear wheel was also driven by the same method. The fully triangulated frame was fitted with a new type of girder front fork, with a central spring, which was the forerunner of later telescopic forks.

Just how far in advance of the time these machines were is shown by the fact that three years in succession (1912, 1913 and 1914) a Scott machine set the fastest lap in the Senior TT.

The roadster and racing models were distinguished by the colour of their cylinders; the roadsters were red, the racers green.

(Britain 1901-69, revived 1987)

Henry Collier and his sons Charlie and Harry Junior were true pioneers of the British motorcycle industry. They began their activities in London during 1901 using De Dion and MMC engines, initially having built an experimental Mathless back in 1899.

Not only did the Collier family build the bikes, they also rode them with great success. Harry Collier Junior won the 1903 ACU 1000 Miles Reliability Trial and Charlie Collier won the Single Cylinder class of the first Isle of Man TT at a record average speed of 49mph, whilst the following year the two brothers finished first and second in the TT – a feat unsurpassed today.

During the Great War production switched to aircraft parts and rifle bayonets. However, post-war saw a return to two wheels – plus sidecars – and even the Model K car (1923). In 1928 the firm officially became Mathless Motor Cycles Ltd. Then in 1930 the famous Silver Arrow v-twin was produced, followed by the even more glamorous Silver Hawk V4 the following year. That same year, 1931, Matchless took over AJS. More expansion followed in 1937, with the acquisition of the Sunbeam marque, and the 'group' being re-registered under the Associated Motor Cycles (AMC) banner.

During the Second World War AMC were a major supplier of military motorcycles to the British armed forces, with the G3L (Lightweight) proving a firm favourite with many wartime despatch riders, using AMC's version of a BMW hydraulically damped telescopic front fork. In the immediate post-war period the bulk of AMC's production was exported. In 1951 the famous 'jam pot' rear suspension units were introduced.

With former racer Jock West as sales supremo, Matchless (and AJS) sold well during the early-mid 1950s helped by its participation in major racing, scrambles and trials events.

Then came a period of further expansion with the purchase of Francis-Barnett, James and Norton. However, this proved to be AMC's downfall. First, the decision to manufacture two-stroke engines for James and Francis-Barnett, second the mix of Norton and AMC parts to create special bikes for the American market. Although the name was revived for an Austrian Rotax powered four-stroke single in 1987 the truly great days of the 'Matchbox' were over.

(Britain 1902-1970)

Ariel first began the manufacture of motorcycles in 1902, although they had been building three-wheelers since 1898. Their first bike came with a 3.5 hp single cylinder motor, and by the outbreak of war in 1914 the Ariel range had expanded to include 498cc side valve singles and ioe (inlet over exhaust) V-twins.

Ariel, then owned by Jack Sangster, was joined in 1927 by the young engineer Edward Turner. Chief designer Val Page was also an important part of Ariel's success, designing new 498cc ohv and 557cc SV singles.

The famous Square Four, at first only in 498cc form, was introduced in 1931. Designed by Turner, larger Square Fours with 601 and 996cc engines followed later in the decade. In 1936 Edward Turner transferred to Triumph in Coventry, following Sangster's aquisition of that factory. During the war, many 347cc ohv Ariels were used by the British forces.

Post-war production centred on 347 and 497cc ohv Red Hunter singles, the Huntmaster vertical twin and a revised 997cc ohv Square Four; the latter often referred to as the Squariel. Other models of the early 1950s Ariel range, included the BSA-derived 198cc Colt single and a 598cc SV single intended mainly for sidecar duties.

Jack Sangster, who had been involved with BSA since the late 1940s, then moved Ariel into the BSA group. This meant that several Ariel models sported BSA components during this era. Eventually Ariel was transferred to BSA's Selly Oak, Birmingham headquarters. There the famous 247cc vertical twin two-strokes, the Leader and the Arrow, were designed. However, the 197cc version was to be the last Ariel (if the Ariel 3 moped is not included) to be built and the marque ceased to exist at the end of the 1960s.

(France 1899-)

Peugeot is one of the famous names in the automobile world, but it has also played an important role in the development of the motorcycle.

Jean Frédéric and Jean Pierre Peugeot opened a small foundry in 1810, which was instrumental in acting as the launch pad of a large family-owned manufacturing empire. In 1885 the brothers Eugéne and Armand, the third generation of the Peugeot family, transformed the company's fortunes, which up to then had produced only bicycles and tricycles, by starting car manufacture.

Peugeot's first motorcycles came in 1899. These were class-leading single and twin cylinder models, whose engines were so highly respected that they were also used by rival manufacturers. For example, the Norton with which Rem Fowler rode to victory in the first Tourist Trophy in 1907 had a Peugeot v-twin engine.

A new era at Peugeot began with the arrival of the Swiss engineer Ernest Henry who, after building successful Grand Prix cars joined Peugeot in 1913 to design a new parallel twin racer with a capacity of 498cc. A novelty was the valve gear, which not only used double overhead camshaft, but four-valves per cylinder.

At the beginning of the 1920s the Rumanian engineer. Lessman Antionescu was hired to redesign the 1913 twin with the hindsight of new technology. The result was a simplified engine with only one camshaft and the number of valves reduced by half, whilst the geartrain now featured bevel gears and vertical shaft. Although these measures appeared a backwards step they worked, resulting in victory for Peugeot in the 1923 Grand Prix des Nations at Monza at an average speed of 75 mph (120 kmh).

On the roadster front Peugeot concentrated upon side valve and overhead singles, plus later two-strokes.

FRENCH PACESETTERS

It may well come as a shock to many present day motorcycle enthusiasts, but France was the first country not only to promote motorcycle racing but also the first to initiate widespread motorcycle production between rival manufacturers.

Well before the end of the 19th century several separate French-based individuals had created organisations to explore the use of the largely untried Otto-cycle engine principle and thus create a fledgling motorcycle industry.

These early pioneers included Count de Dion, his mechanic Georges Bouton, Maurice Fournier, Felix Theodore Millet and Ernest Michaux. In addition, the Russian-born brothers Eugene and Michel Werner had settled in France and become Frenchmen through adoption. Of all these early French efforts the one which had the most profound impact outside French borders was probably the pairing of the aristocratic Count Albert de Dion and the gifted engineer Georges Bouton.

With their headquarters in Paris, de Dion-Bouton was founded in 1882 following a meeting after Count de Dion had admired the workmanship of a model steam engine made by Bouton and his associate Trépardoux.

The collaboration resulted in the de Dion Bouton petrol engine. Their first unit had an aluminium crankcase enclosing a crankshaft and an automatic, suction-operated inlet valve directly over the cam-operated exhaust valve. Unlike the German Daimler engine of the same period, which rotated at 750 rpm, the French engine turned over twice as fast, at 1,500 rpm.

That first de Dion Bouton single was equipped with a small air-cooled cylinder of 50 x 70 mm bore and stroke, giving a capacity of 138cc. The cylinder head and barrel both had cooling fins, whilst the Frenchmen opted for battery/coil ignition thus avoiding the pitfalls experienced by manufacturers like Hildebrand & Wolfmüller.

With an early version of contact breakers their system eventually proved relatively trouble-free. And, combined with a light and simple engine, de Dion-Bouton was able to build on this success and not only build bigger and better engines but created a massive demand at home and abroad.

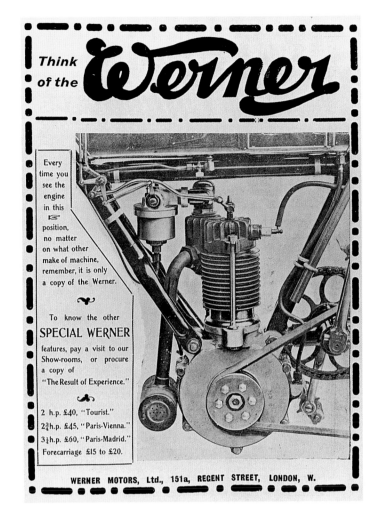

Based in Prague, Josef Walter was one of the self-made men of his era, beginning at the age of 24 as a mechanic repairing bicycles in 1898. Thereafter he built bicycles from parts imported from the British BSA factory and finally in 1902 he constructed his first motorized bicycle. For this he used a single cylinder 3 hp engine set in a conventional bicycle frame. Other features included belt final drive and brakes both front and rear (quite unusual in those days). In 1905 Walter built a twin cylinder machine, the type B. But his main success during this time was with tricycles. After the great War Walter lost control of his own company, so he began making gear wheels and later (after 1925) motorcycles in a new factory. Later still his son Jaroslav became a designer for CZ.

After three years of building motorcycles, the 1906 Puch catalogue listed single and twins in a variety of trims – roadsters, racers, sidecar combinations and even a ladies' model. Puch themselves had a complex history, having been founded in Graz, Austria by Johann Puch in 1891. His first motorcycle appeared in 1900. By 1906 Puch had built a four-stroke v-twin of 904.7cc (80 x 90mm) with beltdrive and 3.5 bhp. These machines ridden by Nikoden and Obruba took first and second places in the 1906 European International Cup race. Puch went on to dominate the Austrian motorcycle scene in the post-war era and beyond.

Opposite: The Hon. C.S. Rolls (of Rolls-Royce fame) in his first motorized vehicle, a French 4 hp Bollée Voiturette tricycle of 1897.

Left: A 1903 advertisement for the French Werner marque. The company was the first to adopt the now normal position of the engine.

Below: Vada Vondrich on a Laurin & Klement machine after his victory in the 1905 Dourdon race.

THE AUSTRO HUNGARIAN EMPIRE

When France began organising the first speed events and long distance road races, the other European nation to mount a challenge to her was Austria, who was anxious to prevent France from monopolising the glory attached to the new sport.

At the end of the 19th century, one of the classic speed events was the Paris to Vienna race. Entrants included specialised racing machinery from France, and products of the Werner brothers. The first machines from the Austro-Hungarian Empire were those from Laurin & Klement, Built at a factory in Mladá Boleslav (now part of the Czech Republic). The first Laurin & Klement machines were built under licence from Werner.

Werners and Laurin & Klements clashed head-on in the 1902 Paris-Vienna. This gruelling 615-mile, four-day event involved the scaling of the Arlberg Pass, some 1,800m (6,000ft) above, sea level, over largely ill-surfaced roads. Klements' leading rider, Derny, led for over half the distance before crashing, but even so of the four finishers, two were riding the Austro-Hungarian machines. This did much to establish the country as a serious motorcycle contender and Laurin & Klement were soon joined by Walter and Puch.

It was also within the borders of the Austro-Hungarian Empire that the FICM (Federation Internationale des Clubs Motocyclistes) was born in the town of Pacov (again now in the Czech Repulbic).

Charlie Collier astride his Matchless-JAP at
Brooklands, 1909.

EARLY RECORDS

As with all forms of motorcycle sport the earliest events were often ill-recorded and none more so than the outright speed record. It was often a case of claim and counter claim as those early speedsters attempted ever faster speeds. Finally in 1909 both the international body the FICM (the forerunner of the FIM) and several national bodies (including the British ACU) officially recognized the holder of the outright two-wheel speed record.

The first to hold the honour was an Englishman, W.E. ('Wee-Wee') Cook who set a speed of 75.92 mph over the flying kilometre on a Peugeot v-twin engined 944cc NLG on 16 June 1909. Cook had already achieved considerable success in racing, including winning the first ever motorcycle event at Brooklands some 18 months earlier. His mount then had been built by North London Garages.

During November 1909 Cook discarded the Peugeot engine previously fitted to his NLG and in its place used one of the huge 2714cc (120 x 120 mm) JAP 90 degree v-twins. This was reputed to turn out 20 bhp and achieve 90 mph, but it was never officially timed.

Cook's record stood for some 12 months before two of the top names of the era – Englishman Charlie Collier (son of the founder of Matchless and the winner of the single cylinder race at the 1907 TT) and American star Jake de Rosier both decided to mount a challenge.

Collier made the first impact when on 20 July 1910 he hoisted the record to 80.24 mph riding, of course, a Matchless (but powered by a JAP V-twin motor); then a month later he went even faster, 84.89 mph.

Jake de Rosier travelled across the Atlantic with his factory Indian to Brooklands, where on the 8 July 1911 he grabbed the world's record under the very nose of Collier by recording 85.38 mph. Later, before leaving England, he upped this figure to 88.87 mph.

In the spirit of the times, the Colliers' laid on a farewell dinner for their American rival. But after de Rosier had sailed for America Collier went back to Brooklands and clocked 89.48 mph on 4 August. Fifteen days later the same rider increased this figure to 91.37 mph.

This speed then stood for several years, until 2 May 1914 when Sydney George sprinted down the Brooklands kilometre at 93.48 mph and thus become the pre-war record holder.

O.C. Godfrey and his Indian motorcycle at the BMCRC trials at Brooklands on 20 March 1911.

(Germany 1901-1967)

One of the pioneers of the German motor-cycle industry was NSU (Neckarsulmer Strickwaren Union), the name coming from the fact that the company was located at Neckarsulm, where the rivers Neckar and Ulm join. It developed first by producing sewing machines in 1880, bicycles from 1887, whilst the first motorcycle was built in 1901; five years later NSU introduced its first car to the public.

The 1901 NSU was equipped with an engine made by the Swiss Zedal company. This was a single cylinder, 234 cc 4-stroke. Basically it was a motorized bicycle, with unsprung frame, the engine being driven by a leather belt to the rear wheel.

Soon NSU switched to engines of its own construction. By the end of the 1914-18 war NSU were building machines with v-twin engines with capacities ranging from 496 to 996 cc, mounted in steel tubular frames.

(America 1901-1953)

Scouts, Braves and Chiefs – yes we're talking Indian, probably the most charismatic of all American bike builders, Harley-Davidson included. The company was founded in 1901 by two former racing cyclists, George M. Hendee and Carl Oscar Hedstrom.

Indian's first production roadster (it also built highly successful racing machines in these pioneering days) was a 4-stroke single with a vertical cylinder. With this design and the famous v-twin which first debuted in 1907, Indian soon developed a reputation for sophisticated design and excellent quality which was to stand for many decades.

One of the twins, a 600cc model was despatched to Britain in the year of its launch and competed in the 1907 ACU Thousand Mile Trial. This event was the fore-runner of the world famous ISDT (International Six Days Trial).

With a further eye to exports across the Atlantic, Indian entered no less than four works riders in the 1911 Isle of Man Senior TT. Scoring an impressive 1-2-3, with the help of its newly created 2-speed gearboxes, Indian's reputation in Europe was cemented and in the following year over 20,000 machines were exported.

The Scout 600cc v-twin appeared in late 1919 and was an instant hit. Designed by Charles B. Franklin, Scouts were renowned for their staying power – witness the factory advertising slogan: 'You can't wear out an Indian Scout'. This was no idle boast, for a Scout set a new 24-hour road record in 1920 covering 1,114 miles (1,792 km) over a closed course in Australia.

The Scout was followed by the 1000cc Chief (1922) and the 1200cc Big Chief a year later. The introduction of the mass produced car in the USA, combined with import tariffs in the UK by the mid-1920s, followed by the Great Depression in 1929, hit Indian sales hard. However, it was still able to acquire the Ace marque but was eventually taken over in 1930 by E.P. Du Pont.

For the remainder of the 1930s and during the Second World War Indian soldiered on with profits still proving elusive. In 1949 a cash injection was made by British entrepreneur John Brockhouse. Brockhouse assumed control of Indian, but this failed to halt the company's financial slide and production was terminated in 1953. Since then many have attempted to relaunch the name, including American publisher Floyd Clymer, but without success.

the Twenties and Thirties

Opposite: A 1930 1265cc Indian four, Model 402. It had a three-speed gearbox and an ioe (inlet over exhaust) engine.

Left: During the 1920s, the huge upsurge in car sales, led by Henry Ford's Model T (shown here) almost killed off the American bike industry.

AMERICA: BIKE VERSUS CAR

Once the guns of war fell silent the US motorcycle industry found itself fighting another battle – against the increasing popularity of the car, particularly in the shape of Henry Ford's Model T. The main attraction of the Model T lay in its bargain basement price, a consequence of the innovative moving production line techniques used by Ford in his Detroit plant. By the end of the Great War in 1918, the Model T had already been on sale for a decade, but its real impact was felt between 1918 and 1927, before it was finally discontinued in favour of more modern types.

Although there was a vast increase in motorcycle sales in Britain and Europe in the first two years after the war (nearly 100 new marques in Britain alone), the huge upsurge of cars headed by the Model T had the effect of drastically reducing the previously large number of American motorcycle producers. Once the dust had settled, only the fittest and biggest survived, names such as Harley-Davidson, Indian, Excelsior and Henderson.

From a total production of 28,189 motorcycles in 1920, Harley-Davidson slumped to just over 10,000 units the following year. But H-D didn't take this lying down and responded by launching an all-new 74 cubic inch (1200cc) 45 degrees v-twin. This basic configuration and displacement was to remain for no less than 65 years until eventually superseded by an 80 cubic inch (1340cc) unit in the mid-1980s.

In 1919 Excelsior (not related to the British marque of the same name) produced its 100,000th bike since production had begun with the Model X in 1905. Excelsior had taken over the Henderson company, builders of the famous inline four cylinder grand touring bikes during 1917 and in 1922 a Henderson had smashed the Trans-America time trial record.

Another milestone was that Excelsior was the first American factory to build a 45 cubic inch (750cc) v-twin in 1925, a format copied three years later, in 1928, by Harley-Davidson.

But all these moves were not enough to prevent the combined strength of Excelsior and Henderson to fold in 1931; brought about by the effects of the Great Depression and fierce competition from market leaders Harley-Davidson and Indian. Of these two great names, that of Indian made the most dramatic news stories during the inter-war period.

Indian's chief designer was the legendary Charles B. Franklin. His greatest achievements were the Scout and Chief, both side valve v-twins.

The 37 cubic inch (600cc) Scout debuted in late 1919 ready for the 1920 season and was an instant hit. Scouts were renowned for their staying power – witness the factory advertising slogan 'You can't wear out an Indian Scout'. (See box on Indians on page 19.)

Following quickly after the Scout came Franklin's next design, the 61 cubic inch (1000cc) Chief in 1922. This too was both a sales (for what was available) and reliability success. A year later came the even larger 74 cubic inch 1200cc Big Chief.

The Indian marque was bought by E. Paul du Pont in 1930. This was at a low ebb in the company's fortunes, thanks to the effect of the Depression. It was not until 1932 that the next model appeared and then it was only a smaller (31 cubic inch) Scout, whilst in 1933 dry sump lubrication was adopted for all the Indian v-twins. With arch rivals Harley-Davidson not opting to use this feature until 1937, Indian stole a march on the competition. The next step was the 45 cubic inch (750cc) Sport Scout in 1934.

For 1938 high performance versions of the Scout and Chief were released in recognition of Ed Kretz's much publicised 1937 Daytona race victory.

With the advent of the 1940s came war rather than peace. Indian found themselves building bikes for the army and after the conflict was over they never challenged Harley-Davidson for the number one spot as they had in the pre-war days.

Right: This is 1930s crime busting with a difference – a sidecar outfit used by the NYPD. The bike is a 1928 Indian Big Chief 1200cc v-twin.

NEWCOMERS

Those that survived the Great War of 1914-18 had a much better understanding of the mechanical world. At its beginning the cavalry went to war with the horse, at the end in a steel motorized tank; it was the same in virtually every other sector of the services, development taking place at breathtaking speed.

Throughout Europe there was to spring a welter of new firms after the war. Some survived only a few months, whilst others went on to become household names, and some are still with us today. Many of the war's biggest armament companies attempted to get a slice of the action, but Krupp, Mauser, Hawker and Sopwith all bombed out; probably the nearest to success was Sopwith's involvement with the ABC 400cc horizontal twin, but although of advanced design with features such as ohv and 4-speed gearbox it suffered from insufficient development and ABC and Sopwith both went bust during the early 1920s.

Much more successful was the German aero engine giant BMW (Bayerische Motoren Werke). BMW had been founded in Munich during 1917 by merging two aircraft engine producing factories, BFW (Bayerische Flugzeug Werke) and Rapp. At first, BMW produced only motorcycle engines; their 493cc twin was supplied to such companies as Bison and Victoria. The first complete motorcycle bearing the famous blue and white BMW emblem on its tank was the R23 horizontal twin launched at the Paris Salon in 1923.

From then onwards BMW were to keep faith with the basic layout of the R23 – horizontally opposed twin cylinder engine and shaft final drive, and still do to the present time – even though they have also built single, three and four cylinder machines.

Germany was rife with motorcycle development during the early postwar era, thanks largely to the terms of the war armistice. Unlike car owners, German motorcyclists were not faced with a pile of documentation before they could take to the road. A consequence of this was proliferation of new motorcycle manufacturers during the first half of the 1920s.

Zündapp was born during September 1917 in Nürnberg. Its original purpose was to manufacture fuses for artillery guns and by the end of the War it employed 1,800 workers. After the conflict was over Zündapp ☞

BMW R23

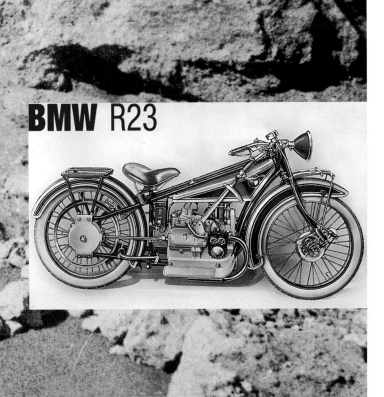

Main picture: In 1924, the Libyan desert was crossed for the first time by a pair of British Dunelt sidecar combinations.

Left: Launched at the 1923 Paris Show, BMW's R23 horizontal twin set a trend for the German company which survives to the present day.

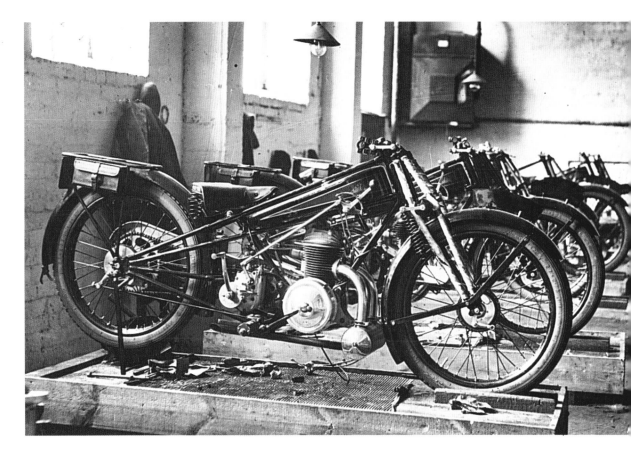

Right: The Cotton factory in Gloucester, England. The company used two-stroke Villiers engines.

Opposite: Three-speed single-cylinder 500cc Moto Guzzi racer which was entered in the 1926 Isle of Man TT.

struggled to find a new identity, but in the autumn of 1921 it had settled on motorcycles. The first model to be put into production was the 211cc Z22. This was powered by a British-made Lewis 2-stroke engine and some 1,000 of these models had been built by October 1922.

The German public first bought motorcycles in high volume in 1924. This boom was greatly helped by a national 17-day touring race which aroused the interest of millions. Zündapp scored some excellent results in this event and the resultant sales (well over 10,000 units that year) set a trend which saw the company follow a special niche in endurance trials which followed the early touring events.

From 1926 onwards Zündapp established branches in all the major commercial centres of Germany. The first was in Berlin, followed by Munich, Cologne and Hamburg. This was the beginning of the establishment of a nationwide dealer and service network which was to set a trend for others to follow. Although they were to continue with their 2-stroke lineage, Zündapp also moved into 4-stroke and the 1930s saw them build horizontally opposed twins and fours.

Other German newcomers included DKW and Horex. Whereas DKW majored on 2-strokes, Horex concentrated upon a range of single and twin cylinder 4-strokes, usually with ohv. Their chief designer Hermann Reeb caused a sensation in 1932 when he created a pair of large capacity vertical twins of 598 and 796cc with chain driven ohc. There had been vertical twins before of course, but not like this.

The Czech Republic had been born out of Bohemia and Moravia, formally part of the Austro-Hungarian Empire, when the map of central Europe had been redrawn at the end of the war. It was to produce a couple of famous marques, CZ and Jawa.

CZ didn't commence motorcycle production until the year 1932, even though the company, Ceska Zbroiovka, was formed in 1918 to manufacture armaments. Ignác Uhl designed the first CZ, the Model 76. This used a 76cc 2-stroke engine and was little more than a motorized bicycle. Today it would be referred to as a moped. Power output was a 2hp at 3,500 rpm, a magneto was provided for ignition and the 'motorcycle' was started by pedalling. The unsprung rear wheel was driven by a chain. Weighing 40kg (88lb), the CZ 76 had a top speed of 25 mph (40 kmh).

From this came the much better CZ 98, which was produced at the Strakonice plant both before and after the Second World War. The company also produced machines with 175 and 250cc engines during the same period; all were 2-strokes.

Jawa began in 1929 by building the German Wanderer 498cc ohv single under licence. Their next move came when the leading British designer George Pactchett joined them in 1930. It was the Englishman who really put the Prague-based company on the map with a string of successful designs, including a racing machine with a 499cc ohv unit construction engine. Patchett even rode himself – racing one of the machines in the 1932 Isle of Man.

In 1932 Jawa introduced their first 2-stroke, a modern looking lightweight with a 173cc British Villiers deflector piston engine. A succession of roadsters followed with 2-stroke and side valve power units. Apart from the Villiers and Wanderer engines (all made under licence agreements), Patchett was the designer. At the onset of the Czech crisis in 1938, Patchett returned to England.

As for the British themselves virtually all the great marques had already made their bow before the 1920s began, including AJS, Ariel, BSA, Douglas, James, Matchless, Norton, OK-Supreme, P&M (Panther), Royal Enfield, Rudge, Scott, Sunbeam, Triumph and Velocette.

So the only newcomers from the British Isles in the days following the First World War of any lasting merit were to be surprisingly few – Brough Superior (1919), Cotton (1920), Francis-Barnett (1919) and HRD – later Vincent (1924).

Italy was the first European country to have a fascist government, when Benito Mussolini and his supporters marched on Rome in October 1922, and the Italian King (Victor Emmanuel III) called on Mussolini to form a new government. By 1928 he had created a one-party dictatorship. But like Hitler in Germany, Mussolini did encourage mechanised transport development, so in general the Italian motorcycle industry flourished during his rule.

Although the Benelli brothers had begun business back in 1911, it was not until 1921 that the Pesaro factory got around to building its first complete motorcycle. That same year Moto Guzzi started its climb to greatness by selling its first production model, the Tipo Normale, following Carlo Guzzi's original 1920 GP prototype, which unlike the production bike, featured 4-valves and overhead cam for its horizontal single cylinder engine.

Sertum began by originally manufacturing precision instruments in its Milan-based factory. But in 1922 its owner, Fausto Alberti, decided it was time to move on to build motorcycles. The marque's first design was a 174cc side valve single, which was soon followed by a cheaper 119cc two-stroke. Thereafter, throughout the mid-and late 1930s Sertum manufactured a comprehensive range of strong, dependable singles and twins with not only side valve, but ohv and even ohc.

The MM company of Bologna, the initials of which stood for the co-founders Mario Mazzetti and Alfonso Morini, began trading in 1924, their first model being a neat little 125cc road racing two-stroke.

After considerable success with the design, a switch in the Italian Highway Code in 1930 meant 125s were more difficult to sell, MM turned its attention from 2-strokes to 4-strokes. The first of these new models, an ohv 175cc, soon became popular and was followed by a sports version with chain-driven overhead cam.

Also, from the early 1930s MM offered a 350cc side-valve tourer and, a little later, a 500cc version intended for sidecar use. Alfonse Morini severed his connection with MM in 1937 to start a rival business, which as Moto Morini went on to greatness, whilst MM was to stagnate, finally closing in 1957.

THE GREAT DEPRESSION

The Roaring Twenties was an era of glamour, excitement and expansion – until the 'Black Friday' of 24 October 1929, the day of the American Wall Street financial crash. America bore the early brunt, but before long the effect was felt worldwide, with millions thrown out of work in all the industrialized countries.

Like the rest of American industry, motorcycle manufacturers took a real beating and by the end of the Depression only Harley-Davidson and Indian would survive and then only by a whisker.

Harley-Davidson had launched its new VL 74 cubic inch (1200cc) v-twin just two months prior to the Wall Street debacle and it was to prove a disaster. Not only was it launched at the wrong time but it was under-developed and unreliable into the bargain. Saddled with this and other problems, H-D went through four bone hard years. And by 1933, with just 3,703 units sold, they were teetering on the brink of oblivion.

There is no doubt that had the depression lasted another year they would have been dragged down. Rivals Indian fared no better. Only the intervention of E. Paul du Pont kept them from bankruptcy in 1930/31. Even after improvements in management and motorcycle design, by 1933 the company was reduced to operating at a mere 5 per cent of plant capacity. It was so bad, that at one stage, there wasn't enough money to meet the payroll! Somehow both Harley-Davidson and Indian did survive but it was a close-run thing.

The situation was no more promising in Europe, particularly in Great Britain and Germany. Then, as now, when America sneezed, the poor men of Europe were likely to catch pneumonia.

In Germany, the crisis led to over 6 million being out of work by 1932, resulting in the closure or near bankruptcy of many of the nation's motorcycle factories.

This crash resulted in Opel switching production exclusively to cars (1930) and Wanderer to radiator production (1931), whilst Windhoff, Neander, Stock, Bekamo, Imperial, Rheingold and D-RAD failed completely. NSU only survived by entering into an agreement with Italian industrial giants Fiat and DKW to become part of Auto Union (as did NSU eventually).

BMW (like NSU), had just completed a major investment programme when the Great Depression arrived and only survived by a policy of diversification and skilled financial management. The other major German marque Zündapp were equally hard pressed, but they too managed to fight through to the Post-Depression era. As a point of interest it was

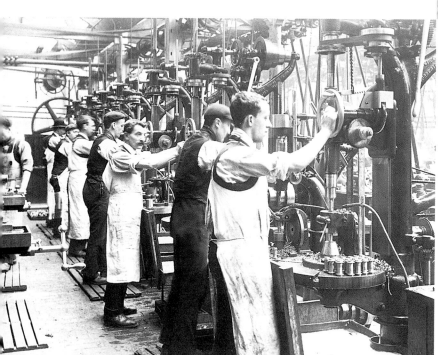

Left: The Tottenham, London-based JAP factory during the 1920s. They produced a whole series of engines, supplying customers like Brough and HRD.

Ariel Square 4

Left: Designer of the Square 4, Edward Turner (at left), with tester Freddie Clarke and Ernie Smith of Ariel's experimental department, at Brooklands in 1936.

Above: the 1937 BSA Empire Star M23 500cc single, a typical product of the British motorcycle industry during the late 1930s.

Zündapp who, together with Porsche, were to create the type 32 car, the father of the legendary VW 'Beetle'.

The year 1931 was to prove disastrous for the famous British marque, AJS. They too had gone for expansion at the wrong moment and the founding Stevens brothers, Harry, George, Jack and Joe, were suddenly plunged head first into a terminal cash flow crisis. The receiver moved in, the result being the Wolverhampton based company found new home in Woolwich, south east London, after being bought out by rivals Matchless.

AJS' problems mirrored much of Britain's ills during the same period, most finding stop-go-stop economics hard to handle. Some firms did however rise to the challenge – either because they had played things safe and not expanded further than their resources or were cash rich. Then again some moved into new territory including automobile construction, whilst others such as Triumph hedged their bets by building cars and bikes.

BSA were one of the strongest companies at that time and were able to launch a new range of attractively styled machines with good performance for 1931. These, built in 348 and 499cc engine sizes, were marketed under the Blue Star name and were the first BSAs to bear what would be a legendary and long-running 'Star' family, headed by its most renowned member, the much loved Gold Star.

Ariel were another success at this time with machines like the Red Hunter single and the first of its Square Fours. The company was also fortunate to have the commercial acumen of managing director Jack Sangster, and the brilliance of designers Val Page and Edward Turner. All three men were destined to play a major part in the success of the British bike industry over the following years.

Rudge, Norton and Sunbeam were other names who coped with the Depression and therefore benefited when the upswing on sales finally came from the middle of the decade onwards.

Trials rider Marjorie Cottle demonstrates a Brough Superior
SS100, which the manufacturers guaranteed a 100mph (160 kmh)
maximum speed, at the 1934 Motorcycle Show at Olympia, London.

(Britain 1919-1939)

Often referred to as 'The Rolls Royce of Motorcycles', the Brough Superior was built between 1919 and 1939 and even though only 3,000 were built in total, they carved a special place in the hearts of motorcyclists the world over.

Based in Nottingham, George Brough benefited from his father William, who had built his own cars and bicycles powered by de Dion engines at the turn of the century. Whilst father William favoured flat-twin engines, George immediately plumped for the v-twin and it was to be seen on the vast majority of his models.

Entering production in 1921, the first Brough Superior was tested by *The Motor Cycle* magazine on 20 January that year in both solo and side-car trim. It was powered by a specially-tuned 986cc ohv JAP engine with Sturmey Archer 3-speed gearbox, Brampton Biflex forks and Enfield cush drive hub. Costing £175 in solo specification it had, for the time, a superb top gear performance which ranged from 8 to 80 mph, whilst its appearance and quality were deemed to be truly excellent. The latter was helped by the heavy nickel plating of many components. The oval bulbous plated tank, which was to be a standard Brough feature was not only a focal point of interest but practical too.

George Brough was ably supported by his right hand man Ike Webb and together they created a line of machines which are still held in awe today. Probably the most famous of all was the SS100 a 50 degree v-twin introduced at the Olympia show in November 1924. It was sold with a guarantee that it would exceed 100 mph (160 kmh) on the track. The design was based on the record breaking exploits of Bert Le Vack and featured a sturdy duplex cradle frame to which were fitted Castle forks, similar in principal to a Harley-Davidson design.

In 1932, a machine designed for sidecar work employed a 800cc Austin watercooled four-cylinder engine with the unusual feature of twin rear wheels and shaft drive. But the most unique of all Broughs was the Dream, a 997cc flat-four engined model which was displayed at Earls

Lawrence of Arabia (astride a Brough SS100) with George Brough, outside the latter's works in Nottingham in 1933.

Court in 1938, but was destined to never enter production, due to the outbreak of war.

Celebrated riders aplenty rode Superiors including Bert Le Vack, Eric Fernihough, Freddie Dixon and Noel Pope. Besides their track successes Fernihough and Pope were also notable speed record breakers.

(Italy 1921-)

Moto Guzzi was founded by Giorgio Parodi, Giovanni Ravelli and Carlo Guzzi who met during the First World War during service with the Italian air arm. A few days after the end of hostilities Ravelli was killed whilst testing his biplane. The winged eagle emblem symbolizes the company's origins. Starting with only ten employees in 1921, including the two partners, Moto Guzzi rose to become Italy's largest and most famous factory, employing hundreds.

Right from the start it took a great interest in racing and until its withdrawal from the sport at the end of 1957, it favoured a horizontal single cylinder engine layout, and with its basic design Guzzi machines and riders won ten TTs and eight World Championships. Although the Mandello del Lario factory achieved numerous continental victories in its early days it was not until 1935, when Stanley Woods won both the Lightweight and Senior TTs, that Guzzi's efforts were crowned with truly international success. Other notable pre-war victories came in the 1937 Lightweight TT and the epic defeat of the mighty DKWs in the 1939 250cc German Grand Prix. During the Second World War Guzzi turned its hand to building military motorcycles, a trend it was to continue when peace finally came, together with police bikes to customers around the world.

(Britain 1902-)

James Lansdowne Norton (often simply referred to simply as 'Pa') built his first motorcycle in 1902, using a French Clement engine. This was soon complemented by another French powerplant, a Peugeot v-twin. It was one of these latter engines with which Rem Fowler won the Twin Cylinder race at the very first TT in 1907. In the same year Norton designed the first engine of its own manufacture. This long-stroke unit, with 79 x 100 mm, 490cc, dimensions, was to become something of a Norton tradition.

In 1911, after a long illness 'Pa' lost control of Norton to the Vandervell family though he remained joint managing director with R.T. Shelley. He died in 1925 at the age of 56.

For much of the 1930s Norton was a major force on the racing scene with riders such as Jimmy Guthrie, Alex Bennett, Freddie Frith and Harold Daniel beating the world and winning no less than 14 TTs. Besides the riders, Irishman Joe Craig, a Norton rider himself during the 1920s, was largely the driving force in a race managerial career which was to span almost 30 years, from 1926-1955. Of course the Second World War stood in the way and Norton became a major supplier to the British Army during the conflict.

The story of this great marque really began with the birth on 30 July 1898 of Jorgan Skafte Rassmussen in Nakskow, Denmark. The young Rassmussen moved to Düsseldorf in Germany in 1904 and then in 1907 to Zschopau, 20 kilometres south of Chemnitz in Saxony. Here, Rasmussen held a number of engineering posts, before setting up his own company in 1919.

A major milestone was reached in 1921, with the introduction of the Hugo Ruppe-designed 122cc 2-stroke engine. By 1922 some 25,000 of these tiny engines had been sold.

This success was followed by a pair of advanced scooters, but these failed to sell. But the SM (Steel Model) put the company back on track. This was another advanced design and its 173cc single cylinder engine was housed in a trend-setting pressed steel frame. It was soon copied by rival manufacturers; even so, DKW was able to stay ahead, and by 1927 it had absorbed no less than 16 of its rivals and had a giant workforce of over 15,000.

Three years later, with even more rapid growth and DKW was able to genuinely claim to be the world's largest motorcycle producer.

DKW
WORLD'S LARGEST
BIKE BUILDER

Above: DKW works rider Waldfried Winkler setting a new class world record for the flying kilo at 102.07 mph (164.23 kmh) in 1937. The machine is watercooled, super-charged 175cc BWK model.

Right: DKW 500cc two-stroke twin on display at London's Olympia show in November 1927

However, the Wall Street crash of 1929 was to greatly affect companies like DKW. But this was partly offset by the innovation in the same year of the loop scavenge system designed by Ing Schnuerle.

This was a major step in the evolution of the 2-stroke engine. The Schnuerle system with its flat top piston offered superior power, improved flexibility and more even firing. It achieved this with angled inlet ports. These allowed the mixture taken in during the induction stroke to proceed up the cylinder, across the combustion chamber and down the other side of the cylinder, taking the course of escaping exhaust gas through its conventional control port. Considerable experimentation ensued before the optimum shape and positioning of the ports was finalised.

But these developments not only allowed DKW to produce a line of high quality modern 2-strokes (some even watercooled) for road use, they were also extremely successful in motorcycle sport in both trials and racing. In the latter their supercharged 250 and 350cc models won several Grand Prix and TT events at were generally accepted as the finest two-strokes in the world.

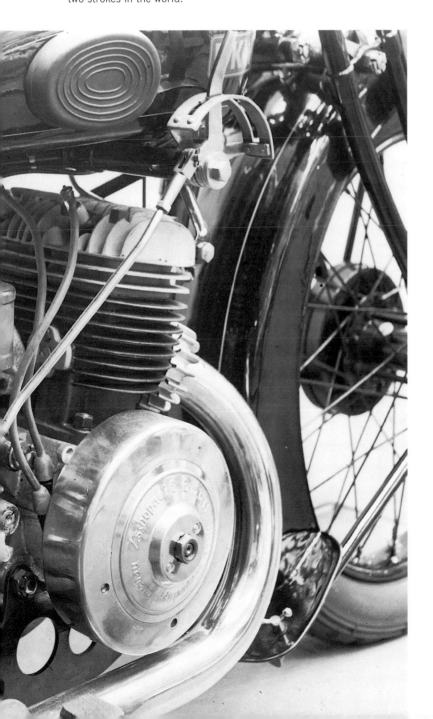

(Britain 1909-1966)

The Stevens brothers, Harry, George, Jack and Joe, began to experiment with internal combustion engines in 1897 at their father's Wolverhampton-based engineering works. They put this to good use by initially building engines which were employed in some of the very earliest motorcycles, cyclecars and even cars. Then in 1909, using Jack's initials (Albert John Stevens), the four brothers created the AJS company.

Having been victorious with their first TT, the 1914 Junior, the firm returned to the racing scene after the First World War to become outstandingly successful in the 350cc category both at home and in Europe.

The marque won three Junior TTs in succession, in 1920, 21 and 22, whilst in 1921 Howard Davies, riding a 349cc ohv AJS, became the first and only rider to win a Senior TT on a Junior machine.

With racing becoming ever more competitive, AJS developed a new overhead camshaft works model for 1927. But somehow even though the bike was extremely robust, it simply wasn't quick enough to challenge its main rivals from Norton, Rudge and Sunbeam.

Like so many others, AJS was deeply affected by the worldwide economic depression which followed the Wall Street Crash. By mid-1931 the Stevens' empire was on the rocks and the factory doors closed. This didn't signal the end for AJS and the company was acquired by the Collier brothers, already owners of the South-East London-based Matchless marque. This new group was to become known as AMC (Associated Motor Cycles), and was to eventually swallow up Sunbeam, James, Francis Barnett and even Norton.

(Italy 1909-)

This famous sporting marque was founded by Giuseppe Gilera, who was born in December 1887, in a small village near Milan. Brought up in a working-class family, even as a schoolboy the young Giuseppe was fascinated by all forms of mechanized transport, which were then in their infant stage of development. He went to work in the Bianchi factory in Milan at the age of 15. Displaying an aptitude far above his age and upbringing, Gilera soon moved on to work as a mechanic with the Italian branch of the Swiss Moto Reve concern. Then after a spell in Geneva with an engineering firm, he returned to Italy in 1908. The following year he began to build his own bikes, the first being a 317cc single with ioe (inlet over exhaust). Like many other fledgling manufacturers of the era, Gilera soon went racing, his first win coming at Cremona in 1912.

During the First World War, Gilera turned his hand to building bicycles for the Italian military. Following the end of hostilities there was a massive demand for motorcycles in Italy, but it was not until 1920 that Gilera was able to capitalise on this, after moving out of Milan to a much larger factory in Ancore.

Besides its roadsters, Gilera throughout the 1920s gained considerable success in long distance trials – thanks in no small part to the exploits of younger brother Luigi, who won many ISDT 'golds' with sidecars.

But the really big breakthrough in bike sport came in late 1937 following the purchase of the four-cylinder Rondine racing and record breaker. As a direct result of this Gilera were European champions in 1939. Then came the Second World War and Gilera, like Norton, switched from the GP circuit to building bikes for the army.

Left: Eric Fernihough after achieving the outright world record of 169.79 mph (273.19 kmh) in Hungary on 19 April 1937, riding a 1000cc Brough Superior.

Right: Joe Wright on Southport Sands, England with the special AJS 1000cc v-twin built to attack the world speed record in 1933.

RECORD BREAKING

On 28 April 1921, Douglas H. Davidson riding a 999cc ioe Harley-Davidson v-twin made history by becoming the first man in Britain to cover the kilometre one-way at over the magic 'ton' – 100.76 mph (162.12 kmh) to be exact. Even though by now two-way runs were needed to qualify for world record status it was still a very impressive achievement.

Exactly 24 hours later, Bert Le Vack on an 8-valve 994cc Indian v-twin beat this figure, when, on the machine he nicknamed 'The Camel', he travelled at 104.52 mph (168.17 kmh). On the same day he went for the world's fastest with a two-way run average of 93.99 mph (151.22 kmh).

Le Vack's great rival Claude Temple responded by taking his Harley-Davidson v-twin even faster over Brooklands' uneven concrete surface and took the record at 99.86 mph (160.67 kmh) – tantalisingly near the 100 mph figure.

Of course, this in turn stung Le Vack back into action and by October, with a new 998cc Zenith-JAP he went even faster, recording a two-way average of 102.80 mph (165.40 kmh).

At this stage it should be mentioned that the American Eugene ('Gene') Walker riding one of the 8-valve Indian v-twins back on 12 April 1920 had been timed on Daytona Beach, Florida at 114.17 mph (183.69 kmh), but this was one-way and wind assisted. Even so he then made the required two-way runs and averaged 103.56 mph (166.62 kmh) on 14 April, but the FICM did not ratify these records for many months, which eventually led to the Americans resigning from the Federation in 1923.

Although this meant that American riders were effectively unable to compete, this didn't extend to their machines and Englishman Freddie Dixon, piloting one of the 8-valve Harley-Davidson vees in the French Boulogne Speed Trials in September 1923, put the record up to 106.80 mph.

Then, on 6 November the same year, Claude Temple put in another blistering performance at Brooklands on his 996cc British Anzani using a 995.5cc (83 x 92 mm) 57 degree v-twin. However, as speeds rose it became evident that Brooklands Railway Straight had run its course in the outright speed stakes and Temple's 1923 effort was the last time that the famous Surrey track was to be used for record breaking.

By 1924 Bert Le Vack appeared on a new 996cc (80 x 99 mm) v-twin (the first JAP with ohv) and in front of 80,000 onlookers took the record for the third time in the Separt Forest, near Paris on the 27 April, averaging 113.61 mph (182.79 kmh) in the process. Three months later in July Le Vack raised the figure again to 119.05 mph (191.55 kmh), which stood for two years.

Le Vack's old rival Claude Temple regained the record at Arpajon in 1926 with an OEC-Temple. Then at the same venue in 1928 Oliver Baldwin, another British rider went even faster at 124.62 mph (200.51 kmh) on a Zenith JAP.

In 1929 a whole group of riders including Le Vack, Joe Wright, Bill Lacey, Baldwin, Albert Denly and Freddie Nicks descended upon Arpajon with Le Vack finally beating off the opposition to clock a two-way average of 129.05 mph (207.64 kmh) on his JAP engined Brough Superior. This

was to be Bert Le Vack's last world speed record as he was to meet his death in a road accident in Switzerland during 1931.

But before this, September 1929 had seen a fresh chapter in the story with a new name and bike – Ernst Henne and BMW as the new holders after blasting down the Munich-Ingoldstat autobahn at 134.68 mph (216.7 kmh) on a supercharged 735cc flat twin. Between 1929 and 1937 Henne was to break the record no less than seven times and is widely seen as the most famous of all the world motorcycle speed record holders – all his achievements being gained on BMWs.

At first his main challenger was Joe Wright who managed to regain, temporarily, the title twice from Henne, first in August 1930 with a speed of 137.32 mph (220.94 kmh) and then with 150.74 mph (242.54 kmh) in November 1930.

Henne retook this last figure on 3 November 1932 at 151.86 mph (244.34 kmh), which was upped to 169 mph (271,93 kmh) dead on a supercharged, fully-streamlined 495cc BMW on the Frankfurt autobahn in 1936.

The following year the well-known English racer Eric Fernihough achieved 169.786 mph (273.18 kmh) at Gyon, Hungary on 19 April 1937 riding an unstreamlined 1000cc Brough Superior. Fernihough also broke Henne's 3-wheel speed at over 137 mph (220.43 kmh).

Fernihough's solo record survived until 21 October 1937, when the famous Italian, Piero Taruffi averaged 170.373 mph (274.13 kmh) with a 492cc water-cooled supercharged 4-cylinder Gilera. But Henne snatched this back a few weeks later with 173.67 mph (279.43 kmh).

But this was to prove the world speed record's pre-war swansong, with Ernst Henne retiring. And in 1938 Eric Fernihough once more made the long journey to Hungary only to meet his death when his beloved Brough went out of control at around 180 mph (290 kmh). Taruffi did attempt some more record breaking in April 1939, but although he covered 127 miles in 60 minutes to take the coveted hour title, he couldn't match Henne's 1937 outright speed.

Below: Piero Taruffi (second from right) makes another attempt to break the record with a 500cc supercharge Gilera four in April 1939. Designer Remor is to his left.

THE ROAD TO WAR

By 1937 the motorcycle had become an accepted part of the overall transport system and in general was much more sophisticated and reliable than it had been only a decade or so previously.

This is well illustrated by 'Torrens' writing in the 6 January 1938 issue of *The Motor Cycle* who had this to say: 'My log book confirms it; for me 1937 has proved a very good year. There has been about the usual number of machines through my hands – just over thirty – and the mileage, although there has been no trip halfway across Europe to add its thousand's, runs comfortably into five figures. What is more, there has been next to no trouble – not even a solitary puncture. It has been an interesting year from my point of view, and from the general standard of the machines exceptionally high.'

Of the hundred of models available on the British market of that time the cheapest was the 98cc Raynal 2-stroke at £18 and the most expensive the 990cc Brough Superior SS100 ohv v-twin at £155.

At the Milan Show in February 1938 the outstanding exhibit was an eight cylinder 2-stroke produced by the Galbusera concern. Although of extremely compact Vee-layout this never entered series production; there was also a 250cc v-four from the same source.

Of more significance to what the general public could realistically expect to purchase were a number of 250cc single cylinder 4-strokes from Benelli, Bianchi, Moto Guzzi, Gilera and Sertum. Several of these companies also offered 500s.

But the really big show that year was in Berlin during the same month. Opened by none other than Adolf Hitler this was truly an impressive event with all the pomp and ceremony of a big state occasion. The Germans effectively managing to turn the Berlin Show into an event of national importance which focused attention upon their motorcycle industry like no other show in the rest of Europe.

Germany, of course, with its controlling Nazi Party, had for a number of years striven to make her youth motorcycle- and mechanically-minded, both by propaganda and tax concessions. The result had been that in a relatively short space of time the number of registrations had risen dramatically (some 1.5 million alone in 1937). Major German marques at that time included DKW, BMW, NSU, Zündapp, Victoria and TWN (Triumph).

The National Cyc-Auto Club's first rally at London's Albert Memorial in 1936. The machines could attain up to 140 miles per gallon.

But even after the Munich Crisis of September 1938 not everyone seemed to realise that war was only a few months away. Two extracts from the editorial leader page of *The Motor Cycle* dated 10 August 1939 shows just how true this is. The first concerned a supply problem which had made it virtually impossible to purchase a new British model due to extra demand.

Another feature of the immediate period prior to the outbreak of the Second World War was the success of multi-cylinder machines in road racing and the effect of causing much thought to be given to the whole subject of motorcycle design. The eight types of engine most promoted were: horizontally-opposed twins (BMW and Douglas); vertical twin with pistons in step (Triumph); v-twin (various); twin 2-stroke (Scott); square-four (Ariel); horizontally-opposed four (Zündapp); narrow-angle v-four (Matchless); and straight four (Gilera).

In the final few days before the outbreak of a conflict which was to last almost six years, there was a welter of sporting events culminating with the ISDT which began in Austria on Monday 21 August 1939. The event, the 21st in the series, had promised to be the most gruelling, and therefore most interesting of all. One journalist who attended commented: 'In the trial – in everything connected with it – there was peace and friendliness. Motorcycle sport had brought nations together and nothing could be more impressive than the helpfulness of one competitor towards another. Of different nationalities they might be, but they were bound together by their common love of motorcycles and by competing side-by-side encountering the same difficulties.' It would be many years before the same could be said again.

Opposite: The Ariel 500cc Red Hunter single.

Left: A 500cc Rudge Ulster sports model being tested at the Brooklands circuit in 1938.

the Second World War

THE HISTORY OF BIKES AT WAR

As a war machine, the motorcycle replaced the horse as an important means of communication and message despatch, whilst in sidecar vogue it established itself as a functional and highly mobile light assault vehicle or transport.

In the Great War of 1914-18 the British with their Douglas 350s, Triumph 550s, Rudge Multis and P&Ms led the way, but they were joined, following America's entry into the conflict, by a host of Harley-Davidsons, Indians and Excelsiors. Other early military motorcycles included FN (Belgium), NSU (Germany) and Puch (Austro-Hungary).

When Germany marched into Poland on 1 September 1939, many countries in Europe had been on almost a war footing for several months since the Munich Crisis of a year earlier. For example, the Norton company had foregone its usual challenge for road racing honours during the 1939 season, concentrating instead on military contracts, thanks to the persistence of its managing director, Gilbert Smith.

The machine Norton was building was the 490cc side valve Model 16H single. This was basically a 1937 civilian model with the military conversion consisting of little more than a crankcase shield, a pillion seat or rear carrier rack, a pair of canvas pannier bags, provision for masked lighting, and an overall coat of khaki paint. The Bracebridge Street, Birmingham factory also built the very similar Big Four with larger 634cc capacity. Some 100,000 16H's alone were built for wartime service, showing how Smith's foresight was to pay dividends.

Preparing for action in late 1939, a section of the Belgian army unit Chasseurs Ardennais mounted on FNs.

NEW DEVELOPMENTS

Many military motorcycles were little more than tarted up civilian models, but modern warfare, as in other areas, was to display a need for more specialized machinery; the powered two-wheeler being no different in this requirement.

In addition each country found it had particular motorcycle requirements: the British concentrated on mainly simple singles, the Germans complex horizontal twins, whilst the Americans opted for heavyweight v-twins. But even in these countries there were many other interesting developments.

Starting with the British, whose staple diet in military bike hardware was usually an ohv or sv single, there were several types which didn't follow this line. Douglas built a prototype flat twin, James and Royal Enfield small capacity 2-strokes, Triumph various ohv twins and AMC constructed another prototype using a 990cc v-twin engine. It is generally agreed that the best wartime British machine was the Matchless 348cc G3L with ohv engine and telescopic forks.

If everyone associated Britain with big singles, then the same could be said of Germany and its big flat twins. But again the truth was somewhat different. Yes, there were large numbers of BMWs and Zündapps using this engine layout, but there were also many other designs. Most of the others were 2-strokes from Ardie, DKW, TWN, and Zündapp. Victoria produced a 4-stroke single, the 342cc KR35WH.

But it was NSU which really came up with something different. This was the extraordinary *Kettenkrad* which was really a small, tracked, personnel carrier that just happened to have a motorcycle front fork. It was powered by a 1478cc ohv Opel 4-cylinder, watercooled engine. Besides its *Kettenkrad*, NSU also built a 122cc 2-stroke and the 2500S and 6010SL models, both with single cylinder ohv engines and separate 4-speed gearboxes.

From Italy came names which were more akin to the race circuit: Benelli, Bianchi, Gilera and Moto Guzzi. Of most interest were the Gilera Marte with 499cc sv engine and shaft final drive and the Moto Guzzi Alce with typical Guzzi horizontal single cylinder engine. The Italians also took their *motocarri* (motorcycle truck) to war including the Gilera Gigante VT in 500 or 600cc form and Guzzi's Trialce.

The most interesting American military irons were not the hordes of Harley-Davidson and Indian v-twins but the unusual Crosley 580cc SV twin, the Harley-Davidson XA flat twin modelled on the BMW 12 and the Indian Model 841 with transverse v-twin engine and shaft drive.

The wartime period wasn't short of ideas.

The German *Kettenkrad* was the strange combination of tracked vehicle and motorcycle. Built by the NSU company, it used motorcycle steering, front forks and wheel.

DISPATCH RIDERS

The motorcycle was in many ways the unsung hero of the Second World War. It was to carry out a truly amazing array of tasks, but it was most widely used by the famous DRs (Dispatch Riders). Although radio communications had taken over from the miles of telephone wire near the front line which had been such a characteristic of the previous war, the bike was still important when everything else failed.

Motorcycles were also commonly used to marshal convoys of vehicles because motorcyclists could direct traffic at one point and then leapfrog ahead, driving along the side of the road, to the next situation.

Another area in which they came into their own was scouting ahead of advancing troop columns. Some, particularly those coupled with a sidecar, carried weapons, usually either a heavy calibre machine gun or even an anti-tank weapon.

Another important reason why motorcycles were so popular was not only the freedom they allowed their riders, but (or should have been!) their relative cheaper costs compared with four-wheel vehicles. The British machines certainly filled both criteria, whereas the large German BMW and Zündapps were to prove more expensive to produce than a small automobile. Then again the bulk of machines built by the Americans (which in practice meant either Harley-Davidson or Indian) were to European eyes large and heavy with their massive construction, foot clutch and hand gearchange. But against this they were well developed and suited to their tasks.

Most bikes intended for DR duties were equipped with pannier frames; often the Americans added to this by equipping their machine with a gun holster, ammunition box and carrier bags.

Motorcycles were also used by other sectors of the military besides the fighting man, such as military police and air force personnel.

Left: WRENS (Women's Royal
Naval Service) dispatch riders
ready for the off on 1942 350cc
Triumphs – the side-valve single
Model 35W.

Right: The ubiquitous German
army sidecar combination, the
BMW R12. It saw service in
all theatres of war.

SIDECARS

By the end of the First World War sidecars had played a vital role in a wide range of military tasks. When war broke out again, sidecar combinations were to play an even more important part than ever. The Allies fitted chairs to American Harley-Davidsons and Indians as well as BSA M20s and Norton 16Hs.

The Norton was unusual in that it was often fitted with sidecar wheel drive which resulted in excellent cross-country capability combined with truly appalling handling when on the tarmac. But generally Allied sidecar outfits were never really developed into comprehensive military vehicles, unlike the Axis powers, and in particular Germany.

This was largely due to the respective national needs for other equipment. For example, the Americans already had the four-wheel-drive Jeep, which was so effective it virtually rendered sidecars redundant for active service. But Germany had no four wheeler comparable to the Jeep. The *Kubelwagen*, their nearest equivalent, was comparatively underpowered. They badly needed a lightweight vehicle, particularly for the heavily mechanised Blitzkrieg method of attack and here the sidecar combination really came into its own.

At first there was the BMW R61 and Zündapp KS600 both with 600cc horizontal twin cylinder engines. Appearing in 1938 they remained in production until 1941, by which time 15,000 BMWs (of which 2,000 were the larger R71) and no less than 18,000 Zündapps had rolled off the production lines.

But the definitive German sidecar tugs were the BMW R75 (745cc) and Zündapp KS 750W (751cc). The Zündapp KS 750W (known as the Green Elephant) appeared first, during the desert war of North Africa in the autumn of 1940. This came at a time when Rommel and the Africa Corps were just starting to push the British out of positions they had recently taken from the Italians. Features included a multi-change four-speed gearbox and reverse gear, sidecar wheel drive, large section 16 inch tyres and a Steib-built chair.

The BMW R75 was originally intended as a towing vehicle for a light gun, but this item proved a non-starter when it was discovered that the towbar weight lifted the front wheel off the ground!

Its specification closely matched that of the Zündapp KS 750W and both units proved extremely robust and effective in servic. However, their biggest drawback was cost of production – it was double that of the four-wheel VW *Kubelwagen*. Even so, 18,600 KS75Ws and 16,500 R75s were built. They saw extensive service wherever the Wehrmacht (German Army) was engaged, but in particular in North Africa with the Africa Korps and on the Eastern Front.

Italy also used three wheel vehicles but these were usually the *moto-carri* (motorcycle fork and engine with a truck rear section).

A formidable trio of British tommies aboard a 1940 Norton 634cc 'Big Four' side-valve single, with sidecar wheel drive

PARA BIKES

With the advent of paratroops it was perhaps inevitably that someone should come up with the idea of dropping a motorcycle that could be quickly assembled in the field.

Although there were others built in Italy, Germany and America (by Volugrafo Aermoto, TWN and Cushman respectively), the British had by far the most success with the concept, with special machines from James, Royal Enfield and Welbike. The two former machines were both fairly conventional 125-class 2-stroke motorcycles.

Royal Enfield's effort was a 126cc (54 x 55mm) DKW-based ultra-lightweight – soon to become nicknamed the 'Flying Flea' in military service. The James was powered by a 122cc (50 x 62mm) Villiers 9D engine with 3-speed hand change gearbox and was known as the Military Lightweight (ML).

But it was the third machine which was the most unusual, and certainly the most interesting. The Welbike was the idea of Lieutenant-Colonel JRV Dolphin and the name came from the creators home town, Welwyn in Hertfordshire.

The basic idea was that the machine must fit in a cylindrical container which could be dropped by parachute and the bike be ready for instant action straight from the crate with the very minimum of fuss. The Welbike was fitted with a 98cc (50 x 50mm) Villiers Junior Deluxe engine. This was an extremely basic unit with a horizontal cylinder and single speed. To fit into the narrow container small 12.5 inch tyres were specified. When assembled but without fuel the weight was 31.75 kg (70 lb). Other features of Lt. Colonel Dolphin's design included a collapsible steering column and handlebars and twin pannier fuel tanks astride the frame.

The Welbike was manufactured by the British Excelsior company (not to be confused with the American marque of the same name), and saw widespread service in two forms, series 1 and 2, but the differences were minimal. In total well over 10,000 were produced in the war years.

An interesting footnote is that post-war the Welbike was produced by Excelsior as the civilian Corgi Scooter with an Excelsior Spryt engine; this too was a sales success in its own right.

Above: British Army airborne transport officer checks motorcycles as they are made fast to the floor of a Horsa glider.

WINNERS AND LOSERS

The Allies won the war but which motorcycles were adjudged to have been the most successful in military service during the conflict? If quantity was the yardstick, then Great Britain would have to be awarded the prize – it built more military bikes during the war than anyone else. Its most popular models being BSA 126,000 (mostly side-valve M20s), Norton 100,000 (side valve 16H), AMC 80,000 (mostly Matchless G3/L series), Ariel 47,600 (W-NG ohv), and Royal Enfield 29,000 (WDRE 2-stroke). These figures do not include Triumph as their factory was destroyed in November 1940, and although production was restarted at a temporary site near Warwick, the main production did not re-start until mid-war with the opening of a new green field site at Meriden near Coventry. Velocette received an order for 13,000 of its MDD-WD 348cc ohv model from France in 1940, but before delivery could really get under way France fell. A total of 1,300 from this order were sold on to the British government, plus another 5,000 (most of which went to the RAF). Added to the above were much smaller numbers from the likes of Cotton, Douglas, James and Welbike, making a grand total of aroudn 420,000 British manufactured machines – a truly staggering figure.

Nobody else could match these figures, the nearest being the United States, followed by Germany, with Italy a distant fourth. Also of interest is Japan who built a total of some 18,000 Rikuo's in either 1200 or 750cc engine sizes. These side valve v-twins were based heavily on the pre-war Harley-Davidson. There was also an assorted array of machines in much smaller numbers from Asahi, Meguro and Cabton; plus some 3-wheelers similar to those built by Italian firms.

Below: British dispatch riders 'at school' in 1941. They are riding Ariel ohv singles.

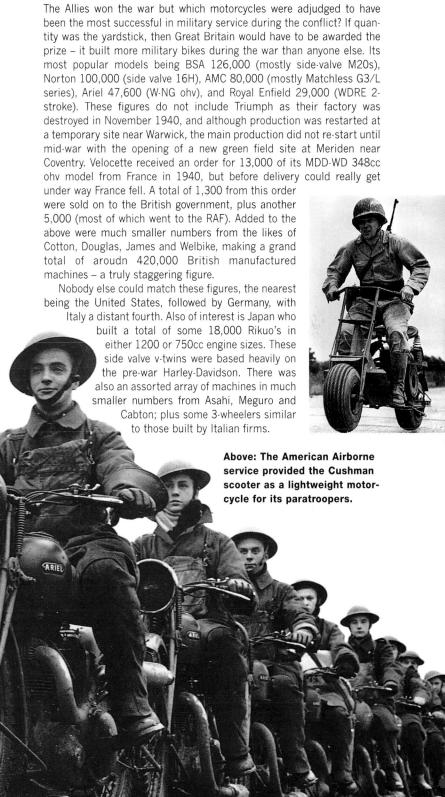

Above: The American Airborne service provided the Cushman scooter as a lightweight motorcycle for its paratroopers.

the Post-War Era

EXPORT TO SURVIVE

Great Britain might have been on the winning side, but when the war finally ended in the spring of 1945 the nation was at a low financial ebb. The long years of conflict had taken their toll and peace brought almost as many problems as had the fighting.

As for the country's motorcycle manufacturers, the questions were what to produce and what markets to pursue. At home, both the general public and the mass of returning young former servicemen with accumulated pay provided what seemed a ready-made opportunity, with the major requirement being ride-to-work machinery.

As for imports, the British economy was in no shape to afford luxury goods from abroad. But in any case the industries of most European competitors had either been bombed off the map or systematically stripped, as in the case of BMW, with materials, machine tools and plant fittings taken as war reparations by the victorious allies.

Although the domestic market appeared to fulfil all sales requirements wider economic forces were at play. The stark fact was that Great Britain Ltd was as good as bankrupt. A combination of overproduction needed to win the war and borrowing from other countries, notably the USA, had left Britain with a massive trade deficit. It was a case of, as the famous phrase from Sir Stafford Cripp's budget speech bluntly put it: 'Export or Bust'.

In motorcycle terms he specifically demanded no less than a staggering 258 per cent of the 1938 export figure by 1948. The manufacturers responded and following the series of measures outlined below, had achieved 278 per cent by November 1947.

How was this miracle achieved? For a start virtually every new motorcycle built went overseas. Models were streamlined so as to make best use of men, materials and production, with Triumph, for example, building only twin cylinder models in the immediate post-war era. But this export drive was not without its problems. The home market had to be satisfied by a combination of pre-war well-worn models and the sale of former WD (War Department) machinery.

Export meant shipping and the resultant need for extra packaging materials and longer transport times than if the bikes had been destined for the home market. When new models or modified models were released first to export markets, it meant any problems were experienced by customers thousands of miles away and were therefore much more difficult to sort out effectively.

Aside from metric instruments where necessary, there was a need for translation of technical and sales literature into a number of foreign languages, which created yet more extra work.

Edward Turner (right), Managing Director of Triumph, with US importer W.E. Johnson Jr.

Quality control was another problem, not only because all British motorcycles of the era used a number of ancillary components from outside suppliers – Smith instruments, Lucas electrical equipment and Amal carburettors for example – but also the major motorcycle manufacturers' own ruthless quest for ever more ways of keeping cost per unit down. All this was at odds with building a top quality product.

But even with all these problems the British motorcycle industry did a lot of things correctly and was a vital part of putting the nation's economy back on a sounder footing. The main overseas markets were the USA, Canada, Australia and Europe, in that order. In fact, it would be true to say that BSA, Triumph and Norton were soon to become household names overseas. Triumph, in particular carved a reputation in north America to rival even the home-produced Harley-Davidson and Indian machines in the eyes of most Stateside riders.

Opposite: A 1949 advertisement for Matchless, when virtually every newly produced British bike went for export.

Left: the BSA works in Birmingham, 20 February 1952, where they were able to produce a new motorcycle every four minutes.

ITALY, HOME OF LIGHTWEIGHTS AND SCOOTERS

After the war the Italians were able to resume peacetime production of motorcycles faster than anyone else. Of the really big companies, only Benelli's facilities at Pesaro on the Adriatic Coast had been extensively damaged during the conflict. In a country starved of personal transport for almost six years, everything on wheels was snapped up in the first few months of peace.

The old-established marques such as Bianchi, Moto Guzzi, Gilera and MM mainly offered updated pre-war designs, except for the tiny Guzzi Motoleggera with its 65cc rotary-valve 2-stroke engine, which soon proved the most popular motorcycle in Italy. Other early sales successes included the 48cc pull-rod 4-stroke Ducati Cucciolo (Little Pup) and 49cc 2-stroke Garelli Mosquito micro-motors, and not least the highly popular Lambretta and Vespa scooters.

The first post-war Milan Show was staged in December 1946, at which several brand new designs made their bow. Noteworthy among these was the futuristic fully-enclosed Miller-Balsamo Jupiter, with a 248cc ohv 4-stroke engine. The remainder of the 1940s saw the motorcycle rapidly establish itself as a major force on the Italian industrial scene with a flood of new marques, such as Capriolo, Motom, Aermacchi, FB Mondial, Rumi, Moto Morini, MV Agusta and Parilla to name only a few.

Many of these new names were large organisations who were unable to build their conventional products after the war. These included Capriolo (Caproni), Aermacchi (Macchi) and MV Agusta (Agusta) – all three of which had played a major role in supplying aviation products to the Italian government during the conflict. Ducati was another similarly affected, although they had supplied radio equipment.

In 1950, three out of five motorcycles registered in Italy that year were Guzzi's. But it was the scooter manufacturers, Lambretta and Vespa who really built the biggest numbers in the two-wheel game. This caused several established motorcycle manufacturers, including MV Agusta and Iso, to enter the scooter field.

If 1950 had been a good year, 1951 was even better with all classes

Above: Ducati launched its 175cc ohv Cruiser scooter in 1952. But its high cost and complexity stunted sales.

Left: Line upon line of Motom ultra-lightweights awaiting delivery from the Milanese factory in 1955.

showing substantial increases. In total there were a staggering 1,112,500 registrations.

Perhaps the manufacturers then became complacent, because in 1952 there were a number of models introduced which proved expensive flops. Notable examples were the Ducati 175 Cruiser ohv 4-stroke scooter, a 350cc vertical ohv twin from Parilla, an FB Mondial scooter with electric starting and the Comet 175cc ohv twin designed by Ing. Drusiani (creator of the triple world 125cc championship-winning FB Mondial). But even so registrations overall continued on an upward spiral.

Two interesting names appeared on the scene in the shape of luxury car specialists Maserati and Ferrari of Milan, although the latter had no connection with the famous car maker. But neither really made a lasting impact, although the Maserati 250 of 1954 had the distinction of being the first ever production motorcycle to sport a disc brake.

The year 1956 was when the Italian motorcycle industry finally reached its first post-war peak in sales, and was followed by the onset of a mini recession. It was also the year when the total number of two-wheelers on Italy's roads passed the three million mark for the first time.

The Milan Show at the end of that year saw the Aermacchi Chimera and IMN Rocket acclaimed as the star exhibits, but both were to prove resounding sales flops. However, there were other models at this show which were to play an important role in the Italian motorcycle industry over the next few years. Heading these was the prototype 175cc overhead camshaft Ducati Sport. This bike was to sire a whole family of bevel drive singles, stretching from 98 to 436cc, over the next two decades. Another was the first Capriolo 124cc with its unique face cam motor.

In 1959 the Italian government gave a helping hand to a beleaguered industry in the form of a new highway code. This meant that both 50cc moped and scooters plus ultra-lightweight motorcycles of certain weight and power restrictions were to be favoured by tax and licence exemptions. So as the decade came to a close there was a new sales boom for this category of machines with Italian manufacturers quickly jumping on the bandwagon.

GERMANY
INDUSTRIAL GROWTH AND DECLINE

Germany's political and economic structure was thrown on its head after the end of the Second World War when four zones of occupation – American, British, French and Russian – were established and the pre-war capital Berlin was divided into four sectors. It was agreed that there should be two states: a capitalist Germany in the West and a communist Germany in the East. Following free elections in West Germany, the Federal Republic was formed in September 1949, with its capital in Bonn. The next month, the Russians proclaimed their occupied zone a state, calling it the German Democratic Republic, with its seat of power in the eastern sector of Berlin.

In West Germany the motorcycle industry rose like a phoenix from the ashes of the Second World War to a position that by the mid-1950s was the envy of the two-wheel world, only to retract drastically before the end of the decade.

The reason for the industry's decline ironically lay in the success of the West German people themselves. German post-war motorcycle production had begun to resume by 1947 at a time when even in the western sector the standard of living was for the majority only just above the very bare existence level. These circumstances conditioned the type of machines purchased, hence they were in the main simple utility models. In the early 1950s the accent switched to technical innovation, performance and luxury, and clearly mirrored the vast improvement in living standards. As a result, the requirements of the West German road user switched from two to four wheels, even though for a short period this was

partially masked by sales of scooters and micro cars (with either three or four wheels). Many of the latter were produced by the traditional motorcycle manufacturers.

Initially a high level of road taxation and insurance rates for cars, plus astronomical German fuel prices, increased the ranks of the motorcyclists. Many professional people such as doctors and lawyers, who in Britain or America would have normally used a car, in Germany rode a motorcycle or scooter.

By the end of 1953, for example, there were more than 2,100,000 motorcycles, mopeds and scooters registered in West Germany. Total output for the industry that same year was 437,500 machines. Not only was this a record for Germany but it was higher than any other country's output of two-wheelers.

All this only served to heighten what was to sadly prove a sense of false security within the entire industry. Many companies over-extended themselves in the headlong stampede for new, more complex (and more expensive) models. The crunch came in the middle of the decade when the majority of these new models were coming on stream.

Even BMW was to be affected, although they had relied on speedy improvements and refinements to their basic 250 single, 500 and 600cc twins, rather than, like the majority, unveiling new designs at a seemingly frenetic pace in a bid to stay ahead of the game. A *Motor Cycle* report in their 25 October 1956 issue said it all in their headline: 'Retrenchment in Germany. Largest-ever Frankfurt show. Serious Over-production: Possible Market for Small-capacity three- and four-wheelers.'

For although the show was a massive, glittering occasion and saw a mass of new and potentially exciting models, the flourish of trumpets was misleading. In truth the industry was alarmed. Not only had the producers overproduced, but their designs were largely unwanted as potential buyers melted away to purchase their first cars – thanks in no small part to the prosperity which was the result of the German economic miracle. By the end of the 1950s very few companies had survived. For those that did, like BMW, it had only been by the skin of their corporate teeth.

Giving BMW as an example, financial problems through 1957, '58 and '59 meant that the company was effectively bankrupt and was saved only by the leadership of Dr Herbert Quandt and support from understanding banking officials. Without doubt, if BMW had been British it would have been thrown to the dogs.

Meanwhile in the regulated East there were no such problems, the state-owned MZ and Simson marques enjoyed stability for many decades until the Berlin Wall came down in 1989, when they experienced almost a repeat of what had happened to the West German bike industry of the late 1950s.

Above: The Heinkel Tourist scooter was a high quality product, which ultimately suffered because of the mass-produced small family car.

Right: DKW advert for the RT350, a deluxe touring model with twin cylinder two-stroke engine.

The German Triumph factory (sold in export markets under the
TWN label) produced a wide range of two-strokes, including the
200cc Cornet.

AM

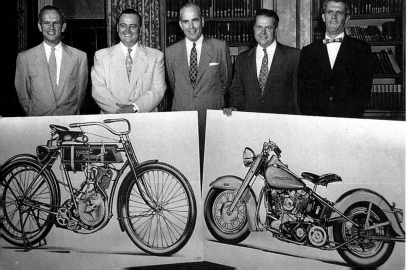

Above: Bill Tuman, on an Indian Scout, after winning the 20-mile National at Bay Meadows on 22 June 1952. He set a new US record for distance, winning in 14 minutes 41.9 seconds.

Left: Second generation of Davidsons and Harleys pictured during the early 1950s, with a then current v-twin and a 1903 model.

Both Harley-Davidson and Indian built many thousands of machines for the American military during the Second World War.

Both expected to make something of a killing post-war, reasoning that there would be a pent-up demand from the vast numbers of GIs returning from wartime service who would be splashing out their accumulated horde of dollars on a new motorcycle.

During the early post-war era in 1946 and 1947, American registrations of two-wheeler motor vehicles did in fact double to around 400,000 units, but growth was made up largely by a massive surge of imports.

This meant that neither Harley-Davidson nor Indian benefited as they had hoped. Of the two, Harley fared the best with its E, EL, F & FL ('Knucklehead') up to 1947, and the EL, FL & FLH ('Panhead') from 1948 onwards. These were v-twins and continued to sell in sufficient numbers to keep the Milwaukee, Wisconsin factory in the black.

Until 1949, all Harleys went by letter or number, or by a nickname (hence Knucklehead and Panhead). But when the company introduced the Hydra-Glide with its new telescopic front forks names took over to denote particular models.

Meanwhile Indian were to be plagued by countless problems. First was that not enough Chief v-twins could be made. Then the new designs promised to dealers didn't arrive in any numbers until 1949 onwards (prototypes had appeared as early as 1946). These included the Arrow single and Scout/Warrior twins. All featured vertical cylinders. Even when these bikes appeared they were not without their faults.

But if all this wasn't enough, in September 1948 the British government devalued the pound sterling from approximately $4 to around $3, which effectively lowered the stateside prices of British motorcycles by between 20 and 25 per cent. This was a hammer blow to Indian and instead of being excited by the prospect of launching their new models

A Harley-Davidson 1213cc Duo Glide, King of the Road in the 1950s, gleaming in US showroom.

they were forced that November to lay off almost a quarter of their 1,000 strong workforce.

The result of this was that company president Ralph B. Rogers went to England the following month to seek a $1.5 million loan from the British company, J. Brockhouse.

In April 1949, as a precondition of the $1.5 million Brockhouse cash injection, Indian agreed to what represented a takeover by the British company. This in turn led the Indian Motorcycle Company to allow the marketing of the following British marques through its existing dealership network: AJS, Douglas, Excelsior, Matchless, Norton, Royal Enfield and HRD Vincent. If ever there was a 'Trojan Horse' deal in motorcycling this was it.

Indian also continued to produce its new singles and vertical twins, but these were effectively sold at a loss as they were unable to compete with the cheaper British imports. The coup was completed in January 1950, when John Brockhouse replaced Rogers as Indian's president.

Chief v-twins continued to be built in decreasing numbers until 1953. In 1954 Indian dealers could only offer the Royal Enfield range and from 1955 until the end of the decade these were offered as badge-engineered 'Indians'. Thereafter, Associated Motor Cycles (AMC), makers of AJS and Matchless and owners of several other British marques (including Norton) acquired the Indian distribution network. Finally in 1962, AMC closed the operation, terminated all American jobs, and sold their distribution rights to the Berliner Corporation of New Jersey. Berliner never used the Indian name.

If all this sounds complicated, the rest of the American industry once H-D and Indian is taken out of the picture certainly isn't, simply because there were no other US marques of any real note. It was left therefore to first the Europeans and then the Japanese to really exploit the American market's true sales potential.

The Berliner Corporation, headed by the brothers Joseph and James, had made their name by importing German makes during the 1950s; notably Zündapp. Besides British imports, the first foreign bikes to hit north American shores were of German origin. These included not only Zündapp, but also BMW, NSU and Horex.

Next came the Italians with a myriad of marques including Aermacchi (marketed by Harley-Davidson), Benelli, Capriolo, Ducati (marketed by Berliner), Garelli, Gilera, Parilla, Lambretta and Vespa. And finally the end of the 1950s saw the arrival of the all-conquering Japanese.

ERICA
STAGNATION OF THE HOME PRODUCT & GROWTH OF IMPORTS

SIDECARS

Once the motorcycle had become firmly established the next question was how could it carry more people? The earliest examples of the 'side-car' arrived just after the turn of the century and by 1903 a couple of firms were already offering them for sale. Most sidecar bodies at this time were of wicker work to cut down on weight.

Following the First World War there was an urgent need to provide motorized transport for the family. This meant that not only were there many specialised sidecar manufacturers, but also that several early motorcycle makers entered into the field. The latter group included such names as BSA, Matchless, Royal Enfield, Sunbeam, Douglas, Phelon & Moore (later known as Panther), Dunelt, Raleigh, Ariel, New Imperial, Chater-Lea and Triumph.

Of the many Continental European manufacturers the two most important names are without doubt both German: BMW and Steib. BMW built their own sidecars for many years, whilst Steib only made 'chairs' and were represented by the dealers Bryants of Biggleswade, Befordfordshire until 1938 and thereafter by Frazer Nash of Middlesex.

In 1936 there were half a million motorcycles on British roads, of which no less than a quarter hauled sidecars. Whilst by 1939 there were three sidecar combinations to every ten solos. The third wheel had proved it was here to stay.

But the sidecar's real heyday was that of the immediate postwar peri-od in the late 1940s and throughout the 1950s. With the ending of the

The British Automobile Association (AA) used the BSA21 and box sidecar in the 1950s as patrol vehicles to help their technicians reach motorists who had broken down.

conflict established sidecar manufacturers returned with renewed energy. With increased demand many new firms sprang up to join the established names such as Swallow, Watsonian, Blacknell, BSA, Garrard and Panther.

The mid-1950s brought the new plastic glass-fibre. One of the first sidecars to enter production using this material was the Watsonian Bambini, a single seater for lightweights and Scooters.

With the advent of the 1960s, sidecar sales began the slump from which they never fully recovered. There were two main reasons: ever more sporting motorcycles, many with frames not suitable for a third wheel and the Mini, which brought affordable four wheels to even the most economy-minded family.

Today sidecars survive only with the committed enthusiast and rep-resent only a tiny segment of the overall bike scene.

COMMUTER BIKES
CHEAP TO BUY, CHEAP TO RUN BRITISH 2-STROKES

Launched in July 1958, the Ariel Leader was a fully equipped 250cc two-stroke twin.

With their role now neatly filled by a second (or even third) car, it might seem unlikely but much of Britain in the 1950s went to work, rest and play on one of the myriad of small capacity two-stroke motorcycles manufactured by domestic bike builders.

When it could last be said that British motorcycles ruled the world, a large percentage of its bikes were not the much loved large capacity sporting single and twin cylinder four-strokes that are so fondly remembered by the classics brigade, but more simple piston port two-strokes from the likes of BSA, Royal Enfield, Greeves, Francis Barnett and James.

Some of the most popular bikes included the various BSA Bantam models. These first appeared in 1948 as the DI and its 123cc engine was an unashamed copy of the DKW RT125. In the next quarter of a century thousands were built, the last B175 leaving the production line during March 1971. The Royal Enfield two-stroke could also trace its origins back to DKW and resulted in a whole series of models stretching from the wartime 126cc RE ML to the 148cc Prince which finally went out of production in 1962. Although many thousands were built a large proportion of these were bought by the British Army or the Royal Mail.

But the vast majority of Brit two-strokes were powered by Villiers engines built in Wolverhampton in the West Midlands. There was a truly amazing array of engine sizes ranging from a 98cc single through to a 324cc twin and an almost unending list of marques which used these power plants, from Aberdale to Tandon.

Towards the end of the 1950s there appeared the Ariel Leader. This was the result, or so it was claimed, of substantial market research. Designed by a team led by the factory's Chief Designer Val Page, the Leader's 246cc (54 x 54 mm) two-stroke twin engine was inspired by the German Adler MB250 and first appeared in July 1958. It combined agile handling and a respectable speed (70 mph/113 kmh) with clean, quiet convenience. But although in many ways a trend-setting machine which offered motorcycle performance and handling with scooter-like weather protection, the Leader never sold in vast numbers.

A true light-weight bike, the 1940 125cc Royal Enfield 'Flying Flea' was a copy of a DKW design, and was later developed as a paratrooper bike.

(Britain 1924-55)

Founded in 1924 in Wolverhampton by TT Winner Howard Raymond Davies, the original HRD Motors manufactured high quality sporting motorcycles using frames produced in-house and specially-built JAP engines. The model 90 featured a single port 499cc JAP motor and the Super 90, a twin port racing JAP unit with a maximum speed approaching the magic 100 mph (160 kmh). All models featured hand change, three-speed Burman gearboxes.

HRD went into receivership in 1927, but machines continued to be built until early 1928. The name and assets were purchased from the receiver by Ernie Humphries, who then sold them on to a young Cambridge undergraduate, Philip C. Vincent. He had long been an enthusiast of HRD bikes and needed an established name for the motorcycle's he was about to produce. These newcomers were Vincent-HRDs, featuring Vincent's own patented rear suspension and using JAP or Rudge engines.

Vincent-HRD continued to use proprietary power plants until a disastrous showing at the 1934 TT, when specially-prepared JAP engines proved unreliable. This prompted Vincent to seek the services of the Australian engineer, Phil Irving and the pair then designed the 499cc engine for the Series A Vincent.

From this relationship came such famous post-war models as the Comet and Gray Flash singles and, most of all, the now legendary Rapide, Black Shadow, Black Lightning and Black Prince 998cc ohv v-twins. Production may have ceased in 1955, but certainty not the legend.

Both before and after their demise, Vincent machines were used to power a number of record breakers. In America both Rollie Free and Marty Dickinson used the Stevenage-made v-twins to set new world and AMA (American Motorcycle Association) records at Bonneville Salt Flats, Utah. Then in Britain George Brown (a Vincent dealer and former racer) created first Nero and then Super Nero to take on and beat the best in the world of sprinting for over two decades.

(Italy 1950-72)

Although it never won a world title under its own name, nonetheless Aermacchi is still one of the most notable names in Italian motorcycle racing folklore. In addition, under the Harley-Davidson tag, Aermacchi two-strokes garnered a quartet of titles in the mid-1970s, with Walter Villa as rider.

The company, based in Varese, had a long history, but much of it in aviation circles. It was not until 1950 that Aermacchi entered the two-wheel arena. For the first decade Aermacchi concentrated its efforts on roadsters, albeit with the odd dirt bike or record breaker thrown in. Then in 1960 two events changed the company's future prospects. The first was a financial tie-up with the American Harley-Davidson concern; the second was teenager Alberto Pagani's results in the Dutch TT and Belgium GP on what was essentially a converted Ala Verde roadster. This was instrumental in convincing Aermacchi to build 'over-the-counter' versions for sale to private customers.

Realizing the limitations of the design, the Varese marque then moved into two-strokes. First came a 125cc single in 1968, followed a couple of years later by the prototype of the twin cylinder model that was to prove so successful in later years.

These developments were mirrored in the street bikes: the Ala Verde (named the Sprint in North America) horizontal four-stroke single and later the SS 350, making way for a variety of two-strokes in the mid- to late 1970s. From 1972 onward these were sold under the AMF Harley-Davidson banner. Finally, in the summer of 1978, Cagiva took over and a new era was born.

(Britain 1904-68)

Percy and Eugene Goodman were the men behind the creation of the Velocette marque. It was Percy Goodman's 1913 206cc two-stroke single which firmly established Velocette on the motor-cycling map. Velocette also went, racing, first with tuned versions of its two-stroke before becoming converts to the four-stroke.

Sporting success throughout the 1920s and 1930s did much to publicize the Velocette marque and sales of production roadsters flourished. Models such as the KTS and the KSS overhead camshaft models were highly respected, whilst the famous KTT was the customer version of the factory's race-winning 350. In fact Velocette was the first machine to win the 350cc World Championship, when Freddie Frith took the title in 1949, with Bob Foster continuing the feat the following year.

During the 1950s the Hall Green factory, Birmingham, developed the 349cc Viper and 499cc Venom ohv singles. In 1961 one of the latter, Venom Clubman, with an Avon fairing and megaphone exhaust, but otherwise remarkably standard machine, averaged over 100 mph at the Montlhéry circuit near Paris for 24 hours, to set a new world record for the distance.

Viper and Venom machines did well in Sport Machine racing and then, in 1964 Velocette introduced its ultimate sporting roadster, the Thruxton.

Although its sports singles were revered by enthusiasts all around the globe the company's management did not always get it right. Notable failures were the small capacity machines such as the Victory Scooter and the Vogue enclosed motorcycle. Even the more successful LE and Valiant models failed to attract customers in the numbers originally anticipated. This, combined with the relatively small sales of the expensive Thruxton, so weakened Velocette that it could not recover and the company went into liquidation in 1968.

(Germany 1920-)

Although BMW (Bagerische Motoren Werke) can trace its history back to the 19th century, the first BMW motorcycle did not appear until after the end of the First World War. Its first efforts began in 1920 with development work on a machine using a proprietary Kurier 148cc two-stroke engine. Named the Flink, it was not a commercial success. Next, in 1921, came the introduction of an engine which was to map out BMW's two-wheel future. Designed by Martin Stolle it was a 493cc horizontal twin side valve four-stroke. Besides being used by BMW to power its own Helios machine it was also supplied to rival firms like Victoria.

The first true BMW came in 1923, when the R32 was launched at the Paris Show, powered by a direct descendant of the 1922 M2 B15 engine from the Helios. A major difference was that it was mounted transversely, in unit with a three-speed gearbox and shaft final drive – the Helios featured fore- and aft-mounting and chain drive.

The R32 was the beginning of a virtually unbroken line which still exists today, albeit in modernised form. The only other engine layouts were various vertical singles which spanned the late 1920s through to the late 1960s and the K-series three-and four-cylinder models which began with the K100 of 1983.

From 1928-50, BMW built supercharged racers for a number of riders, including Georg Meier and Walter Zeller. When Germany became a member of the FIM in 1951 and was unable to use superchargers, a special version of the horizontal twin using overhead cams instead of overhead valves was built. It found a niche in sidecar racing and went on to win no less than 19 world titles. Drivers included Florian Camathias, Max Duebel Klaus Enders, Fritz Hillebrand and Fritz Scheidegger.

SPAIN
A NEW INDUSTRY IS BORN

No country in Europe has changed so dramatically over the last half century as Spain. From a rural, pre-industrial society ruled by a Fascist dictator, the country has become a modern, thrusting democracy and an integral part of the European Community.

The key to this change was the unique combination of stability under one leader, the promotion of industrialisation, and a protectionist system that was maintained throughout Franco's reign. And nowhere was this to act to such good effect as in the motorcycle sector during the immediate post-war period.

At the end of the Civil War of 1936-39, won by General Franco's Nationalists, Spain was a country almost broken in two by strife, but unlike the majority of other Western European nations, it managed to escape involvement in the Second World War. It was during this period, when other nations were committed to the vast expense in lives and money that was the result of total war, that Spain took its first hesitant steps on the road to modernization.

Prior to the war, although Spain was still largely a rural country, it had been able to import luxury goods such as cars and motorcycles from France, Britain and Germany. But with these countries committed to war production, Spain became unable to meet its transport requirements. The need for self-sufficiency created a climate ideal for it's early motorcycle producers to grow and prosper.

The first two companies, Sanglas and Montesa, had already laid the foundations for their respective ventures well in advance of VE (Victory in Europe) Day in the spring of 1945. This gave the emerging industry both an excellent start, and when war in Europe finally ceased Franco imposed strict import controls to prevent foreign competition from posing threats to the its local manufacturers.

By the end of the 1940s, Montesa was well established and sufficiently confident to send a race team (with 125cc bikes) to the Dutch TT in 1948. Sanglas meanwhile were as modern a concern as could be found anywhere in the world, being one of the first manufacturers to fit telescopic forks to all its production models.

But it was the 1950s which really saw the expansion of Spain's bike builders. The boom began with the arrival of the Derbi and Osso marques, followed quickly by a proliferation of other, smaller producers often using Hispano-Villers engines (British Villiers designs built under licence). By the end of the

Derbi 250cc Super

Jawa-influenced Derbi 250cc Super, the Spanish company's first real motorcycle which started production in 1950.

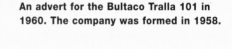

Left: The highly successful pairing of Jorge Sirera and Eduardo Werring racing their 125cc Montesa and sidecar in the late 1950s.

An advert for the Bultaco Tralla 101 in 1960. The company was formed in 1958.

decade, the major players had been joined by Bultaco and Mototrans (the latter licence-builders of Italian Ducatis) to complete a picture of a relatively large motorcycle industry which had taken only 15 years to evolve from nothing.

Of all the Spanish marques, Bultaco is perhaps the most famous, founded by Francisco Xavier Bulto. Probably uniquely in motorcycle history, the company had its origins following events in another company's boardroom. In May 1958, a meeting of directors was called at Montesa, then the largest of Spain's bike builders. There had been heated disputes for some time over a single, central issue – to race or not to race – and this meeting was to be the watershed.

Together with Pedro Permanyer, Bulto had founded Montesa in 1945, and the pair were its largest shareholders. Now they found themselves at opposite sides of completely unreconcilable views. Permanyer was backed by other company directors in the opinion that the factory should withdraw from racing, whereas Bulto believed that the firm's racing involvement and reputation were interlinked and without it he saw no future for himself at Montesa.

So he left to pursue other business interests until persuaded by a group of former Montesa engineers to set up a rival company This was to build a 125cc road bike, which could not only be sold in satisfactory numbers as a means of transport, but would also form the basis of a simple, effective racer. And so was born Bultaco, who over the next quarter of a century were to not only build some of the best Spanish roadsters and racers, but title-winning motocross and trial bikes too. Bultaco's sporting successes convinced its rivals to follow suit.

With a 594cc engine, the BMW R60 (made from 1955 until 1969) was equally suitable for solo or sidecar use.

BMW TWINS

During the years 1954 to 1955, BMW had carried out a mini-redesign of their long-running horizontally-opposed twin cylinder range. Essentially the German company needed something new and exciting to offer the public in the face of flagging sales. The new models had to be different and this was difficult for are a manufacturer committed to a certain design philosophy.

So, for 1955 the new models had a completely redesigned frame, the most striking features of which were the Earles-type fork of the front and swinging arm rear suspension. The 19-inch wheels of the older models were replaced by 18 inch items and were equipped with twin-leading shoe front brakes. The new models were the same internally as their fore-runners – 494cc (68 x 68 mm) and 594cc (72 x 73 mm) – but they were re-designated R50, R60 and R69. The trio were launched in a blaze of publicity at the 38th Brussels Show in January 1955.

Besides the frame and suspension there were other major changes to the bikes: an enclosed shaft drive within the offside leg of the swinging arm, a deeper fuel tank with a lockable toolbox whose lid formed the left knee grip, interchangeable wheel hubs, new silencers and mudguards; however, the bikes still wore the traditional sombre black finish with white pinstriping. Engines were largely unchanged, but there were some improvements and the transmission now featured a diaphragm clutch and a new three-stage gearbox.

An R69 was tested by *Motor Cycling* in April 1956 and recorded a maximum speed of 102 mph (164 kmh). But the real bonus of these machines was comfort – they felt like the kind of bike you could ride all day without getting tired.

At the end of the 1950s the R50S and R69S were introduced. The bigger of the two benefited from some engine technology gleaned from BMW's racing experience. There was a vibration damper at the end of the crankshaft and the main bearings were designed to cope with whip and flex in the crank. The top-of-the-line R69S produced 42 bhp at 7,000 rpm and was good for 110 mph (177 kmh). The suspension was also uprated and the larger model received a steering damper.

These machines remained unchanged until replaced by the telescopic forked 5 models a decade later, but for 15 years they gave sterling service to their owners.

A couple of 1962 ISDT 'works' BMW Twins. These machines were basically standard production roadsters specially prepared for the event.

POLICE SERVICE

As far as Europe was concerned, it was not until 1921 that the streets of London reverberated to the sound of a police motorcycle engine. Scotland Yard, increasingly concerned by the rising number of criminals using either cars or bikes as a means of getting away from the scene of a crime, were looking for a way to fight this new trend.

Their answer was a prototype squad of officers equipped with BSA sidecar combinations who roared around searching out criminals at work and enforcing the then mandatory, 20 mph (32 kmh) speed limit of Britain's capital.

Although four wheeled patrols were a common feature of police work in the 1920s, the Metropolitan Police did not go fully operational on two wheels until 1931. That was when over 60 BSA and Matchless sidecar outfits took to the streets for the first time: the Metropolitan Police Traffic Division was born.

The success of the British police motorcyclist led to other European countries taking the idea on board and during the early post-war period they had become very much an established part of life in almost every country of the world.

In fact national prestige was often at stake and many patrol forces were truly famous, including Sweden's 'White Mice' on BMWs, West Germany's *Traffic Schutzpolitzei* who also used BMWs, Italian autostrada police with their Moto Guzzi Falcone singles and of course the various American State Highway patrols with their giant Harley-Davidson v-twins.

As for the Metropolitan Police, they, like the rest of the British constabulary were by now kitted out with Triumph twins for highway patrol and the famous Velocette LE 'Noddy Bike' for local duties, a task that during the next few years would almost disappear, being replaced instead by 'Panda' patrols in small cars.

Finally, in today's safety conscious world, it may come as something of a shock to recall that British police riders did not have crash helmets until 1953; before this a conventional police flat cap was all that was expected to be worn.

A pair of British Police Triumph Speed Twins on escort duty in the City of London during 1958.

RECORD BREAKING EXPLOITS

To many the supreme challenge of motorcycling is not wheel-to-wheel racing against others on road or track but a constant endeavour to create new speed records in solo and sidecar categories designated by the FIM (Federation Internationale Motocycliste).

Eventually, neither Brooklands nor Montlhéry, the French track near Paris, was suitable for the attempts on the most important record of all, the world's motorcycle 'fastest', which at the end of the Second World War stood to the credit of Ernst Henne on a supercharged BMW twin at 174 mph (280 kmh). He had established this in 1937 and it was not until fourteen years later, in April 1951, that a successful attempt to break it was made.

Then as before, the record was snatched by a German rider on a German machine. The man was Wilhelm Herz, his machine a streamlined 499cc supercharged NSU twin and his speed of 180.17 mph (289.8 kmh) on the Munich to Ingoldstadt *autobahn* broke the previous record by 6 mph.

In the same week that Hertz blasted the solo record, his NSU teammate Hermann Böhn broke the three-wheel record with another machine fitted with a 'spatted' braced wheel. But his 125 mph (201 kmh) speed didn't satisfy the rider or NSU and six months later he beat his own record by a clear 29 mph (47 kmh) to raise the world's fastest sidecar speed to 154 mph (248 kmh).

These figures stood for some two years whilst factories and private owners alike worked on how to beat NSU's figures. Then, in 1954, there began a three year blaze of activity which was destined to prove, to everyone's amazement, that the world's motorcycle outright speed record could not only be beaten by private owners but also by basic road-going machines.

It all began when Edinburgh-born New Zealander Robert Burns brought out his basically 1951 streamlined Vincent HRD 998cc Rapide V-twin and sidecar and added an extra mile an hour on Böhn's three-wheel speed by recording 155 mph. On the surface this might not seem much of an increase, but in truth it was a wonderful achievement when you consider it was done on a virtually standard machine in New Zealand without any of the elaborate factory backing or organisation which had accompanied the NSU records.

If all this wasn't enough another New Zealander, Russell Wright, attained 185 mph (298 kmh) on a famed Black Lightning Vincent to break Herz's four-year-old NSU solo record by 5 mph.

Of course the Germans were hardly going to take his lying down. First up was BMW and on the Munich-Ingolstadt *autobahn* the ex-world sidecar champion Wilhelm Noll recorded 174 mph (280 kmh) to establish a new three-wheeler best.

On the solo front American Johnny Allen achieved 193.7 mph (311.6 kmh) on the famous Utah Salt Flats, only for this to be disallowed by the FIM.

By 1956, NSU had realised that if it wished to improve its speeds it too would have to go to Utah, so at the end of July 1956 the Germans arrived to do battle. And battle they did, ultimately setting a new record of 210.64 mph (338.9 kmh) average for the two-way run. This represented a 25 mph increase over Wright's speed. It was also 18 mph faster than the unofficial speed set by Johnson.

Remolo Ferri successfully breaks the world record over a kilometre on a Lambretta on 10 August 1951.

Other notable exploits of the time include Luigi Cavanna's 137 mph (220 kmh) on a 248cc Moto Guzzi sidecar in 1952, Ray Amm's heroic one-hour record at 133 mph (214 kmh) on a 'Kneeler' 499cc single cylinder Norton at Montlhéry in 1953 and the Ray Amm/Eric Oliver records of up to seven hours at over 120 mph (193 kmh) on a 348cc 'Kneeler' Norton in the same year.

Then there were the never-to-be-forgotten records created by the brilliant rider/designer Gustav Baumm on the 'Hammock' rear-engined NSU – surely the ultimate in streamlined efficiency – in 1954 and 1955. On the 49cc version he covered a mile at 93.5 mph (150 kmh); with a 98cc engine the same distance was clocked at over 111 mph (178 kmh) and with the 124cc behind him he registered a fantastic 135 mph (217 kmh), which beat many existing records in classes right up to 350cc.

But probably the greatest of all record-breaking stints of the era was Bob McIntyre's incredible 141 miles (227 kmh) in one hour at Monza in the autumn of 1957 on a 349cc Edera four cylinder road racer. What made this so difficult was the state of the bumpy track, with the machine often leaving the ground.

Of course others came later and bettered all these figures, but considering the technology and the conditions, all the records set here were superb achievements in their own right.

Designer Gustav Baum tries out the NSU 'Flying Hammock' record machine at Hockenheim in 1954.

Flying **Fish**

The 1953 Norton 'Flying Fish' record bike was ridden by Ray Amm and Eric Oliver with which they broke many records at Montlhéry.

BRITISH SPORTING SINGLES & TWINS

When hostilities ended in 1945 Britain was at a low financial ebb and virtually everything manufactured in the first four years of peace had to go for export. But by 1950 the situation was stabilizing and new designs, previously only available to foreign buyers, began to be available on the home market.

The Isle of Man the previous summer had provided potential buyers several things about which to get excited. That period showpiece for the finest in British iron, the Clubman's TT, had seen a trio of winners guaranteed to make any red-blooded enthusiast's heart beat faster in the shape of the various class winners.

The 1000cc race attracted 10 starters, of which nine were 998cc Vincent-HRD v-twins, the winner being the Watford & Bushey club member, D.G. Lashmar. The 350cc race saw victory go to one of the new BSA Gold Star models ridden by Manchester Eagle clubman H. Clark.

But the real interest centred on the 500's. Here it seemed likely to be an epic battle between the wily old veteran Allan Jefferies on a Triumph Tiger 100 twin and the youngster Geoff Duke who was already being tipped as a future world champion, riding a single cylinder ohv Norton International. Both the 350 and 500cc entries were much larger than the 1000cc category, with 70 and 60 starters respectively – and not a foreign model in sight!

From BSA came not only the 348 and 499cc Gold Star singles, but also the pre-unit ohv twins in the shape of the 497cc A7 and 646cc A10, the sporting versions being Shooting Star, Road Rocket, Super Rocket and Rocket Gold Star. The most sporting of these models were the pair of Gold Star singles and the Rocket Gold Star; but the latter was only offered for two years, and then during the early 1960s.

In September 1949 the first three production models of Triumph's new Thunderbird made the headlines by each running at over 92 mph (148 kmh) average speed for 500 miles (800 km) and then did a flying lap of over 100 mph (160 kmh). The Thunderbird was a larger 649cc version of Edward Turner's masterpiece, the Speed Twin which had first appeared in 1937 to such acclaim.

Like their BSA counterparts there were to be several sporting models developed from these two, basically, tourers – the Tiger 100, Tiger 110 and the most famous of all, the T120 Bonneville.

Unlike BSA with their Gold Star, Norton sadly failed to develop their International models, even though the final variant got as far as having Featherbed frames and Roadholder front forks. Instead it was left to the Dominator twin.

Like its BSA and Triumph counterparts the 'Dommie' was produced in more than one engine size. In fact there were more models and engine sizes than the other two marques together, if one discounts the later BSA/Triumph unit construction models.

The first Norton twin was the Model 7 in 1948. This, like the later 88, used a 497cc engine capacity. Next in 1956 came the 77 and 99 with a larger 596cc engine. It should be noted that only the 88 and 99 of these models sported the Featherbed frame, originally conceived for the factory's Manx dohc single racers. Finally in 1960 the engine grew again to 646cc. (later still it was to grow still more to 745cc for the Atlas in 1962, originally purely for export).

Other sports roadsters of the era included the 998cc Vincent-HRD v-twin in its various states of tune and the AJS and Matchless 498, 593 and 646cc vertical twins; of which the CSR variants were the quickest. Royal Enfield also built a number of vertical twins, with 495, 496, 693 and 736cc sizes. Not to be outdone, Ariel offered 497 and 646cc twins which owed a lot to the BSA A7/10 series.

On the singles front, besides the Gold Star and International, the best of the bunch were the Ariel Red Hunter, Royal Enfield Bullet, the Vincent-HRD Comet and the Velocette Viper and Venom duo.

Sales in Britain peaked in 1959 with record registrations of some 300,000 units. But this was to prove the high water mark for the home-based industry.

Left: The 1959 Velocette Viper Clubmans 350, a much prized machine now and then.

Above: The BSA Gold Star Clubman, which was available with either 348cc or 499cc single cylinder ohv engines.

Built from 1950 through to 1963, the BSA 646cc A10 Golden Flash was typical of many British vertical twins of the same era – it was what the industry made best.

the Rising Sun

THE EARLY YEARS

Today, Japan is universally accepted as the world's foremost industrial power in many sections of engineering, not least motorcycles. It has vast production facilities, cutting edge technology, worldwide sales and plays a major part in all forms of motorcycle sport. To the casual observer marques such as Honda, Suzuki and Yamaha have been there for ever.

But this unchallenged leadership is strictly a post-war phenomenon. Before the Second World War, very few people outside Japan even knew motorcycles were manufactured in the land of the rising sun, and even fewer had been seen, much less ridden one.

In fact, Japan could almost claim to have been something of a pioneering country in the history of powered two-wheelers, the first machine which might be classified as a motorcycle being imported from Germany in 1899. This was a steam-powered device with a pair of large wheels mounting solid rubber tyres, with two tiny outrigger wheels, imported by the Toyko-based Iizuka Trading Company.

Then followed a period when a handful of more conventional internal combustion-engined motorcycles were taken to Japan by foreigners between 1901 and 1905. In 1907, another trading company, this time Isikowa, imported a number of British Triumphs and the same year saw motorcycle racing staged in Japan for the first time. This took place during November, when a number of riders took part in an informal race over the bridle path that circled Veno's Shinobazu lake, following an organized pedal cycle race.

The following year, 1908, Narazo Shimazu designed and built the first ever motorcycle engine manufactured in Japan. This was fitted into one of the imported Triumph frames.

Shimazu's creation was quickly followed by several more, including complete machines, some of which utilised imported engines. Finally, formal official permission was granted from the Japanese government in 1909 to import several different marques on a commercial basis.

Although mainly of British origin, these also included NSU and Progress from Germany and Indian from America. This effectively opened the flood gates and soon companies in both Kyoto and Tokyo were set up to manufacture motorcycles for sale to the public – but again using imported engines.

Japan's second motorcycle race took place in conjunction with a bicycle event at the Chikko Grounds near the harbour in Osaka during 1911. A similar situation arose the next year when motorcycles and bicycles raced (separately) at the Hanshin Horse Race Course in Naruo. Finally, in 1913, the motorcyclists became independent of other sporting bodies when they organized a meeting themselves.

The first all-Japanese 'production' bike appeared in 1913. Built by Miyata, it was powered by a two-stroke engine and was sold under the Asahi (Sunrise) name, but the vast majority of local riders chose imported Western brands. One has to remember that in those far off days only the relatively well-off could afford the luxury of a powered two-wheeler. These young Japanese invariably were only interested in the latest things from America and Europe – it was not fashionable to be seen on a locally-produced product. Due to this state of affairs, the Miyata company was forced to suspend production in 1916. During those four years, a mere 40-odd bikes had been sold!

This was the era when the most popular models were large-capacity Indians and Harley-Davidsons, but from 1920 onwards, British and European marques took over at the top of the sales charts. By the middle of the decade, however, some of Japan's car makers decided to produce motorcycles that would offer a viable alternative to imported types.

In 1926, the nation took motorcycle racing to its heart. Vast crowds watched riders take part in dirt track and road races. Up to 50,000 spectators witnessed hard-fought competitions which were often sponsored by the nation's leading newspapers. In 1957 Kenzo Tada became the first Japanese rider to part in the Isle of Man TT, riding a 350cc Velocette. It was also at this time that many motorcycle clubs were formed. The result was that motorcycling became accessible to a much wider range of people. Motorcyling had become an established part of the nation's life.

Left: The very first Honda motorcycle – the Type A of 1947.

Right: The Hurricane single of 1956 – the cycle parts were modelled on a British Triumph.

(Japan 1946-)

Soichiro Honda was born in 1906, the eldest son of a village blacksmith in Komyo, long since swallowed up by the urban sprawl of modern-day Hamamatsu. He left school in 1922, taking up an apprenticeship in Tokyo as a car mechanic. Later he returned to Hamamatsu, opened his own garage business and with his new found source of income went auto racing. This came to an abrupt end after a serious accident at the Tama River circuit, near Tokyo, in July 1936.

Following this unfortunate incident he sold his dealership and entered the world of manufacturing with a piston ring company. Then came the war, which saw the Honda organisation making aircraft propellers.

In 1946 Honda came back into the business world setting up the Honda Technical Research Institute. At total odds with its grand-sounding title, this venture was based in a tiny wooden hut, little more than a garden shed, on a levelled bomb site on the fringe of Hamamatsu. For once luck was on his side and after uncovering a cache of 500 war-surplus petrol engines, Honda launched himself on the path of motorcycle manufacture; something he was to do with unparalleled success.

The rapid sale of those initial bikes encouraged him to move into motorcycle design. Shortly, after the incorporation of the Honda Motor Company in 1948 it produced over 3,500 98cc Model D two-strokes and by 1953 had built 32,000 Model E four-strokes.

Despite increasing production numbers, Honda realised that to survive the company would have to export bikes on a grand scale. To achieve this Honda used a combination strategy based on clever advertising, producing world championship winners and manufacturing smaller, efficient but reliable bikes at affordable prices. This recipe for success worked to perfection and by the mid-1960s Honda's production levels had reached 130,000 bikes per month. And it has continued its growth to the present time, with not only overseas manufacturing plants being added, but cars too. This latter area has represented a majority in the company's annual turnover, since the mid-1980s.

(Japan 1952-)

Suzuki's origins stem from the year 1909 when Michio Suzuki, its young and aspiring founder, created the Suzuki Loom Company in Hamamatsu, Japan. Business prospered as Suzuki supplied weaving looms to the burgeoning Japanese silk industry. In 1937 the decision was taken to diversify and it negotiated with the British Austin car concern to build the Austin Seven under licence but the outbreak of war dashed these plans.

Following the hostilities, pedal cycles became Japan's main source of personal transport. Following the lead set by Soichiro Honda, a number of companies began to offer small 'clip-on' petrol engines which could be attached to the customer's own bicycle.

Suzuki followed this trend in 1952 by offering their own micro-engine, effectively acting as the spur for a new era in the company's history. Within a year the Power Free was succeeded by the 60cc Diamond Free, the larger engine helping to cope with Japan's mountainous provincial roads.

In 1954, Suzuki announced their first real motorcycle, the 90cc Colleda, which was also their first four-stroke. Then followed a myriad of models featuring both two and four-stroke engines from the 50cc Selped moped to the 250cc Colleda twin.

Besides motorcycles Suzuki also built cars from the mid-1950s, the first examples powered by a small capacity two-stroke. But although Suzuki was becoming a force to be reckoned with on the home market, they were all but unknown outside Japan.

Following once again in Honda's footsteps, Suzuki entered a team in the 1960 Isle of Man TT. Success was not immediate, but after the East German MZ works star Ernst Degner defected at the end of 1961, the company quickly signed him up bringing not just riding skills, but technical information. The result was Degner won Suzuki their first world championship (50cc, in 1962). Many more titles followed, including motorcross.

Track success led to showroom sales and soon a string of new models began to appear, a trend which continues today. Highlights include T20 (1966), GT750 (1971), GS750 (1978), GSX1100 (1981), GSXR750 (1984) and RGV250 (1989).

American Kevin Schwantz and Englishman Barry Sheene are probably the two most famous Suzuki riders, but there are plenty of others who have helped cement the legend.

YAMAHA

(Japan 1954-)

Yamaha conjures up a sporting image with any bike buff, although if its successes in racing, motocross and trials are combined, both Honda and Suzuki could probably boast as many, if not more, victories.

The reason for this image lies in Yamaha's unwavering commitment to racing since the early 1960s, which has included both pukka works machinery and the offering of production 'over-the-counter' bikes for club and national riders around the world.

The company has also manufactured musical instruments (including some of the best pianos in the world), snowmobiles, industrial engines, marine engines, lawnmowers, unmanned helicopters, Formula 1 car engines, industrial robots and even swimming pools!

Although Yamaha only started building motorcycles in the 1950s, its origins actually go back to the last century when Torakusa Yamaha started repairing organs in 1887. It was this that set Yamaha on a course that would eventually lead his company, Nippon Gakki, to become one of the world's foremost manufacturers of musical instruments. Before the turn of the century the company was not only a major supplier on the home market, but had already begun an export drive, which included shipping some 80 organs to Britain in 1892.

Although Torakusa Yamaha died in 1916, Nippon Gakki continued to expand even when its production facilities were badly damaged by Allied bombing in 1945. They were able to slowly struggle back to making musical instruments by 1948.

During 1950 control of the company passed to Genichi Kawakami, then 38 years old. One of his first moves was to take the decision to begin motorcycle production even though the company had no previous experience. Their first model closely followed the German DKW RT125 (as did BSA in Britain with the Bantam).

From this came a long line of ever-improving two-stroke models culminating with the RD-Series in the 1970s and later the LC (Liquid Cooled) range. Running parallel to these developments was a policy of racing similar bikes (TD and TZ).

Like Suzuki, Yamaha have largely switched production to four-strokes, but even today the company still build a number of two-strokes, albeit lightweights.

ENGINES

1957年型

トーハツ

トーハツ

TOKYO HATSUDOKI CO., LTD.

DEPRESSION, WAR

Left: Page from the 1957 brochure of Tokyo Hatsudoki Co. Ltd, manufacturers of the Tohatsu range of motorcycles.

Right: A 1957 125cc Fuji two-stroke single, showing definite German influences.

The Wall Street Crash and the Great Depression were felt in Japan, too, with consequent unemployment and hardship, but the country's comparative isolation gave it some protection.

When the economic situation improved, the Miyata company resumed production in 1933 and in April 1935 the firm began what could be termed quantity production. The machine was a 175cc two-stroke single. Once again, this used the Asahi brand name, but unlike the previous effort, the newcomer proved a good seller. The major reasons for this were its good reliability record and excellent performance.

During the same year that Miyata began mass production, the newly formed Rikuo Internal Combustion Company commenced licence manufacture of the 1934 American Harley-Davidson 750cc v-twin. These were sold in Japan under the Rikuo (Road King) label.

Foreign motorcycle racers visited Japan for the first time in 1934, the initial event being a dirt-track meeting at Inogashira, Tokyo. The five riders, all of whom were American, were headed by the well-known Pitt Mossman, and had been invited to Japan by the organisers of the Yokohama Port Festival Exhibition.

The Stateside racers used pukka Martin competition models powered by British JAP engines. These proved so much faster than the standard roadsters used by the Japanese riders that, within days, the Americans found themselves motorcycling heroes. This also had the effect of changing attitudes towards competition in Japan, and soon the home manufacturers began to turn their attention to building proper racing machines.

The Second World War changed everything and left Japan a shattered country, with the vast majority of its production facilities and cities little more than piles of rubble. From this scene of desolation in a few short years Japan was to create the biggest economic miracle witnessed in modern times.

First into production after the war were Meguro, Miyata and Rikuo. Soon these were joined by Tohatsu, Pointer, Abe Star and Mishima. Other early post-war marques included Mizuho, Hosk, IMC, Olympus, Showa,

AND THE MIRACLE

Cruiser, Gas Den and others with such quaint names as Pearl, Queen Bee, Jet, Pony, Hope Star and even Happy! The number of manufacturers reached a peak of around 120 companies by 1952. By the late 1950s few of these had survived. Those that did were headed by Honda, Suzuki and Yamaha, plus the Meguro company (later taken over by Kawasaki), Tohatsu, Pointer, Bridgestone, Lilac, Liner and Rabbit.

But although there were fewer marques the survivors built more bikes and the full extent of this can be gauged by recalling that in 1945 only 127 motorcycles were built in Japan, but by 1950, production had risen nearly twentyfold to 2,633. Five years on and these figures had increased to 204,304. By 1960, the figure had reached an amazing 1,349,090 machines. Much of this last figure was thanks to the phenomenal success of one model, Honda's C100 Super Cub.

Introduced in October 1958, the Super Cub sold in vast numbers straight away and in 1959 production reached an incredible 755,589 units. The Cub was the brainchild of Honda's super salesman – manag-

Above: The best-selling Honda C100 Cub. By 1959 sales figures had exceeded 750,000 units.

ing director Takeo Fujisawa. Until this time all the world's motorcycle makers had concentrated upon enthusiast models which only a limited number of people would buy. But the new Step-thru 50 enabled Honda to open a vast new market for the man (and woman) in the street.

Looking at the vast majority of Japanese motorcycles of the 1950s one sees British and German influence, but by the following decade Japan had created its own recognition points. This coincided with not only going Grand Prix racing with new multi-cylinder bikes, but also introducing such innovations as electric starting, mirrors and direction indicators as standard equipment.

Although it is true to say that although Honda largely led the export drive and the subsequent entry into Grand Prix racing, the other surviving Japanese manufacturers soon jumped on the bandwagon and the result was a vast sales boom which benefited the whole industry.

The resultant growth saw these companies plough back a good percentage of their revenue into research and development which fed down into the standard street models. This in turn was to the manufacturers' advantage in their attack on the European and American markets. Whereas British, European and American makers had allowed their profits to go to shareholders, the likes of Honda, Suzuki and Yamaha put theirs back into generating more sales, allowing success to build on success.

The Lilac MF39 300cc shaft-driven twin of the late 1950s – almost the japanese BMW.

Lilac sales catalogue showing production and office facilities.

It's Coming **LILAC** Time

We are much pleasure to introduce you about our productions.

Recently, the number of the motorcycles have been increased remarkably and they are being used by many people for recreational purpose, office works and other use.

Hitherto chain system drive device were used both in tricycles and four wheelers, but now this chain system has been entirely replaced with shaft drive one.

In motorcycles too the improved system has been adopted resulting in making them stronger than before.

Under such the circumstances, our company was adopted the shaft drive system since our factory established in 1948.

In order to our pioneering mechanics won recongnition from the user, our "**LILAC**" has been much selling all over the world.

Now, we produce 4 type of motorcycles, MF-39 Type 300 c.c., MF-19 Type 300 c.c., LS-18 Type 250 c.c. & C-81 Type 125 c.c.

All of them are adopted the shaft drive, electrical & kick starter, V-type twin 4 stroke engine.

Please ride on a **LILAC**.

We know that our **LILAC** will give you the best of satisfaction.

Hamamatsu Factory

Head Office

Right: The original 1959 four-cylinder Honda Racer, forerunner of the marque's Grand Prix racing dynasty.

Below: Japanese rider Toshio Matsumoto racing a twin cylinder two-stroke Suzuki in the 1960 125cc TT; he finished 15th.

VICTORIA
Avanti

The stylish sports moped and light weight motorcycle

Les vélomoteurs sportifs de rasse et motocyclettes légères

the Swinging Sixties

THE EUROPEAN SALES DECLINE

The seeds of the decline in the sales of European-built motorcycles can be traced back to the mid-1950s. Following a decade of unprecedented demand for all forms of cheap mechanized transport to fill the vast gaps left in the personal transport sector due to the ravages of war, European manufacturers had enjoyed the good times. Unfortunately these were not to last for ever.

In Britain, 1955 marked the end of the road for Vincent-HRD, the Stevenage-based marque becoming a victim of its own search for perfection, unable to make a sufficient level of profit on an expensively manufactured range of machines. Remember that when Vincent went under, its products were viewed as the 'Superbikes' of the era.

A year earlier, in 1954, Soichiro Honda had toured Europe, visiting, among other places West Germany, England and the Isle of Man. At the last location his enduring impression was of the display put on by the German NSU team. There is little doubt that his trip sowed the seeds of how Honda were best advised to go about things. Just as NSU and other Europeans were thinking of cut-backs, Honda and the rest of the Japanese industry were planning their first steps into the big-time.

It wasn't that nobody took the Japanese seriously. For example, Triumph boss Edward Turner visited Japan in 1960 on a fact finding expedition. He reported that 'Japan has 90 million highly intelligent, very energetic, purposeful people, all geared to an economic machine with an avowed object of becoming great again, this time in the world of business and industry, and nothing apparently is going to stop them.' Turner ended by saying: 'The trip was a dynamic experience and a somewhat frightening spectacle.' Unfortunately, neither his company's board, nor that of any other British motorcycle manufacturer acted in a positive manner. Instead the entire industry continued to build the same type of machines as it had in earlier years, whilst any profits went to the shareholders rather than being ploughed back into research and development.

At the same time there were several takeovers and mergers which, if anything, only made things worse. AMC (Associated Motor Cycles), based in Woolwich, London, had by the early 1960s acquired Norton, Francis Barnett and James, to add to their existing AJS and Matchless marques. The end result was a spate of badge engineering, which was convenient for the manufactures but took little account of the buying public. Design suffered too, but several less than imaginative products such as the AJS/Matchless lightweight ohv singles, the Norton Jubilee, Navigator and Electra twins and, perhaps most disastrous of all, the AMC-designed two-stroke engines for Francis Barnett and James.

The BSA/Triumph Group fared better, but it to wasn't always given the best leadership or the required funding for new research.

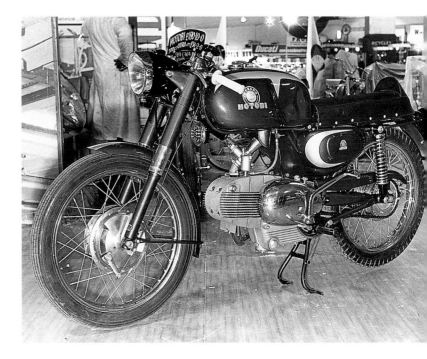

Above: Typical Italian lightweight of the era, a 1963 Motobi Catria 200cc ohv single.

Nevertheless, it had a loyal following and a firm export base to offer some stability and continuity when it came to assessing future demand. The same was true of Royal Enfield, who for a time saw its 248cc unit construction ohv single in its various forms sell well, but the larger Bullet single was becoming dated (although this was later to find a new lease of life in India). The 692cc Constellation and its ultimate replacement, the 736cc Interceptor received an initially favourable reception but had little significant impact on the overall market.

Looking back, people still find it astonishing than an industry which was once dominant in the world market came to dwindle into nonexistence. But the fault perhaps lies not wholly within the motorcycle industry itself. Britain, like the rest of Europe, had just recovered from the austerities of the post-war years and memories of rationing were fresh in people's minds. As the then Prime Minister Harold Macmillan famously put it "Britain had never had it so good". Complacency was as rife with politicians and working people as it was with management. Unemployment was virtually unknown and if you lost one job there were plenty of others you could walk into. The Trades Unions were demanding higher wages and shorter hours and why should the workforce disagree? It was the Swinging Sixties and the motto was 'live now and pay later', but few people realized just how much there would be to pay when the bills finally came in.

By the end of the 1960s the British factories, or at least those that remained, plus their German and Italian counterparts, were fighting a rearguard for their lives and the jobs of their employees in the face of falling demand and the seemingly unstoppable onslaught of the Japanese industrial juggernaut.

choose TRIUMPH for 1960

The NEW 500 c.c. "TIGER 100" £247.17.9 (incl. £42.7.9 P.Tax)

A magnificent new model in the star-studded Triumph range — the NEW Tiger 100, combines refinement, silence and stylish appearance with all the exciting performance of its famous predecessors. High compression pistons, special camshafts and many other advanced features give this light and easily handled model a quite out-of-the-ordinary performance.

The Best Motorcycle in the World

An advert from 1960 proclaiming the new 500cc Triumph Tiger 100 unit construction model.

THE JAPANESE ADVANCE

As the 1960s dawned the Japanese, led by Honda, made their international debut, more or less simultaneously, on the racing circuits and the marketplaces of the world. It would be true to say that, initially, they amused instead of amazed motorcycle enthusiasts, both in Europe and America. Their racing machines were only moderately fast and not always reliable, whilst their standard production models, although loaded to the full with technical goodies, appeared somewhat weird to the western eye.

Yet within a few short years the picture had been absolutely reversed, with not only virtual race dominance by the Japanese, up to and including Grand Prix level, but the likes of Honda, Bridgestone, Suzuki, Yamaha and Hodaka were well respected names enjoying the strongest dealer base within the industry.

So what had caused such a reversal of fortunes? Firstly, the Japanese had created a firm foundation within their own domestic market which by the end of the 1950s was one of the strongest and fastest growing in the world. Next, they had planned a properly-founded export drive which included a yen-rich racing budget and had recruited the right people within the various countries which they had targeted for their showroom sales invasion. Never in the entire history of motorcycling had one nation achieved such dramatic inroads into worldwide markets in so little time and with such all-round determination and efficiency.

But this was no mere marketing exercise. There were sound reasons behind the Japanese success story. Without exception, Japanese motorcycles featured good performance, good handling, good build quality and a high level of technical refinement – sophistication, even – that neither the European and American bike builders could match.

The top selling motorcycle of the first generation of Japanese exports was without doubt Honda's CB77, known in the USA as the Super Hawk. Even though the CB77 was a sport machine this didn't mean it was uncivilised. Far from it indeed, as amongst its comprehensive specifications were such features as electric start, twin mirrors, large silencers, 12 volt electrics, a comfortable dual seat, combined speedo and rev counter, a proper air filtration system and comprehensive mudguarding.

Add to this a 100 mph-(160 kmh) plus maximum speed (*Cycle World* got 105.2 mph/169 kmh in a 1962 test), a 305cc all-alloy vertical twin with overhead camshaft at 180 degree crankshaft, two-leading shoe brakes, a frame which used the unit construction engine as a stressed member, and fully enclosed suspension both front and rear, the total package was a very advanced machine for its day. Its nearest competitor, at least in the performance stakes, was the Triumph Tiger 100 – but this was some 200cc larger in engine size and also weighed a third more. The British product also had a much inferior technical specification, which included ohv engine with dry sump lubrication, 6 volt electrics and single leading shoe brakes.

Other notable Hondas of the same era included the CB72 (essentially a 247cc version of the Super Hawk), the CB92 (a superb 125cc ohc sports twin) the Super Cub (a commuter step-thru) and a range of touring C-models in 124, 150, 247 and 305cc engine sizes.

The other Japanese manufacturers were quick to follow Honda's lead. The first Suzuki to be exported in any real numbers was the twin cylinder two-stroke 246cc T10. Notable features included electric start, hydraulically operated rear brake and direction indicators. Yamaha's early export mainstay was the YD3. This was very similar to Suzuki's offering but without the hydraulic rear stopper. There were also the YG1 (80cc single with rotary valve induction) and the YDS2 sportster (using a tuned version of the YD3 engine).

Other notable Japanese bikes of this first generation included the Lilac 500cc flat twin, the Bridgestone 90 and 175cc (both with rotary valve engines), the Tohatsu 125cc (a unique two-stroke twin with three crankcase sections) and the Hodaka range of on-off road two-stroke singles. Their most popular model was the 90 Ace. Hodaka was unique in being a Japanese-built, American market-only product. And very successful it was, too, for several years giving the likes of Honda, Suzuki and Yamaha a run for their money in sales performance.

Unfortunately for the Europeans, Japan was here to stay.

Right: Englishman Bill Smith pilots his Japanese Honda CB72 during the Thruxton 500-mile race in 1962.

Left: When it appeared in 1959, the Honda C92 124cc ohc twin set new standards with its deluxe specification.

YAMAHA 100 TWIN
MODEL YL-1
with Yamaha Autolube

EST 1887

Discover the swinging world of YAMAHA

Compared to European ultra-lightweight motorcycles, Yamaha's YL1 100cc twin offered real sophistication.

Jawa's impressive 350cc ohc twin first appeared in 1949, and was built for much of the 1950s.

IRON CURTAIN DEVELOPMENTS

Motorcycles were not made in any great numbers in Russia until 1928, when a few experimental roadsters were produced in Izhevsk. Much of this was because under the Czar industrial development wasn't greatly encouraged. The First World War had a devastating effect on the country closely followed the October Revolution of 1917 and its aftermath. These events, and the fact that the Soviet Union remained a largely rural, peasant economy, made it difficult for Russian engineers to undertake the design and construction of motor vehicles alongside their European contemporaries.

The first Soviet machine to enter anything like series production was the M21, which went on sale in 1930. Powered by a 300cc single cylinder two-stroke engine which was similar to the German DKW of the period, the M21 launched the USSR onto two wheels.

There then followed a period of imitation, resulting in various American and British machines being copied. For example, in 1935 something closely resembling a 595cc BSA Sloper was introduced under the code name TIZ-AM-600, whilst a Harley-Davidson lookalike was produced in Podolsk, sporting coil ignition with gear primary drive, a three-speed gearbox and a pressed-steel frame.

However, Russian engineers were also beginning to display the fruits of their own homegrown research. The first signs of this really began to show by the end of the decade with a definite improvement in quality and several ingenious new designs, including a 250cc two-stroke with an enclosed pressed steel 'shell' which came from the from the Kharlov factory.

In 1940 – Germany did not declare war on the Soviet Union until June 1941 – came the Izhevsk, which appeared to be virtually a direct copy of a 350cc DKW. Another face seen before with a different coat of paint was the M72, a 750cc horizontal four-stroke twin, with shaft drive, telescopic forks and plunger rear suspension that was really a thinly-disguised BMW R71.

At the end of the Second World War many of the previously industrialized parts of the Soviet Union had suffered the greatest damage. A large rebuilding program was required, but it was one which was undertaken without the US assistance available to the West. The Communist Party and its officials responded by launching a rebuilding programme to satisfy the country's many needs. High on the list of these was a cheap and reliable means of transport.

Since motorcycles were less costly to build than four wheelers, the Soviets chose this path to satisfy much of its private demand for transport in the immediate post-war era. One consequence of the Allies victory was an increased sphere of Soviet influence, and this included areas which had formerly been in the forefront of the motorcycle industry. Consequently, the Soviets began to build their own versions of DKW and BMWs, both of whom had factories which ended the war in the eastern sector of Germany which was now under Soviet control. Of course, there was no need at all to worry about patent or copyright law.

The two main types to be mass-produced were the 125cc Moskva two-stroke – the DKW RT125 design (also copied by BSA in Britain and Harley-Davidson in the USA amongst others) – and the M75, the Soviet version of the flat-twin BMW.

But there were also more interesting spoils to be had. At the termination of the hostilities in 1945, the troops of the Soviet Union overran the production facilities of the DKW marque at Zschopau. Here they discovered a wealth of special research and experimental projects, including all the necessary tooling and manufacturing equipment. Together with the blueprints, everything was shipped back to Moscow where it was evaluated at the Central Construction and Experimental Bureau and ultilised for both current production and in future projects. Amongst these goodies were racing versions of the RT125, which set the Russians up in the sporting field and with the pre-war supercharged, four-piston, twin-cylinder, watercooled two-stroke DKW.

By the late 1950s several Soviet engineers, including S. Ivanitsky and A. Meshkovsky, had begun to design a new breed of motorcycle, which included a dohc twin for racing. These had appeared fleetingly outside the Iron Curtain in Finland during 1957, but by the early 1960s even more ambitious racing designs were to appear, culminating with the four cylinder 350cc C-364. This machine caused a minor sensation when it appeared in public for the first time at the East German Grand Prix in July 1964.

But no such exotica ever appeared on the street, instead the Soviets made do with a staple diet of 125/175cc single and 350cc twin cylinder two-strokes and the BMW-derived flat twin four-stroke. However, the factories could never make enough, which led to a thriving trade for the Communist satellite countries such as Poland (WSK), Hungary (Czepel), East Germany (MZ and Simson) and Czechoslovakia (Jawa and CZ). Even then there was always a long waiting list for the general public.

Above: Production facilities at the Izhevsk motorcycle plant in Soviet Russia in 1947.

Below: Jawa's production line in 1966. The machine in the foreground is a 175cc single.

f the Sixties meant anything in Britan, it was the beginning of 'youth culture'. For the first time, young people had money in their pockets to spend on fashion and, more importantly, a pair of wheels to give them the freedom they yearned for. But what sort of wheels? The answer to that question placed you inevitably in one of two camps. Choose a motorcycle and you were a 'Rocker'; cut the style with a scooter and you were a 'Mod'. There was no middle ground.

Press reports were of twin sets of hooligans battling it out at seaside resorts each Bank Holiday or outside pubs and clubs on Saturday nights. The Rockers wore their hair long, sported black leather jackets covered with studs and badges and heavy boots with white socks showing over the top. Mods had smarter haircuts, wore parkas and smart shirts and trousers. Weapons varied from coshes to chains, knives or broken bottles. Although it is true that there were some very unpleasant incidents, the full truth was not quite as black and white as the newspapers liked to report it. Alongside the hooligan tip of the iceberg there were thousands more who simply enjoyed their motorcycling or scooting pleasure.

Cafés and coffee bars were the Rockers' traditional meeting places. Cheap (and unlicensed to sell alcohol), they were perfect haunts. There was no obligation to buy more than a single cup of Espresso coffee, no matter how long you stayed. Bar-billiards and a jukebox stacked with the latest rock 'n' roll chart toppers were additional attractions. This was the lifestyle for many sixties bikers, but it didn't survive into the following decade. Other crazes took over and the venues that the Rockers used all but vanished due to a combination of more upmarket roadside restaurants and new roadbuilding programmes. Nevertheless, several of the old café's had become almost a byword of the era and they're still remembered with fondness by bikers of a certain age.

As for the machines themselves, it was very much a case of 'anything goes', from a humble Bantam or Tiger Cub with clip-ons and home-made rear sets to a mighty Norvin (a 998cc Vincent HRD engine shoehorned in a Featherbed Norton chassis). And apart from those lucky souls who

MODS AND ROCKERS

could afford to commission the likes of Baldock, Hertfordshire-based Doug Southwell to build one of his superb Southwell-Tritons (usually a pre-unit Triumph Bonneville motor in a set of Norton cycle parts), owners had to carry out their own work. 'Homebrewed' bikes ranged from a light customising job with basic engine tuning right through to highly ambitious and creative super-specials. Perhaps the ultimate dream-bike of the era was a Clubmans BSA Gold Star. The standard specification included either a 348 or 499cc pre-unit ohv single cylinder engine, housed in a welded, full-duplex steel-tubed frame, and round tubular swinging arm. The fuel tank was either the standard chromed-steel item or an aftermarket Lyta five-gallon alloy component. Then came the famous Burgess-BSA 'Goldie' silencer with its distinctive whistle, swept back exhaust pipe, chrome-plated mudguards, matching Smith's speedo and tacho, clip-ons, rear seats and chrome-plated wheel rims. The close ratio gearbox allowed 70 mph (113 kmh) in first gear and much slipping of the clutch – not exactly ideal for town work! But Sixties youth loved the Goldie. It was just about the hottest thing on two wheels, with a reputation which included a 100 mph (160 kmh) lap at Brooklands, Clubmans TT race victories, scrambling and trials winner, it came close to the magic ideal bike in many observer's eyes. Of course it had its faults, but what motorcycle of that period didn't? But it is as a café racer that its best remembered, being the nearest most riders came to owning a

street-legal racing machine in the 1960s. After production ceased (in 1962), BSA tried to offer various twin-cylinder models as its replacement, including the Rocket Gold Star, Lightning and Spitfire, but none really managed to match the charisma of the big single.

To supplement his bike, the Rocker had a number of go-faster goodie shops, headed by the likes of Paul Dunstall, Dave Degans (Dresda Autos), CR Speed Shop and Taylor Dow (run by ex-racer Eddie Dow).

The 'Mods', much to the great contempt of the Rockers, rode Lambretta, Vespa or similar small-wheeled scooters. Often these machines were bedecked with lashings of chrome plate, masses of extra lights, spare wheels, mirrors and even handlebar tassles. Other variations included stripped down creations whose frames were bereft of almost any bodywork whatsoever. Noisy sports silencers were mandatory and, instead of outright speed, the scooterist's aspiration was to corner his machine with the footboards raising sparks from the tarmac. As far as Mods were concerned, image was more important than the technical specifications of the machine he rode.

The battles fought on the seafronts of Brighton, Southend-on-Sea, Great Yarmouth and other coastal resorts now seem part of a bygone age. Motorcycling today no longer carries with it ideas of threat and rebellion. But in truth, that was probably the case for the majority of riders even at the height of the Swinging Sixties.

Above left: Mods on the seafront at Clacton, Essex under the watchful eye of the police, circa 1964.

Above: Made in 1979, the film *Quadrophenia* revisited the Mod culture of the 1960s.

Left: These 'pudding basin'-helmeted rockers were typical of Sixties youth in Britain.

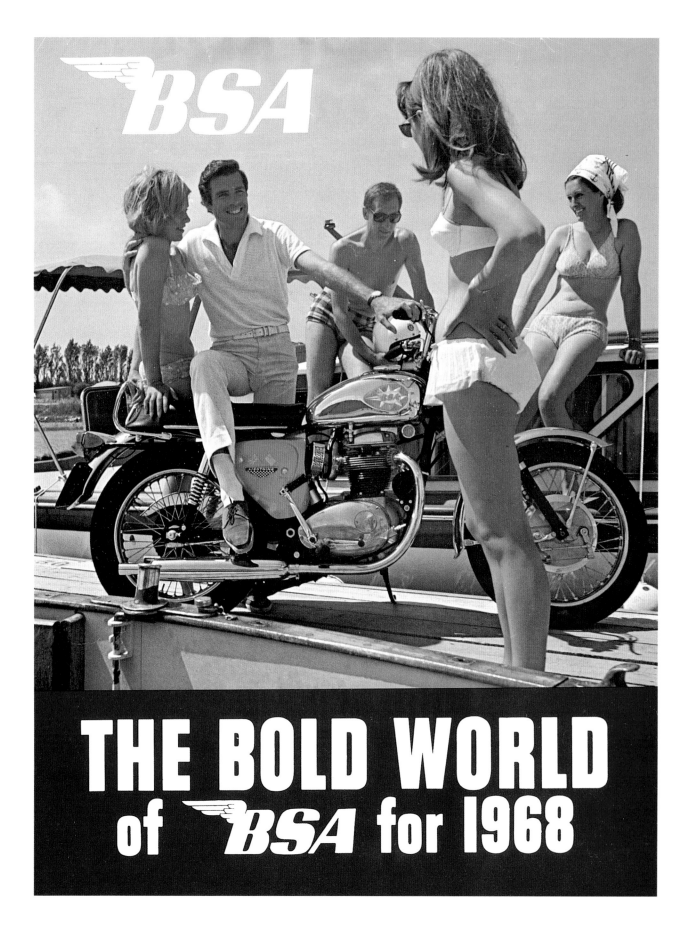

BSA EXPORT DRIVE

In the immediate post-war period, the biggest market for the BSA Group's products was the United States, and this became true for the Triumph marque when it became a member of the BSA Group in the Spring of 1951. But Triumph had already had a long history of involvement with the US before this.

The story of Triumph's entry in America began in the 1930s and was principally the result of the efforts of two men, Bill Johnson and Edward Turner. The story goes that while on honeymoon in Hawaii in 1934, Johnson came across an Ariel dealer who had one of the legendary Ariel Square Fours in stock. A keen motorcyclist and something of an engineer, Johnson bought the bike and had it shipped home to California. There followed a correspondence with the Ariel factory in England and with the machine's designer, Edward Turner.

Johnson set up as an Ariel importer for the US West Coast, while Turner moved to Triumph as Managing Director, persuading Johnson to add Triumph to his stocks. The two men maintained contact during the war years and in 1946 Turner travelled to the US and met Johnson personally. A close personal friendship developed and from then on Triumph's penetration into the US market increased spectacularly. British machines enjoyed an especial popularity throughout the country.

Following the war, the American motorcycle movement simply grew and grew. By 1960 Bill Johnson's organisation, together with the recently created Triumph Corporation, headed by Denis McCormack who handled the East, imported over 6,500 Triumphs. By 1965, this figure had shot up to well over 15,000 units.

Perhaps when one considers that Bill Johnson died in 1962 and Edward Turner retired in 1964, the ultimate demise of the BSA Group a few years later is more easily understood. What is certain these two men established Triumph as a major force in probably the most difficult market in the world.

Left: A typical 1960s BSA advert aimed at the American market.

Top: Eighty per cent of Triumph motorcycles were exported in the 1950s and 60s, mainly to the USA.

 (Britain 1902-)

To many, Triumph epitomises the very best in British motorcycling and today, under the guidance of John Bloor who purchased the name in the 1980s, it is once again a major marque.

The company's illustrious history stretches back to the early years of the century, but perhaps the true glory days began when it was bought by Ariel owner Jack Sangster in 1936. He immediately set the design talents of Edward Turner to work, creating one of the most important motorcycles of all time, the Speed Twin. The Speed Twin was often copied by its rivals over the next quarter of a century, but rarely bettered.

In 1951 the company was sold to the BSA Group and a new era began which saw Triumph as a major dollar earner with not only the latest version of the Speed Twin, but other models including the 649cc Thunderbird and 499cc Tiger 100. Later with the introduction of the twin carb Bonneville even more sales success came Triumph's way.

But even the introduction of the 740cc Trident three-cylinder model in the late 1960s couldn't stop Triumph and its parent BSA hitting the financial rocks in the early 1970s. There followed a the workers' co-operative, which failed in the early 1980s, before John Bloor rescued Triumph and recreated the legend.

 (Britain 1906-71)

BSA were major players in the British motorcycle industry from the earliest days. In the inter-was years its reputation was founded upon success in trials, six day events and early scrambles. In all three disciplines the Birmingham company made a considerable impact and, at the same time displaying the excellence of its standard product, it also entered machines in demonstration tests, including the famous Maudes Trophy.

By the end of the 1920s, BSA was able to claim that one in four motorcycles was a BSA, figures helped at that time by such excellent showroom sellers as the Round Tank and the Sloper.

But it was the end of the 1930s which saw the arrival of a machine, or at least a name, which was to provide BSA with its enduring image – the Gold Star. Few motorcycles can be everything to everyone but the Goldie came closer than most – a 100 mph (160 kmh) lap at Brooklands, Clubmans TT winner, scrambles, trials and of course its famous café racer role – BSA's single could cope with almost anything. Production, to the regret of a host of admirers, finally ceased in 1962.

BSA built a truly vast array of models during the 1950s and 60s, the best-known being the Bantam, A-series twins in both pre-unit and unit guises, C15/B40 singles and the Rocket 3 triple.

The whole group floundered as the 1970s dawned, bringing the demise of this once grand marque.

 (Italy 1911-)

The Benelli company had established itself as a racing manufacturer before the war, but withdrew from competition in 1951, following a fatal accident to one of its riders during practice for the French Grand Prix. They returned to the fray in 1959 with an updated 250cc single, with Duke, Dale and Grassetti at the controls. These had little success, so the company concentrated on developing a 4-cylinder GP bike, efforts which were crowned when Benelli won its second world crown in 1969, with Australian Ken Carruthers the rider.

After De Tomaso took over the company in the early 1970s, Benelli built and marketed a series of Japanese-inspired ohc fours and sixes, from 250 through to 900cc. There was also a series of 2-stroke lightweights, scooters and mopeds.

In 1989 De Tomaso sold Benelli to a local machine tool manufacturer who subsequently produced a new range of 50cc models from a fold-up mini-bike to an out-and-out sportster called the Devil.

THE CAFÉ RACERS

Café racers were very much a phenomenon of the 1960s. But these leather-jacketed flyers of the Swinging Sixties weren't the first, or the last, of their kind. Less well-remembered were the 'Promenade Percys' of the pre-war era, and during the 1970s the United States had an intense but short-lived love affair with an updated version of the Sixties café racers. But in all three eras, the machines and their riders were viewed by both the public at large and other motorcyclists very much as rebels against the establishment.

The first coming of the café racer was during the early 1930s, when the world was slowly pulling itself out of the Great Depression. After years of gloom, there was at last money enough for almost any youngster in work to get a motorcycle. This new-found wealth and freedom allowed these young men to make runs to the coast (hence the title 'Promenade Percys'). The runs usually made use of A-class roads such as the Southend arterial highway, leading from England's capital.

In those far-off days the machinery was truly varied, from a series of home-built specials using a cocktail of components from several manufacturers through to classics such as overhead camshaft Nortons or Velocette singles. Either way, items such as lighting equipment, tool boxes, mudguards and stands were cheerfully binned in the quest to squeeze out a few vital extra mph.

Those 'Promenade Percys' with an eye to fashion and a tinge of respectability would opt for a Brooklands 'Can' (a fish-tail silencer). Those with less regard for the public's eardrums would simply gut the original silencers or fit a suitable length of copper pipe. Riding gear in those days, except for leather coats or ex-army greatcoats and perhaps a pair of goggles, was largely non-existent.

Then came the Second World War and the errant speedster exchanged His Majesty's highways for the altogether less carefree days of His Majesty's armed forces.

Various events contrived to create the café racers of the 1960s, together with the more widely-publicized Mods and Rockers. New motorcycles, notably the BSA Gold Star, the Norton Dominator, the Royal Enfield Constellation, the Triumph Bonneville and the Velocette Venom created a new breed of enthusiast, while films such as *The Wild One* (1953) and *The Leather Boys* (1964), publicised the type. Add to this the potency of that supreme pop music phenomena, rock 'n' roll, an increasing affluence, and the mushrooming youth culture and the ingredients all fell into place.

But what really distinguished the café racer from the rest was the influence that British short circuit racing had, inspiring as it did many owners to attempt to recreate a street version of the track racers. In addition, certain manufacturers built clubman's racers, many of which ultimately found their way on to public roads. These, together with suitably modified standard production machines, were to form the nucleus of the era's 'ton-up' fraternity. Road racing equipment such as lightweight alloy

or glass fibre petrol and oil tanks, clip-on 'bars, rear-set foot controls and the like soon became the hallmark of the café racer.

As for the riders themselves, they often frequented all-night transport cafés and coffee bars ('coffee bar cowboys' was another name for the cult), sipping frothy cups of Espresso coffee to the blare of rock 'n' roll from the inevitable brightly-lit jukebox. To stop boredom setting in, riders devised the practice of death-defying 'burn ups' from one café or coffee bar to the next. Another thrill was the out-of-town high-speed trip, for example to spectate at race meetings. Riding garb was usually a leather jacket, Levi jeans, leather flying boots and pudding basin or sometimes 'space' helmet.

A focal point for many café racers was the London-based Fifty-Nine Club. Founded by the Reverend Bill Shergold, it was a haven for young motorcyclists and for over a decade Father Bill was to be seen in the midst of the action in typical riding gear astride his Triumph Speed Twins – he was a man of his time as well as a man of the cloth.

Although the café racer scene had lost much of its support in Britain by the end of the decade, it found a new home across the Atlantic for a short period in the 1970s. Searching for a new direction, several state-side custom builders perceived the scope offered by the road-racer styling, and the café racer gained an extension of its life span. Of course, in America the concept was modified to suit home market tastes. But underneath the flamboyantly painted full fairing, behind the tinted wind-shield and between the modern cast-alloy wheels and disc brakes, the café racer was alive and kicking. Even the mighty Harley-Davidson factory joined in, with its own offering, appropriately named the Café Racer, which debuted in 1977.

Left: Clubmans 499cc BSA Gold Star in café racer trim; its many modifications included dolphin fairing, Norton chassis, plus glass-fibre tank and seat.

Above: Paul Dunstall marketed cafe racer 654cc BSA Lightning twin in the mid-Sixties.

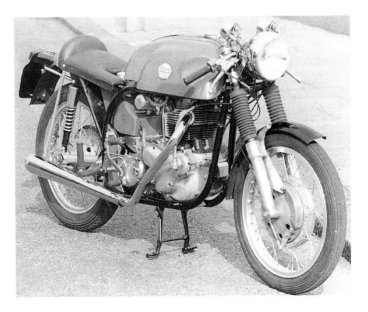

Above: Dunstall Domiracer with tuned engine, swept back pipes and Oldani front brakes.

Associated Motor Cycles of Plumstead Road, Woolwich, London, more commonly know under the abbreviated AMC banner, were a prime example of just why the once dominant British motorcycle industry was to crumble away and ultimately collapse.

The hub of AMC was Matchless and AJS. In 1938 they acquired Sunbeam (which was then sold on to BSA in 1943) and used the trading title of AMC for the first time and, as such, survived both the pre-war slump and post-war austerity, absorbing those companies that did not: Francis Barnett (1947), James (1952), Brockhouse (1959), and also, in 1952, the big daddy of them all, Norton. The latter operation did not, however, move from its original Bracebridge Street, Birmingham home, to Plumstead itself until 1963. By then the rot had already begun to set in. The following is just why and how it happened.

AMC can be adjudged as being a classic case of the process known as 'badge engineering'. This is where models which are apparently different from one another are produced by the simple expedient of substituting one logo for another on the tank and elsewhere. This might appear to be a totally wasted exercise, but the motorcycling fraternity are a largely conservative group of people which likes to stick with what they

AMC
HIT THE ROCKS

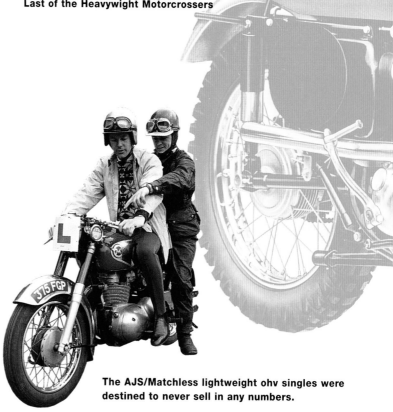

1965 Matchless G80 CS
Last of the Heavywight Motorcrossers

The AJS/Matchless lightweight ohv singles were destined to never sell in any numbers.

AMC (Associated Motor Cycles) didn't move with the times and when this Matchless 350 Mercury was shown at the Blackpool Show during 1963, the design was totally outdated.

know rather than move on to untested waters. So the name itself may command selling power, whether or not some other firm now owns it and controls the product. Certainly badge engineering appeared to work well enough for AMC in the 1950s.

Then came the 1960s and market expectations changed. After many years of profit AMC suddenly lost almost £250,000 in 1960. It was even worse the following year. In an attempt to stem the rising tide of losses the AMC board decided to jazz up its ageing line of models with flashy new tank badges and two-tone colour schemes, when what it needed was fresh ideas and new models.

This lack of vision could perhaps be traced back to the death in 1954 of Charlie Collier, the 70-year-old co-founder and former racer of Matchless motorcycles. A man with motorcycling in his blood, he was virtually irreplaceable. But perhaps even he would have been unable to stem the tide of the times.

But not all was amiss within the good ship AMC. For example, before his death Charlie Collier had initiated a £1 million pound re-tooling investment programme. This not only enabled increased production, but also improved quality. And whilst the manufacture of its in-house two-stroke engines was never too successful, AMC's own gearbox for its four-stroke models was a real success (previously the company had used bought-in Burman assemblies).

Like much of the British industry, AMC's various lightweight motorcycles (and scooters) were largely unsuccessful. Certainly from a performance viewpoint they were sadly lacking when compared to Continental

Together with Suzuki's Super Six, the Italian Ducati Mach 1 was the fastest 250cc street bike of the 1960s, with 100 mph (160 kmh) plus performance.

THE TON-UP 250S

In the war of the 'ton-up' (100 mph) 250s it was a straight fight between Japan and Italy – which in practice meant a war between two bikes, Suzuki's Super Six and Ducati's Mach I.

The Italian bike appeared first, in September 1964, debuting in Britain on the eve of the London Earls Court Show, where it caused an instant sensation. It was clearly based around the earlier 248cc Diana (the Daytona in the UK) which itself had been launched back in the spring of 1961 and had featured the Bologna company's well-tried ohc single with unit construction, bevel drive and wet sump lubrication. Compared to its forerunner, the Mach I featured five-speeds, a three-ring Borgo high compression piston, larger valves, a higher lift cam and a 29 mm Dell'Orto racing-type carburettor. Other features included rear set foot controls, a distinctive red and silver finish and optional rev counter.

Testing a Mach I in *Motor Cycle News*, Pat Braithwaite wrote: 'In a Lightning jet fighter Mach I (plus a bit) takes you through the sound barrier. The new-for-1965 Ducati Mach I takes you through the 'ton barrier'. And it's only a two-fifty!' This was very much a racer-for-the-road as the following test comments reveal: 'A fast corner looms up. The gear ratios are as close as a racer's ... change down twice and keel over to sample steering and roadholding second to none'. But away from the engine, chassis and brakes and things were not as perfect; the electrics and kick-start operation were the biggest headaches.

Compared to the raw boned Ducati, the Suzuki was a far more civilised piece of equipment. With the T20 Super Six, Suzuki took a big step into the future and it was to be the forerunner of their modern range of twin cylinder two-strokes for the next decade and a half. With it came pump lubrication, six gears, a tube frame and super-sports performance. All that remained from the earlier T10 model was the basic unit construction layout, horizontally split crankcases, inclined cylinders and a few minor components.

The Suzuki appeared just over a year after the Ducati and the two machines were not just rivals in the showrooms, but on the race track too. They locked horns in events such as the Brands Hatch 500 mile race and the Manx Grand Prix and honours were pretty well shared. At the end of the day it was very much down to personal choice – Italian flair or Japanese sophistication. You paid your money and took your choice.

European and later Japanese types. The big singles and vertical twins were well-made and largely durable. Unfortunately, development from the mid-1950s onwards was largely nonexistent. And although AJS, Matchless and Norton machinery was often seen winning road race, motocross or trials events, this glory never seemed to transfer itself to increased showroom sales.

Another problem was competition from the BSA Group, AMC's main rivals. Whereas the BSA and Triumph singles and twins largely became unit construction engines, those of the AMC, AJS, Matchless and Norton remained old fashioned pre-unit. Except, unfortunately, failures such as the lightweight 250/350cc AJS/Matchless singles and lightweight 250/350/400cc Norton twins.

After the transfer of Norton to Woolwich, the AJS/Matchless machines began to utilise Norton components such as Roadholder forks and front wheels and even Norton's 745cc Atlas engine. This was to be the final straw for long-suffering supporters, who, after all, were the customers. They rightly felt that if they wanted a Norton they would go and buy one, or maybe a new make not associated with AMC at all. The result was unsold motorcycles and big discounts to bribe what sales there were. Of course, this state of affairs couldn't continue long and on 4 August 1966 it was announced that the Directors had asked the company's bankers to appoint a receiver. It was the end of an era.

HONDA'S CB450
THE 'BLACK BOMBER'

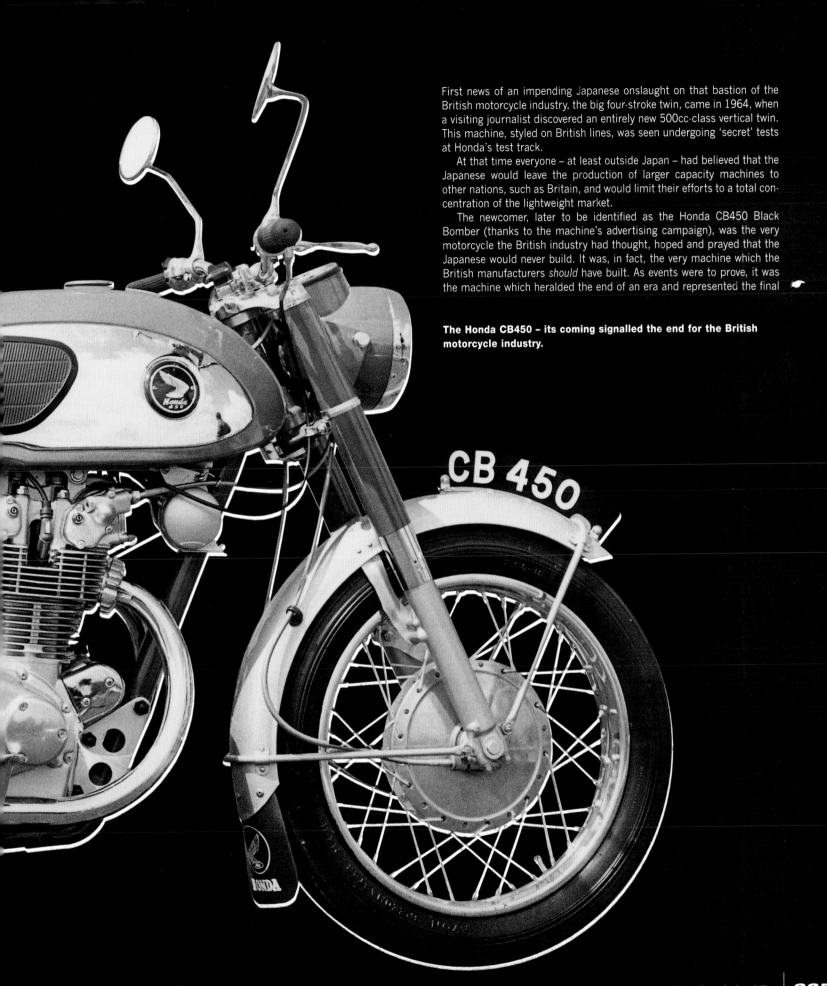

First news of an impending Japanese onslaught on that bastion of the British motorcycle industry, the big four-stroke twin, came in 1964, when a visiting journalist discovered an entirely new 500cc-class vertical twin. This machine, styled on British lines, was seen undergoing 'secret' tests at Honda's test track.

At that time everyone – at least outside Japan – had believed that the Japanese would leave the production of larger capacity machines to other nations, such as Britain, and would limit their efforts to a total concentration of the lightweight market.

The newcomer, later to be identified as the Honda CB450 Black Bomber (thanks to the machine's advertising campaign), was the very motorcycle the British industry had thought, hoped and prayed that the Japanese would never build. It was, in fact, the very machine which the British manufacturers *should* have built. As events were to prove, it was the machine which heralded the end of an era and represented the final

The Honda CB450 – its coming signalled the end for the British motorcycle industry.

push for market supremacy by the industrial giants of Japan. It was the beginning of a trend culminating a few years later with the really big guns, headed by Honda's CB750 four cylinder Superbike.

For firms such as BSA, Triumph and AMC, the 305cc CB77 had been the assumed benchmark signaling the limit of how far the Japanese had intended advancing. The CB77 (the Super Hawk in USA) was really only an overbored CB72 two-fifty and no match in the grunt department for the larger 650 and 700cc British twins.

But the complacent British management were in for a nasty shock. Honda, having successfully attacked the lightweight sector, were not setting an upper capacity limit. Having set their sights higher they needed a flagship and saw the CB450 as just such a machine. It was something which could perform against the opposition on both motorways and back roads, the dreaded Black Bomber or Dragon, as it was sometimes called, was just that – at least on paper.

When it first appeared it was not an out-and-out sportster, but really a sports tourer. Its ultra modern engine design, outstanding brakes and a high standard of reliability made it a formidable opponent. The only fly in the ointment was in the handling department, where there was still plenty of room for improvement.

For most engineers in the 1960s, tradition was something to be followed – but not at Honda. Their earlier designs had shown that they were far too enterprising to take anything as given. With the engine of their CB450 this love of technical innovation had been taken a stage further, in the shape of several features which departed from the engineering norm. Most obvious were its twin overhead camshafts. Next came their method of drive, namely by a long chain from a sprocket in the centre of the crankshaft. Then there were torsion bar valve springs, a 180 degree crank and – for the time – a mind-blowing peak rpm of 8,500.

Another controversial aspect of the CB450 was Honda's corporate marketing campaign for the model, at least in Britain. A string of aggressive ads appeared depicting Honda's newcomer compared to certain British bikes – examples included an ancient 1952 BSA plunger-framed twin and worse still, to many British bike fans, a Vincent v-twin (which had gone out of production over a decade earlier). Comparing the cheeky Japanese invader to a BSA was bad enough, but with one of the legendary Vincents, that was simply sacrilege! Phone lines were soon buzzing at Honda's Chiswick headquarters.

In the USA, the CB450 (and later the 500T) gained more respect than in any other world market. The popular 450CL variant was introduced in 1967 and reflected the street scrambling craze of that time sweeping the North American continent.

The year 1968 saw Honda produce its ten millionth bike, and Soichiro Honda himself rode the garlanded machine off the production line in a blaze of publicity. It was fitting that the machine was a CB450. The past celebrated by the hopes of the future.

In racing, the model's most notable successes came in the 500cc Production TT in the Isle of Man during 1969 and 1971. In the first year a Le Mans-type start was held and Graham Penny thumbed the electric button to make an instant getaway while the rest of the field were still getting ready to kick their machines into life. Penny eventually won after race favourite Tony Dunnell (riding a Kawasaki Mach III) crashed out. Then in 1971 Honda scored a one-two with Penny finishing runner-up behind race winner John Williams.

But time was not on the CB450's side with new four cylinder Honda models taking over its mantle. Nevertheless, the CB450 holds a vital place in motorcycling history as the first of a tide of larger capacity machines from Japan that were to sound the death-knell for the moribund British motorcycle industry.

MOTO GUZZI V7
ITALY'S FIRST BIG BIKE

Few motorcycle engines have had a stranger beginning than the large capacity Moto Guzzi v-twin. It was also destined to have the honour of being its country's first true large capacity motorcycle of the modern era. Its origins lay entirely with a contract from the Italian military authorities for the extraordinary 3 x 3 go-anywhere tractor. The 3 x 3 must surely rank as one of the most bizarre-looking vehicles of all time. However, it used a 90 degree pushrod v-twin of 754cc – and this was to spawn the classic range of Guzzi v-twins.

The original 3 x 3 project began back in the late 1950s when the Italian Defense Ministry in Rome conceived a requirement for a go-any-where, lightweight tractor to operate under almost any conditions, over any terrain, including deep sand and snow. The result was a vehicle which was able to achieve some truly amazing feats – including the ability to climb almost vertical surfaces!

It was Italy's military (and civil) authorities which were to play a vital role in the v-twin engine, with their need in the early 1960s for a suitable replacement for its ageing Guzzi flat single Falcone models, used in con-

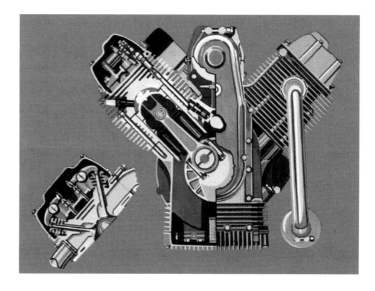

Above: Partial cutaway of the Moto Guzzi engine showing details of the V7's cylinder head.

Below: A Moto Guzzi V7 700cc v-twin near its birthplace, Mandello del Lario, on the shores of Lake Como in northern Italy.

siderable numbers throughout Italy for both military and police work. Work on the original prototype of what was to emerge as the V7 motorcycle began in 1964. Early the following year, the first pre-production models were being presented for governmental approval. Even at this early stage, the Guzzi management realized that here was a machine destined for success in the wider field of everyday riding. The first civilian prototype appeared in public during December 1965 at the 39th international Milan Show. Hailed immediately by journalists and show-

goers alike as the star exhibit, its commercial future was assured.

The V7 title was taken from its original engine capacity of 703cc. The ohv power unit had over-square dimensions with bore and stroke dimensions of 80 x 70 mm. This engine layout gave the big Guzzi its own trademark, and its simplicity and initial soft state of tune endowed it with a long and usually trouble-free life. It was these characteristics which were to prove why the design has outlined most of its competitors and still lives on in updated form today.

BSA AND TRIUMPH TRIPLES

During the latter half of the 1960s, rumours abounded concerning a planned new series of larger capacity models from the BSA and Triumph factories that were under development. In fact, work on such a project had begun early in the decade, but it was not until 1968 that firm details of the two newcomers were finally released to the press and public. Up to this time both companies had built 650-class ohv parallel twins, at first with pre-unit construction engines, but from 1962 (BSA) and 1963 (Triumph) using the more compact unit layout.

Essentially the two marques built their new bike as a joint venture and the engine, which was a parallel three, had a capacity of 740cc (67 x 70 mm), ohv, unit construction and four speeds. This was designed at the Triumph plant and its chief architects were Doug Hele, Bert Hopwood and Jack Wicks. It was perhaps to be expected that the engine followed Triumph, rather than BSA practice and was designed by adding a third cylinder to the existing twin. Valve gear followed the pattern set by Edward Turner, with two camshafts fore and aft of the cylinder block, driven by gears and operating pushrods enclosed in vertical tubes lying between the cylinders.

Upright cylinders and a different frame were the distinctions between Triumph and BSA threes, named the Trident and Rocket Three respectively. They used common suspension, brakes and electrical equipment. Although both versions achieved considerable publicity from their prowess on the race track (wins at Daytona, the Isle of Man TT, the Race of the Year at Mallory Park and the Thruxton 500-mile endurance race) showroom sales were less spectacular.

Initially all production went for export and it wasn't until 1969 that the home market saw any supplies. By then Honda had announced their mould-breaking CB750 four cylinder, which, together with largely unpop-

ular styling, consigned the BSA and Triumph triples to virtual also-rans in the sales war.

Later restyled and with five-speeds they soldiered on after the BSA Groups' financial crisis in 1971, but never really sold in great numbers. Had they been launched five years earlier, who knows what they might have achieved.

Above: The great Mike Hailwood on a 750cc BSA Rocket Three during qualifying for the 1970 Daytona 200.

Left: Canadian Roger Beaumont racing one of the very first T150 Tridents in the autumn of 1968.

Road Racing

Left: The Isle of Man TT (Tourist Trophy) began in 1907. This picture dates from the Senior Trophy race, 5 July 1911.

Right: Ulsterman Joey Dunlop holds the record for the greatest number of TT victories. Most have been achieved on Hondas.

TT ORIGINS

In the early years of this century an ever-increasing band of enthusiastic motor-bicyclists had established themselves as a fraternity as well organised as the sporting motorists. Founded on the lines of the Automobile Club of Gt. Britain and N. Ireland (later the RAC), the Auto Cycle Club was their governing body, and it was at their 1906 annual dinner that the idea of a motorcycle Tourist Trophy race was first proposed.

The suggestion came from one of the after-dinner speakers, H.W. Staner, the editor of *The Motor Cycle*. While proposing the toast he mentioned the Tourist Trophy races for cars, which were being held in the Isle of Man. Why, he asked, could there not be a similar event for motorcycles? He suggested limits on engine capacity and machine weights, with the object of demonstrating the reliability and efficiency of roadsters.

The ACC committee took up the idea, but decided that a better way of exploiting the touring aspect would be to put the emphasis on fuel consumption so as to demonstrate and develop not only the reliability of motorcycles, but also their economy.

The choice of the Isle of Man was a logical one. With a 20 mph (32 kmh) speed limit enforced in Britain, the most practical venues for speed events on public roads were therefore Continental Europe or Ireland. But the Isle of Man, with its own parliament, were able to close its roads and its authorities were by then accustomed to collaborating with the organisation of such events and welcomed 'racers'. Furthermore, the ACC folk were no strangers to Manxland; the previous year they had held speed selection trials over Manx roads in preparation for the International Cup Race in Europe. On being approached, the Island government readily gave consent to a motorcycle TT, and the ACC set about organising it.

Except that the motorcycling press of the time almost invariably described him as 'the well-known sportsman', not much is known about the Marquis de Mouzilly St Mars. How he – presumably a Frenchman – came to link up with the TT project is not clear, but we know the practi-

cal outcome, for it took the form of the Tourist Trophy itself. Given by the Marquis for the best performance in the single cylinder category of the race, this handsome and valuable 2ft 10in. high silver figure of Mercury, poised on a winged wheel, later became the Senior Trophy. In its life it has been repaired many times, and in 1939 it disappeared into Germany, turning up in Italy in 1945 when it was found by Australian TT rider, Arthur Simcock. For the twin cylinder class a silver rose bowl was presented by another sportsman, Dr Hele-Shaw, who was a member of the ACC committee. His award disappeared permanently very early on in TT history.

To select a suitable course a party of club officials, led by the Secretary, F. Straight, visited the island early in 1907. The car racers were then using a circuit that started in Douglas, went direct to Peel, then to Kirkmichael and Ramsey and back over the Snaefell Mountain. This was judged too steep for motorcycles. Instead, a triangular 15 miles, 1,430 yd. circuit was chosen. It started and finished in St John's by the Tynwald Hill. The route ran anti-clockwise to Ballacraine, along the present course by Glen Helen, up Creg Willey's Hill to Kirkmichael where it took a u-turn left, following the coast road via the awkward Devil's Elbow, to Peel and back to St John's. In short, the 'Short Course' – and this set the scene for the event which began the TT series.

On the morning of Tuesday, 28 May 1907, 17 singles and eight twins paraded at St John's to have their petrol measured out. Class 1 bikes (singles) were allowed one gallon for every 90 miles, the twins, one for every 75. They had to cover ten laps of the 15.8 mile course and machines started in pairs every minute. Pedalling gear was permitted!

Charlie Collier (Matchless) won the Class 1 event at 94.5 mpg. Collier averaged 38.22 mph, his brother Harry put up the fastest lap of 41.81 mph. before retiring. Rem Fowler (Norton) won Class 2 at 36.22 mph, with a quickest lap of 42.91.

A TRADITION ESTABLISHED

In 1909 the two-class system was abandoned in favour of a straight race for singles up to 500cc, and multis up to 750cc. Fuel consumption restrictions were also axed.

In 1911 the Coronation Year Jubilee TT races moved to the Mountain Course of 37.75 miles (60.73 km) from Crony-Mona through Edge's corner and Willaston, to St Ninian's Church and down Bray Hill. Junior and Senior classes were introduced and the races were spread over two days. O.C. Godfrey led an Indian one-two-three in the Senior.

In 1913 on the last lap of the Senior the leader, Frank Bateman, crashed at Keppel Gate and died in hospital – the first TT fatality. The following year safety helmets were made compulsory.

Racing resumed in 1920 after the First World War and in 1921 for the first – and only – time the Senior was won by a 350, Howard Davies taking the trophy on the same machine he'd used to finish second in the Junior. In 1922 a Lightweight (250cc) race was introduced, followed in 1923 by a sidecar event. Then in 1924 an Ultra-Lightweight event (for 175s) was held, along with a mass start. This latter innovation was not used again until 1948.

Walter Handley, riding a Rex Acme became the first man to win two TTs in a week in 1925, whilst in 1926 controversy reigned when at the Lightweight presentation it was announced that the winner Pietro Ghersi (on a Moto Guzzi) had been disqualified for using a spark plug of a different brand than that stated on his entry form.

In 1931 Norton took the first Senior one-two-three since Indian in 1911. Jimmy Simpson (riding a Norton) was the first man to break the 80 mph (48 kmh) lap speed. Norton repeated its Senior one-two-three the following year whilst Stanley Woods took Junior and Senior victories, a feat he copied in 1933. The 1935 Lightweight TT saw the first win on a foreign bike, Woods was the rider, setting a 74.19 mph (119.37 kmh) class lap record on his Italian Guzzi. He then did the double yet again (on a v-twin Guzzi) in a dramatic 4-second win in the Senior over Jimmy Guthrie's Norton.

In the last TT before the onset of war, Stanley Woods won his tenth victory (on a Velocette in the Junior), whilst Georg Meier won the Senior on a BMW.

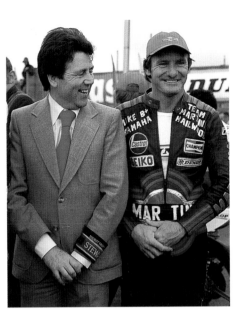

Geoff Duke and Mike Hailwood in 1978 – both great World Champions and multi-TT winners.

Racing resumed in 1947 and in 1949 a lad called Geoff Duke won the Senior Clubman's event. By 1951, when Duke rode factory Nortons, he was in a class of his own to snatch a decisive Senior/Junior double.

When Duke left Norton for Gilera at the beginning of 1953, Rhodesian Ray Amm won both the Junior and Senior on a Norton in the face of stiff opposition from Duke and the rest of the Gilera squad.

For 1954 the 125 and Sidecar races were run over the much shorter Clypse circuit, whilst the Senior was stopped after four of the seven laps due to dreadful weather conditions, Ray Amm being declared the winner. In 1955 Duke set a new lap record of 99.97 mph (160.85 kmh) whilst winning the Senior, whilst Bob McIntyre went one better two year later during the Golden Jubilee Senior TT on a dustbin-faired Gilera four by setting the first of five ton-up laps, the best at 101.12 mph (162.7 kmh).

Back in 1956 John Surtees had scored a MV Junior/Senior double, an achievement he repeated in 1958. Next year saw the first appearance of Japanese machines in the event, when a trio of Honda won the 125cc team prize.

In 1961 Mike Hailwood became the first man to win three TTs in the same week. Then in 1962 the newly-created 50cc class saw Beryl Swain become the first woman to compete in a solo class. More records were set in 1963 – the biggest attendance and the first Japanese rider to win (Itoh on a Suzuki).

Phil Read became the first competitor to break the 100mph 250cc lap barrier in 1965 on a Yamaha, whilst Mike Hailwood showed great resilience to win the Senior, despite a high-speed crash, two lengthy pit stops and a machine only running on three cylinders for the last lap.

A seaman's strike delayed the TT until August in 1966, then in 1967 the TTs Diamond Jubilee saw Hailwood again win three in one week (250, 350 and 500cc).

Over the next three decades the TT declined, at least in its attraction to world class stars, although from time to time it hit the headlines, usually for the wrong reasons. High points came in the form of for Hailwood's magic 1978 comeback, Steve Hislop's lap record breaking form and Joey Dunlop's record number of victories.

But even so, to many the TT remains *the* premier motorcycling event of the year. In recent times it has attracted a large numbers of visitors even without the world class stars of yesteryear. Maybe it's the Manx tradition, the lure of Mona's Isle, but whatever the reason, the TT is still alive and kicking.

Opposite: Bob McIntyre on a Gilera, after his record win in the Senior TT in 1957.

Opposite, inset: Stanley Woods is congratulated by Joe Craig after winning the 1933 Junior (350cc) TT.

Left: Beryl Swain, during the 1962 Isle of Man TT 50cc, was the first woman to compete in a solo class.

THE BROOKLANDS LEGEND

Brooklands, near Weybridge, Surrey, had the distinction of being the world's first purpose-built motor-racing circuit. It was opened to the four-wheel brigade in June 1907, but motorcycles didn't feature until the following year, when they were introduced to broaden its appeal. In fact, the first bike contest at Brooklands was a private match between W.G. McMinnies (Triumph) and Oscar Bickford (Vindec) on 25 February 1908 and victory went to McMinnies at a shade under 53 mph (85 kmh).

The first full scale motorcycle meeting was held a few weeks later on Easter Monday, attracting 24 entries, ranging in engine size from 331 to 986cc. This was won by a NLG (North London Garages) Peugeot.

One of the most famous of all Brookland contests was held in 1911, when Matchless-mounted Charlie Collier took on the American Jake de Rosier's Indian v-twin. De Rosier emerged the victor but later that year Collier had his revenge and in the process set a new Brooklands lap record at 91.37mph (147 kmh).

Although 100mph had been attained before the war by racing cars at Brooklands, the bike brigade had to wait until 1921 before one of their number exceeded the magic 'ton'. The distinction went to Douglas H. Davidson on a Harley-Davidson, who reached 100mph over a measured kilometre. The first to achieve a complete lap at a hundred miles an hour was the legendary Bert Le Vack riding a Zenith – and it was raining heavily at the time!

In fact Le Vack became the leading record breaker at Brooklands during the early 1920s using a variety of machinery. Le Vack was also the winner of the most important race at Brooklands during the period, the 500 miles (800km) of July 1921. Le Vack's Indian averaged 70.24 mph (115 kmh).

Vociferous opposition from local residents foreshadowed the introduction in 1924 of compulsory silencers, and thus the famous Brooklands 'fishtail' can came into being.

Besides Le Vack other famous riders at the Surrey track in the 1920s included Horsman, de la Hay, Lacey, Judd and O'Donovan. The 1930s saw Brough Superior riders dominate. The first of these appeared in 1930 and was the work of E.C.E. (Ted) Baragwanath and was capable of 110 mph (177 kmh) with a sidecar fitted. Later, in the hands of Noel Pope and in solo form with a more powerful engine, it exceeded 160 mph (258 kmh) and became the first machine to lap Brooklands on two wheels at over 120 mph (193 kmh).

It was Pope who was later to achieve the ultimate two-wheeler lap at Brooklands in 1939, lapping at 124.51 mph (200 kmh), a record that will stand for all time as, five months later, the track closed for ever.

Above: Brooklands Clubman's Day in 1939, the last year of racing at the famous Surrey circuit.

Right; Norton's success at the 1921 Brooklands meet is proclaimed in the advert.

EUROPEAN CHAMPIONSHIPS

As in motoring, Grand Prix races were organised for motorcycles. The first of these was the Grand Prix de France held in 1904 and won by Laufranchi on a machine powered by a 598cc v-twin Peugeot engine.

But generally Grand Prix racing did not begin in earnest until the early 1920s, partly because of the First World War which caused stagnation in both civilian motoring and motorcycling. After the conflict there was a switch by the large arms-producers to peacetime manufacturing, resulting in the rapid development of new models. This in turn led to a need to go racing both from technical and publicity viewpoints.

In the early 1920s, British motorcycles and riders were largely dominant. After years of racing at Brooklands and the Isle of Man they were well prepared. The British concept was also widely accepted throughout Europe, and sales and publicity were greatly helped by racing victories. Road races patterned on the Tourist Trophy were organised, including the famous Lario race in northern Italy.

The first European Championship was held at Monza, also in Italy, on 7 September 1924 and victory went to a local manufacturer, Moto Guzzi, ridden by Guido Mentasi. Other famous events soon followed, such as the Belgium, Italian, Ulster and German GPs, plus the Dutch TT. The 500cc class was the major event at these meetings and it was usually supported by 175 (later 250cc) and 350cc races. But there were often so few competitors that all three classes raced together, each capacity group starting at intervals of a minute or so. Race distances were usually between 200 and 300 miles and some GPs lasted over five hours.

As speeds went up and the popularity of the sport grew, so the organisation of the meetings took on a more professional air. To provide spectators with more exciting programmes race distances were cut. This meant that the various capacity classes could be run as separate races – thus star riders were able to appear more than once.

The riders often used to travel to events by train – bikes and tools were loaded into baggage vans while riders and mechanics settled down in comfort. So comprehensive was the rail system of Europe in the interwar years that travelling times compared very favourably with those by road today. The racing fraternity of the day were referred to as the 'Continental Circus'.

British and Italian riders and bikes were soon joined by a third party, the Germans, who, helped by a Nazi government, were anxious to impress the world with sporting victories and were soon challenging for all the major honours.

For 1938, the FICM (forerunners of today's FIM), the sport's international governing body, saw fit to introduce an official European Championship series. That year the results of the eight most important European races counted. These were the Isle of Man and Dutch TTs and the Belgian, Swiss, French, German, Ulster and Italian GPs.

Then came the war and the end of international racing for over six years, and with it the end of the old European championship system.

Toricelli, with his Austrian Puch two-stroke, celebrates winning the 250cc class at the German Grand Prix in 1931. The venue was the famous Nürburgring circuit.

SIDECAR RACING

Sidecar racing made a hesitant start to its life during the early 1920s when racing pioneers such as Bert Le Vack added a third wheel to their racing machines to add flavour to racing at the famous Brooklands circuit. The first sidecar event at the Isle of Man TT came in 1923 when 14 outfits lined up to do battle. Eight different marques took part, Douglas being the most prolific with three machines, while Norton Scott and Sunbeam had two outfits each.

Three laps around the 37.75-mile (60.73-km) Mountain circuit was the test and Freddie Dixon (Douglas) took the victory. The same man was also destined to go down in the record books four years later as the only rider to win both a solo and a sidecar TT.

Sidecar entries declined the following year to only ten, but the future looked bright enough in 1925 with an entry of 18, with 11 different makes represented. The revival didn't last, however, and sidecars were deleted from the TT programme in 1926, when not enough entries were received to stage a race. They didn't return until another 30 years, when in 1954 Eric Oliver won on a Norton outfit.

By then, sidecars had benefited from the considerable prestige of being included from the start in the world championships, which had been inaugurated in 1949. British machines and riders dominated the

Above: The German Helmut Fath during the Dutch TT in 1969. He created history by becoming the first world champion to win with an engine of his own design.

early years of the world sidecar championships, with Eric Oliver and Norton proving a virtually invincible combination.

But although Oliver caused a sensation when he appeared on a much streamlined Norton 'Kneeler' during practice for the Belgian GP in 1953, even this major step in the evolution of the racing sidecar couldn't stave off the challenge from the German manufacturers the following year.

Phenomenal is the only word for BMW's success from the mid-1950s to the mid-1970s. In 21 years from 1954 until 1974, the BMW outfits took the title on no fewer than 19 occasions. Breaking their hold in 1968 came Helmet Fath, who created history by not only winning, but by actually designing his own four-cylinder engined sidecar.

Next came König, another German company, whose watercooled four-cylinder outboard engine was transformed into a championship-winning sidecar racer, which won in 1975 and 1976.

After this the likes of Yamaha and Krauser came onto the scene, and also the Swiss engineer/rider Rolf Biland who invented the longer 'worm'-type outfit which relied heavily on F1 car technology.

The first sidecar TT was held in 1923 and the winner was Freddie Dixon with passenger T.W. Denney. The outfit used a 600cc Douglas twin with a banking sidecar.

SUPERCHARGING

By the late 1930s many of the world's racing factories were either using, or contemplating the use of supercharging to extract extra performance.

And it wasn't just in GP events where the supercharger came into its own, as witnessed by a blown Triumph Speed Twin running at Brooklands to set a new 500cc lap record at 118 mph (190 kmh) with Ivan Wickshead in the saddle.

On the Continent NSU, Gilera, Moto Guzzi and BMW all campaigned supercharged bikes in the dying days before the outbreak of the Second World War; with Georg Meier becoming the first foreign rider on a foreign bike to win the coveted Senior TT, when he took his supercharged BMW twin to victory in June 1939.

Had the war not intervened a whole host of newly designed supercharged bites would have appeared, including the Velocette twin cylinder 'Roarer' and Bianchi four.

But when the conflict finally came to an end the sports governing body, the FIM, banned the use of supercharging. Only Germany continued to use it, with machines such as the 500 BMW and 350/500 NSU being raced in the post-war era. These were only allowed to compete within the confines of the German state, and then only till 1951 when the new West Germany rejoined the FIM.

Dorino Serafini, on a four cylinder Gilera, during the 1939 Ulster GP. He won the race, averaging 97.85 mph (157.4 kmh).

WALTER KAADEN
FATHER OF THE MODERN TWO-STROKE

Walter Kaaden was a true engineering genius. He was also a man of the old school – humble, honest and loyal. He was born on 1 September 1919, the same year that the DKW factory was founded. His father was chauffeur to both Dipl. Ing. Carl Hahn, who oversaw DKW in the 1930s, and Jorgan Skafte Rassmussen, DKW's founder.

When he was only eight years of age, the young Walter was able to accompany his father and Rasmussen to the opening of the famous Nürburgring circuit. As this doubled as a racing circuit and industry test ground. the track was vital to the development of motor vehicles in Germany.

Walter Kaaden entered the Technical Academy in Chemitz, some 15 miles from DKW's base at Zschopau. Chemitz was a centre of industry and commerce for the German state of Saxony; other motorcycle marques were based in the area, including Wanderer. The Second World War broke out when Kaaden was 20. His engineering prowess saw him posted to the famous Peenemünde research centre where he was to work under Wernher von Braun. At that time Germany was leading the world in rocket design and Kaaden is generally acknowledged to have built what was the prototype cruise missile, the 4S 293, which is today on permanent exhibition at the Deutsches Museum, Munich.

After Peenemünde was virtually destroyed by the RAF in August 1943, the research centre was relocated and work on the V2 rockets continued. Then, in May 1945, Kaaden was interned by the advancing American forces and later handed over to the Russians. Zschopau meanwhile was in the part of Germany controlled by the Communist authorities and eventually in the early 1950s Kaaden returned and was soon to enter the employ of DKWs successors, MZ (Motorraderwerke Zschopau).

From 1953 Kaaden took charge of the MZ racing department, which meant he controlled all the factory's sporting activities. Kaaden then developed a series of engines where the carburettor was mounted to the side of the crankcase, where it supplied mixture by means of a disc valve mounted in the crankcase wall. He was also a pioneer in utilising the now widely-used square 54 x 54 mm dimensions (on a 125cc single) with expansion chamber exhaust.

By 1961 the 125 single and 250cc twins were offering the equivalent of 200 bhp per litre – an amazing figure for the time – and MZ looked like taking the 125cc world title. But it was not to be. Their chief rider, Ernst Degner, defected to the West and went to work for Suzuki.

Coincidentally enough, Suzuki won their first ever world championship the following year. Kaaden had been approached by the company earlier, but had refused Suzuki's advance, putting his family and country before personal freedom or wealth. However, Kaaden's research has been reflected in all subsequent racing two-strokes, not just those from Suzuki, but throughout the rest of the industry.

Walter Kaaden died on 3 March 1996, but his technology has outlived him and acts as a constant reminder of the man who is universally acclaimed as the 'Father of the Modern Two-stroke'.

Left: MZ engineering genius Walter Kaaden (at left), with riders Mike Hailwood, Alan Shepard and Ernst Degner in 1961.

Above right: Stanley Woods after the 1935 Isle of Man TT.

Stanley Woods
(1905-1993)

Many would argue that the greatest rider of the inter-war period was Irishman Stanley Woods. He was born in Dublin in 1905 and competed in the TT for the first time in 1922 as a works rider for Cotton in the Junior race. Woods had gained the ride by writing to Cotton and saying how good he was; the story goes they were so surprised to receive such a letter they simply caved in and loaned him a bike! His Isle of Man debut was in quite spectacular style: not only did his bike catch fire whilst refuelling in his pit at half distance, but he recovered from this setback to finish a very creditable fifth!

The following year Stanley Woods entered all three TTs, but retired in the lightweight and Senior. The Junior, like the other two, was over six laps, giving a total race distance of 226.5 miles. After an action packed race which saw several favourites retire, Woods emerged the winner at an average speed of 55.73 mph to give Cotton its first TT victory.

After two barren years of no finishes, he returned to the TT as a Norton works rider in 1926 and repaid them handsomely by winning the Senior race in convincing fashion. Here was where his career took off. He stayed with Norton for eight years, from 1926 to 1933, bringing them victory in the TT in 1926, 1932 and 1933. The latter two years he was supreme, winning both Senior and Junior events. He did the double yet again in 1935 aboard Italian Moto Guzzi machines.

Towards the end of his career Woods moved to Velocette and in 1936 finished runner-up on the Senior, but set a new outright TT lap record at 86.98 mph.

His final tally was ten TT victories which even to this day has only been bettered by two men, Mike Hailwood and Joey Dunlop.

Geoff Duke
(1923-)

Geoff Duke was born in St Helens, Lancashire in 1923, the son of a baker. At the age of 19 he volunteered for the Army and after a spell as a trainee mechanic became a dispatch rider. On leaving the Army his first move was to purchase a new BSA B32 trials machine, his first victory on the machine coming shortly afterwards. His success and a good slice of luck saw him meet up with Artie Bell, then the number one rider in Norton's road racing team. This was to result in the offer of a job at Norton and the chance to ride the newly developed 500T trials model. The Norton job brought about an entry of a standard 348cc Manx Norton for the 1948 Junior Manx Grand Prix. He retired half way through the race with a split oil tank whilst leading his first ever road race!

Next came a third place in the 1949 Irish North West 200 on the same Manx, followed the next month by victory on a production International model in the Senior Clubman TT. Then came more glory with a win in the Senior Manx GP and a second in the Junior event following a crash. Geoff was promoted to the full Norton works team, managed by Joe Craig, for the 1950 season.

A series of tyre problems meant that Norton didn't have a very good 1950 season, but Geoff went on to score a double 350/500cc world championship the following year; and retain the 350cc title in 1952. But by now the four-cylinder Italian models were outpacing the single cylinder Nortons. So Geoff signed for Gilera, winning, the 500cc title for the next three seasons, 1953, 54 and 55.

Politics and accidents did much to restrict his efforts in 1956 and 1957, and then Gilera quit. Geoff followed two years later after racing a mixture of Norton, BMW and Benelli machinery.

TRANSATLANTIC TROPHY

Legend has it that the Anglo-American Transatlantic Trophy match race series was born in the bar at Daytona's Plaza Hotel in February 1970. At that time, Formula 750 racing had just commenced on both sides of the Atlantic, the bikes to beat being the superb-sounding, BSA/Triumph triples.

The United States had only just rejoined the FIM after a break of almost half a century. So the outside world had no real idea of what, if any, talent the Americans had for European style racing.

With the arrival of the BSA-Triumph racing organisation in the States things began to change. It soon became obvious that, in spite of their inexperience, the 'novice' Americans possessed a genuine talent. So, the friendly rivalry between British and American racers began.

It was agreed that the event should be staged in Britain where the road racing circuits were acknowledged as being the more suitable at that time. The Easter weekend of 1971 was the date settled on for the

Barry Sheene (left) and Kenny Roberts on parade for the Transatlantic Race at Mallory Park, Easter 1980.

first contest and the circuits chosen were Brands Hatch, Mallory Park and Oulton Park.

The British team included Ray Pickrell, John Cooper and Paul Smart. The only recognised tarmac racer in the American team was the veteran Dick Mann, who had won at Daytona in 1970 aboard a 750 Honda after the American captain Gary Nixon had been sidelined just prior to the event by injury. And although the Americans tried hard enough, Britain finally won by 183 points to 137.

By 1972, the publicity earned by the Transatlantic match series was sufficient to attract some major sponsorship. Also, the American team was much stronger and included the country's top racer, Cal Rayborn. He amazed British crowds with his race-winning performances aboard a XR750 Harley-Davidson v-twin. Although Britain won again the margin was much smaller.

The following year saw fantastic racing, with not only larger teams but many stars appearing for the first time, including Barry Sheene and the Canadian Yvon du Hamel. It was so close that the event was not settled until the last race, Britain narrowly retaining the title.

In 1974 the event was dominated by American Kenny Roberts and the Americans won for the first time. From then on the two countries constantly swapped places. But although it was still staged in the 1980s, the 1970s were the best years, as later works contracts conspired to limit the top stars from taking part.

ITALIAN LONG DISTANCE RACES

The decision taken by the Italian government to cancel by decree the 1958 running of the famous Giro d'Italia (Tour of Italy) and the Milano-Taranto road races, robbed not only Italy, but the whole motorcycling world of two of its greatest spectacles.

The Giro was staged for the first time in 1953 and was limited to machines of not more than 175cc. The gruelling contest contained spectacular point-to-point stages run over nine days and covering some 1,300 miles (2,090 km) of ordinary Italian country roads (this was before the country was effectively criss-crossed with motorways). The stages varied from a mere 50 miles (80 km) to almost 300 (480 km) in a day. Considering that many of the bikes taking part were little more than tuned lightweight roadsters or mopeds this was a feat in itself, but under racing conditions it was a real challenge. Add to that, running the event in early spring invariably meant several days of unfavourable weather and the 'Giros' claim to have been the toughest motorcycle road race ever conceived has to be taken seriously.

In 1957, the final year of the race, the weather provided snow, hail, sleet or rain on seven of the nine days and the top six places were occupied by five different makes (MV, Morini, Mondial, Gilera and Bianchi).

If the Giro wasn't tough enough, then there was the even more demanding Milano-Taranto, run in a single leg from one end of Italy to the other. Unlike the Giro, the Milano-Taranto was open to machines up to 500cc, sidecars, and, at one time, scooters. The event's history stretched back to 1919, when it was called the Milano-Napoli and the first event was won by a 350 Garelli two-stroke at just 24 mph (39 kmh). From then to 1936, it was won by a variety of machines: Harley Davidson and Indian from America and Frera, Bianchi and, for three years running,

Moto Guzzi from the home country. Guzzi continued this form by winning the first running of the new full-length Milano-Taranto in 1937.

From then on the famous race became almost the preserve of Guzzi and Gilera, at least as far as the outright winner. Only in 1954 was there an outsider – Venturi, riding an FB Mondial, took the race with a winning speed which was the lowest since 1933, simply because all the leading Guzzi's and Gilera's fell by the wayside.

Post-war, one man dominated: Bruno Francisci, a Roman Moto Guzzi dealer. His victories in 1951 and 1952 for Guzzi were crowned in 1955 by a fantastic ride for rivals Gilera. That year he rode a pukka GP four cylinder, adopted just enough to comply with the rules.

In 1956 there were no less than 36 marques represented, many of which were official factory entries. Then came the tragic accident in the Mille Miglia car race, resulting in the death of a whole group of spectators, who, like the spectators at bike events, insisted on lining the roadside. The tragedy caused such a public outcry that the politicians acted by banning all such events, both four and two wheel.

So came to an end an era when Italy's towns and villages were able to witness the thrills of real road racing at close quarters.

Left: The programme cover for the last Giro d'Italia (Tour of Italy) staged from 6 to 14 April 1957

Below: Overall winner of the 1954 Milano-Taranto Classic, Remo Venturi pushes his 175cc FB Mondial into life.

GRAND PRIX

In 1949, the FIM finally adopted the structure of an official series and the first Grand Prix World Championships, with a total of six venues took place. However, only the Blue Ribbon 500cc solo class was staged at all six circuits; the 350cc had five, 250cc four, whilst the 125cc and sidecars only took place at three.

Englishman Les Graham took the coveted 500cc title riding an AJS Porqupine twin. Another Englishman and English bike took the 350cc – Freddie Frith and a Velocette KTT single. If Britain dominated the larger classes, then Italy did the same in the smaller ones: Bruno Ruffo (Moto Guzzi) and Nello Pagani (FB Mondial) taking the 250cc and 125cc categories respectively. The sidecar crown went to Eric Oliver and passenger Denis Jenkinson with their Norton outfit.

In those days all the leading contenders employed four-stroke engines, usually with either single or double overhead cams. Also the norm was one or at the most two cylinders. But this pattern was to undergo considerable change over the years.

As the 1950s began to progress the first developments seen were multi-cylinder Italian bikes from the likes of MV Agusta and Gilera arriving on the scene. This meant that British marques such as Norton and AJS were soon under pressure. It also began a migration of British riders, including Les Graham (from AJS to MV Agusta, 1950) and Geoff Duke (from Norton to Gilera, 1953).

In the lightweight classes Italian bikes and riders were usually dominant, although the German NSU marque made its mark from 1953 to 1955 period, its top riders being Werner Haas, Ruppert Hollaus and H.P. Müller. Also, NSU were one of the first companies to exploit aerodynamics, together with Moto Guzzi and Norton.

Guzzi usually campaigned ohc horizontal singles, but also built a

In the first year of the World Championship series in 1949, Freddie Frith won the 350cc title on a Velocette.

watercooled inline four and, most significantly of all, a V-8! Guzzi, together with Gilera and FB Mondial retired from the scene at the end of 1957.

But it was MV Agusta who were to really make their mark. This began in 1956, when Carlo Ubbiali secured the double, winning both the 125cc and 250cc championship titles. Although vanquished in every class during 1957, MV, led by John Surtees, came back to win all classes in 1958 – an astonishing feat which it was to repeat again in 1959 and 1960. Surtees quit bike racing in 1961 for four wheels, eventually entering the history books as the first and only man to win World Championships with both motorcycles and cars. The role Surtees played in the technical development was undoubtedly a key factor in MV's successful evolution as the world's premier racing team.

If Surtees had been instrumental in establishing MV in the 350cc and 500cc categories, his team-mate, Italian Carlo Ubbiali, was equally important in the 125cc and 250cc classes. It is perhaps strange that he, too, chose the end of 1960 to announce his retirement, but unlike Surtees this was to be the final curtain on a career which had begun at the end of the 1940s. He could rightly claim to have been a 'champion of champions', carrying off no less than nine world titles in 14 seasons.

Count Domenico Agusta had signed the Rhodesian (now Zimbabwe) rider Gary Hocking as his replacement for both riders. Hocking had sprung to fame as a privateer on Nortons, and had scored his first Grand Prix victory on an East German MZ two-stroke in Sweden during 1959. Then, in 1960 he was runner-up in the 125, 250 and 350cc classes on MVs.

Geoff Duke on works Norton 500cc winning Ulster Grand Prix in 1952.

Left: German Werner Haas winning the 1954 250cc Dutch TT. Victory gave him and NSU the world title for a second year.

Below: John Surtees at the Belgian GP in 1957 with fully streamlined four cylinder MV Agusta.

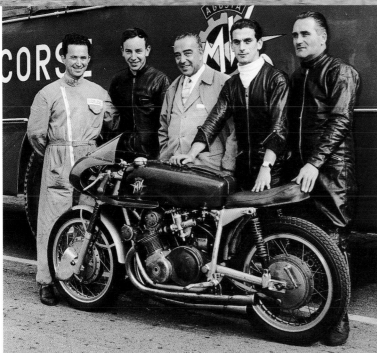

Count Domenico Agusta (centre) with riders John Surtees (left), Umberto Masetti (second from right) and Carlo Bandirola in 1955.

Although Hocking scored an MV double in the two larger classes in 1961 he sensationally quit bikes for cars after winning the Senior (500cc) Isle of Man TT in June 1962 following the death of his close friend Tom Phillis. Phillis was an Australian who had been one of the first non-Japanese riders to race for Honda. Honda had arrived on the scene of the 1959 TT, when they took the team prize in the Ultra-Lightweight (125cc) TT. Phillis had signed midway through 1960 and in 1961 was the first man (with Mike Hailwood) to win a title on a Japanese-made machine, when he piloted his 125cc Honda twin to take the crown.

THE 1960S AND 70S

The beginning of the 1960s saw a rash of 'foreign' signings by the Japanese manufacturers eager to take Grand Prix glory. Jim Redman, Tommy Robb, Bob Intyre, Bob Brown and Luigi Taveri contracted for Honda; Paddy Driver, Hugh Anderson and Frank Perris joined Suzuki; and later Phil Read and Mike Duff were on Yamaha's books.

Besides these there were also Mike Hailwood, Ernst Degner and Derek Minter. Hailwood won his first world title on a Honda 250cc four cylinder in 1961 and then left to join MV Agusta. Degner had previously ridden for the East German MZ factory. When he defected in 1961 there was some controversy because he was alleged to have given his former employer's secrets in the art of the two-stroke engine to his new employers, Suzuki. Whatever the truth of the matter, the following year Degner and Suzuki became the first ever two-stroke road racing championship holders (albeit in the newly-created 50cc category). Minter holds a place in history, but for the wrong reason. His 'sin' was that he rode an older Honda four to victory, beating the official factory riders in the 1962 Lightweight (250cc) Isle of Man TT. The Japanese top brass were so offended that the Englishman was never allowed to race for Honda (or for that matter any other Japanese manufacturer) ever again.

Back in 1961, MV had cut their racing budget and entered its bikes under the 'Private' banner. As events were to prove this was a fortunate move, because the Japanese were to dominate the smaller classes for much of the decade. But the Italian company still retained its grip in the larger (350cc and 500cc) classes. In fact, MV Agustas were to remain the machines to beat until 1974, going no less than 14 straight 500cc Championships in that period alone. This was assisted by having top riders like Mike Hailwood, Giacomo Agostini and Phil Read as pilots.

By 1967, Honda had scored 16 Championship titles and nearly 140 Grand Prix victories. Along the way, it had raised the stakes in motorcycle racing to incredible levels, spending a truly awesome amount of money. Stymied by MV Agusta during 1966 and 1967 in the 500cc category, Honda announced its withdrawal from racing. Suzuki followed at the same time, and Yamaha reduced its efforts. Yamaha finally quit at the end of 1968, after Phil Read and Bill Ivy had given them a 125/250cc double on their latest four-cylinder two-stroke models.

Yamaha would probably have quit in any case because for 1969 the FIM introduced new rules concerning the 50cc and 125cc classes, limiting the former to single cylinder, the latter to twins. Both capacities were to have a maximum of six gears. The 250cc class was to be limited to twin cylinder and six speeds a year later. Effectively this outlawed the hyper-expensive Japanese multi-cylinder machines. But in this net was also caught the small Italian Benelli factory with their four-cylinder 250. Slowly developed over a ten year period, its finest hour come in 1969 when the Australian Kel Carruthers piloted the eight speed dohc across-the-frame four cylinder model to the 250cc world title. It was the last four-stroke to achieve a World Championship.

Then came a period during the early 1970s when Yamaha production-based twin cylinder two-strokes ruled the class, before the Italian Harley

Far left: Giacomo Agostini during the 1973 Dutch TT. The Italian holds the record for the largest number of world championships, a staggering 15 in total.

Left: The Honda camp at the Dutch TT in 1961. The Japanese were just about to press the explode button on the opposition.

Below: Walter Villa won four world titles during 1974, 75 and 76 on Italian-built Harley-Davidson two-strokes. He is here in action at the Austrian GP at Salzburg in 1976.

Davidson (formally Aermacchi) factory won a trio of 250cc championships in 1974, 75 and 76 (they also took the 350cc title in 1976), before Morbidelli (1977) and Kawasaki (1978, 79, 80 and 81) took over.

Kawasaki had also won the first 125cc title year under the new twin cylinder/six-speeds rule in 1969, when Englishman Dave Simmonds gained their first ever world crown. Other championship winning marques in the first decade of the new formula were Suzuki, Derbi, Yamaha, Morbidelli, MBA and Minerelli.

The smaller category, the 50cc, saw an equally exciting contest for honours with Derbi, Kreidler and Bultaco sharing the honours during the 1970s.

Meanwhile, the 350 and 500cc championships, seemed a much more difficult agenda. The four-stroke MV Agustas ruled supreme until the mid-1970s – not even the mighty Honda could break into the larger class (although Honda won the 350cc title from 1962 to 1967 inclusive).

Then MV achieved the 350/500cc double in 1973 when Agostini was 350cc champion and Read 500cc top scorer. In 1974 Agostini signed for Yamaha and promptly won the 350cc championship. But ill-luck dogged him in the 500cc class, depriving him and Yamaha of the double. That same year Phil Read and MV Agusta defied the two-stroke juggernaut for the last time, winning in France, Belgium, Finland and Czechoslovakia. But although MV were to gain an occasional victory in the next couple of seasons, with the last one coming at the Nürburging in the 500cc race in late 1976, it was the end of the championship line for the famous Italian marque – and for four-strokes in Grand Prix racing. Agostini and Yamaha took the 500cc title in 1975.

500CC CLASS CHAMPIONS

In the blue ribbon 500cc class it was now the turn of Suzuki with their RG500 square four (two-stroke, of course) and a brilliant young Londoner named Barry Sheene. To Sheene must go the title of the man who brought motorcycle races to the attention of the wider British public, with his excellent riding skills and attention-grabbing PR – some, it must be said, thanks to his amazing ability to survive the most dreadful accidents. Sheene won the 500cc championship back-to-back in 1976 and 1977.

Next came Kenny Roberts, the first American world champion who also transformed racing by applying his flat-track riding style to the tarmac and in the process helped further motorcycle racing tyre technology.

Although still competitive in the smaller classes, Europe had largely been sidelined in motorcycle racing development by the end of the 1970s. Only in the 50cc (replaced by the 80cc from 1984, until its own demise at the end of the decade) and 125cc categories did the likes of MBA, Minerelli, Garelli, Krauser and Derbi make any impact.

The 500cc now came down to a straight fight between Suzuki, Yamaha and Honda. Kawasaki, who won several titles in the 250cc and 350cc classes in the late 1970s and early 1980s with Kork Ballington and Anton Mang, never made the same impact in the bigger class although they tried hard enough.

Honda attempted a return to racing with a four-stroke with oval pistons and massive engine revolutions, but in the end the NR500 simply couldn't match the two-stroke opposition, so Honda gave up and built their own two-strokes. At first this was a three-cylinder design, but later Honda joined rivals Suzuki and Yamaha with a four-cylinder model.

In 1984 American Freddie Spencer became the first man in history to win both the 250cc and 500cc titles in the same year, and both his bikes were Hondas. A year earlier, the 350cc class had been axed, its last winner being the Kawasaki rider Anton Mang, with the final development of that company's successful inline twin.

In the big class, the Americans had begun their dominance as riders, whilst Japan became unstoppable as engineers. In fact, the only non-Japanese manufacturer to challenge for honours in the 500cc class in the 1980s and 1990s has been the Italian Cagiva marque and many see Cagiva's financial problems of the mid-1990s as stemming directly from the vast amounts of money they spent in trying to match the Japanese.

Then, from 1978 to 1994 – with brief interludes in 1981 by Marco Lucchinelli, 1982 by Franco Uncini, 1987 by Wayne Gardner and from 1994 by Mick Doohan – every 500cc championship has been won by an American. After Kenny Roberts came Freddie Spencer (1983 and 1985), Eddie Lawson (1984, 86, 88 and 89), Wayne Rainey (1990, 91, 92) and, finally, Kevin Schwantz (1993).

In the almost five decades since the World Championship was first staged in 1949 there has been a complete transformation in racing. The early riders raced largely on road circuits; now only purpose-built venues are employed. Safety has been a major issue, not just on the circuits themselves, but also in the riders' protective clothing. Technology has moved on apace, so that besides two wheels and an engine, the racer of yesteryear would recognize little in today's machine specification. Two-strokes have replaced four-strokes, disc brakes are used instead of drums, whilst suspension, tyres, exhaust and electrics have all undergone incredible changes. Streamlining is now almost an artform and the use of lightweight materials such as carbon fibre was unthought of years ago. But technology marches on. No doubt in the 21st century motorcycle racing will see yet more radical changes. But there are two things which have not changed. Grand Prix racing is still the premier motorcycle sport and demands the highest of skills of the riders.

Above: The brilliant Londoner Barry Sheene in action at the Venezuelan GP in 1977. He was the last Briton to win a solo road racing world title, being 500cc champion for Suzuki in both 1976 and 1977.

Left: In the mid-1990s Australian Mick Doohan, on the Honda NSR500, was the man to beat in the blue ribbon 500cc class. He won yet again in 1996.

THE BOL D'OR

One can trace the Bol d'Or 24 hour race right back to 1922, and this French classic is easily the longest-running day and night event in the motorcycle racing calendar. In fact it would be true to say that it dominates the endurance racing scene, carrying with it the biggest prestige and the richest prizes, almost equalling a full Grand Prix world championship meeting.

The very first Bol d'Or saw the two-wheelers racing non-stop for some 48 hours. This was followed by a similar event for cyclecars and sidecars. This extravaganza ran from the 27 to the 29 May 1922, and in the motorcycle solo event there were separate categories for 250cc, 350cc and 500cc machines. As this event was staged some 12 months before the first 24-hour car race at Le Mans, it means that it was motorcycles which sparked the great French passion for long distance racing.

That first ever Bol d'Or was held at the Vaujours circuit and was won by a Motosacohe. From 1923 through to 1936 the race was staged at St Germain, except for 1927, when Fontainebleau was the venue. Then in 1937, the Bol d'Or moved to the legendary Montlhéry circuit. During the inter-war period, besides the original Motosacohe success, victories were secured by: Sunbeam (three), FN (one), Giliet-Herstal (three), Monet-Goyon (one), Velocette (three), Jonghi (one), Norton (two), Harley-Davidson (one), Motobécane (one) and another by Motosacohe.

The Bol d'Or was reinstated after the war at St Germain in 1947, where it was won by Gustave Lefevre on a plunger-framed 500 International Norton. Lefevre went on to record another six victories, the last one in 1957, making him the most successful rider in Bol d'Or history. During the 1960s, with motorcycling in decline, there was no Bol d'Or race from 1961 through to 1968.

What saved the event – and most probably endurance racing – was the advent of the modern Superbike, in the shape of Honda's magnificent four pot CB750. Montlhéry was again the setting for the re-launch of the famous French marathon and in 1969 there were several factory-backed entries. Works Triumph Tridents contested the 1970 race and duly took the chequered flag, piloted by Paul Smart and Tom Dickie.

Then came the big intercontinental battles of the 1970s, between European and Japanese manufacturers. As Montlhéry could no longer cope with the growing importance (and sheer size) of the Bol d'Or, the race was moved in 1971 to the Bugatti circuit at Le Mans. This move was largely instrumental in the Bol d'Or's rise to pre-eminence amongst today's endurance races.

Le Mans, because of the shape of the town and circuit, was an ideal setting. Added to this is the atmosphere built up in the days preceding the annual event – the racing is only a part of what is virtually a week-long carnival. The circuit itself features a wide array of amenities with everything from a comprehensive camp site, through bike shows to

discos. The organisers cleverly combine the thrill of racing with an unmatched array of other attractions in a way no-one else has achieved, even at Grand Prix level.

Although another British victory was chalked up in 1971 (Pickrell/Tait on a BSA Rocket Three), the 1970s were largely the era of the Japanese aircooled four-cylinder bikes from Honda and Kawasaki. Often these were entered by individual teams such as Japauto of Paris, and Godier and Genoud. These usually sported special chassis' from the likes of Dresda or Egli.

But by the end of the decade direct factory involvement had become the norm. The manufacturers could see that endurance racing made a genuine contribution to the road riders' everyday motorcycling in areas, such as engine reliability, chassis design and stability at high speed.

It would be true to say that Kawasaki were the first of the Oriental bike builders to realise the link, but they were quickly followed by Honda and, eventually, Suzuki and Yamaha. European factories joined in with BMW, Ducati and Laverda all entering official teams during the 1970s.

Then in the 1980s everything moved up a gear, with new technology including water or oil-cooled engines, monoshock rear suspension, floating disc brakes, as well as huge improvements in tyres, chains, electrical systems and lubricants.

Many of today's Superbikes owe much to prototypes which have first appeared at events such as the Bol d'Or; notable examples being the Suzuki GSXR 750/1100, Yamaha FZ750/FZR1000, Honda RC30/RC45 and Kawasaki ZX series.

Above: Frenchman Jean-Claude Jaubert winner of the Bol d'Or in 1981 on a 977cc Honda.

Left: The Kawasaki France team in April 1996. One of their riders, the Scot Brian Morrison took the world endurance title that year.

Above: The 125cc twin-cylinder two-stroke Rumi scooter, class winner in 1957, 58 and 59 Bol d'Or.

SPRINTING DOWN THE LINE

Above: John Hobbs on a double-engined 1340cc Weslake takes off in spectacular fashion.

Of all motorcycle sports, sprinting is the oldest and record attempts over short, measured distances were made very soon after the turn of the century. Britain was the sports' original home, and although sprinting has since spread around the globe, it is still seen as a 'British' sport. In other countries, notably the US, it became known as drag racing.

Legendary names In Britain down through the years have included: Noel Pope, Freddie Dixon, Ernie Woods, George Brown, Alf Hagon and John Hobbs. In the United States, men such as Tom Christenson and Russ Collins were the leading exponents of drag racing during the same era. Famous venues for sprinting have included Marine Drive, Brighton, Greenham Common airbase, Oxfordshire and the purpose-built Santa Pod. In the US sprinting began in the 1950s at places like Daytona and the Bonneville Salt Flats in Utah and graduated to purpose-built strips.

Whether it's sprinting or drag racing the requirements are largely the same – maximum engine power for the capacity, light weight, a massive rear tyre for the best possible drive and, today, an aerodynamic stream-lined shell for maximum penetration at high speed.

The NSA (National Sprint Association) was formed in Britain during 1958 and it arranges sprint meetings with competitions for varied machine types and capacities. Sweden, Holland and Germany have followed this trend. The Dutchman Henk Vink was a great sprinter in the 1970s riding Kawasakis. Another famous exponent was E.J. Potter, the Michigan Madman, who rode a five-liter Chevrolet car-engined monster.

HOW TO START RACING

Everyone has to start somewhere and for most people this usually means club racing. In Britain there are several clubs with which the budding race star can begin his career on the tarmac. Some clubs, like New Era, hold meetings at virtually every venue, whilst others, such as EMRA (East Midland Racing Association), only stage events at one circuit, in their case Mallory Park.

Before entering a meeting the rider has to obtain a racing licence. In Britain this is issued by the ACU (Auto Cycle Union). The first stage is novice. This means having to take part in at least the first ten meetings with a novice orange jacket.

The next stage is gaining a Restricted licence. This means that you can take part at any club event (provided you belong to the particular club in question) without the need to wear an orange jacket. Once another ten signatures from race meetings are gained a full National licence can be yours. This entitles you to take part in any meetings (other than International) in the country.

Finally, there is the International licence, but even this does not automatically entitle the holder to contest the World Championship series, for which you have to be on a country's approved grading list.

For a novice, the first requirement is approved riding gear, including one piece leathers, helmet, boots and gloves. Before actually entering a meeting it is important to take part in a practice session (run at most circuits) or to enrol with a racing school.

The next important issue is to select the best class of bike for your needs. Today there is a wide range of machinery. As a novice you will not normally be allowed to race certain categories including machines exceeding 600cc (excluding singles, twins and classics). Two very good 'learner' classes are either 125cc open or Formula 400. There are also budget classes, including Ministockers (road-based 125s), MZ and formula LCs.

One way of attracting potential sponsors early in your career is the SuperTeen class. Run at national events, these are for 125cc road-based machines such as Aprila and Cagiva and provide an excellent start for any youngster between 15 and 19 years of age.

Whichever class you finally chose remember the golden rule – only proceed at your own speed – every newcomer's pace and style of development is different.

Below: The class of 1995, SuperTeens at Snetterton race track in April 1995. Machines are Medd Aprilia (left) and Mick Walker Racing Cagiva.

THE DAYTONA 200

The first ever Daytona 200 race was run in 1937, but Daytona Beach has been the home of American speedsters since the turn of the century. At that time the sprawling Ormond Hotel was a popular haunt for wealthy northern industrialists who travelled south to enjoy the clear blue skies of Florida. Amongst these men was Ransom Olds, founder of Oldsmobile and his friend Alexander Winton, another American pioneer auto manufacturer. And it was not long before both were sampling the delights of speeding up and down the gleaming silver sands of Ormond and Daytona beaches.

Legend has it that both clocked almost 60 mph (97 kmh) during a highly unofficial burn-up in 1902. This event reminded the Hotel proprietors of a proposal they had received some four years earlier, to stage a cycle week on the beach with the Ormond as its base. This was to be the catalyst for an event which still takes place today.

First it was men like Glenn Curtiss who set Daytona on fire, building a V-8 motorcycle which (although never officially recorded) achieved over 136 mph (219 kmh) on Ormond Beach in 1907.

During the 1920s and 1930s the Florida beach witnessed a number of speed record attempts as men such as Sir Henry Seagrave and Malcolm Campbell fought for the glory of the world's fastest on four wheels, powering their British-built monster cars along Daytona's thin strip of silver sand. But soon the record breakers departed, forced out when speeds proved simply too great for such a narrow course. But this made space for another form of motor sport – the Daytona 200 motorcycle race.

The first event took place on 24 January 1937 in front of some 15,000 spectators. From a field of 98 riders the winner was Ed Kretz riding a Indian v-twin.

The original course south of Daytona town was 3.2 miles long, with a flat-out blind down the beach, a 180-degree corner on sand, then full throttle again along a narrow, undulating tarmac road which ran parallel to the beach behind the sand dunes and back to the beach via another 180-degree turn.

This combined road-beach circuit ran until 1960 and it was no easy trip, The 1940 event saw only 15 of the original 77 starters still running at the end. After America's entry into the war in December 1941 no Daytona races were run until 1947. The course was 'moved' down the beach in 1948 as part of the old section was being affected by new development. The basic layout was the same, but the overall length of a lap was now 4.2 miles. The same year also saw the last victory by an Indian machine.

Realising the potential of the Stateside market, the British factories (notably Norton) began to take an interest and in 1949 Norton-mounted Dick Klamfoth set a new race record at over 86 mph (138 kmh) when he won in front of over 16,500 fans.

Norton went on to scoop three more Daytona victories in successive years. All this was too much for American pride and the AMA (American Motorcycle Association) promptly banned Norton's Manx racers, despite the fact at 499cc they were giving away half their capacity to the locally-built 750cc Harley-Davidsons.

In 1961 the Daytona 200 was transferred to the new purpose-built International Speedway venue, with the main race supporting a number of motorcycling events over a full week for the first time.

Roger Reiman, on a Harley-Davidson, became the first winner, averaging just under 70 mph (112 kmh). Throughout the 1960s it was a straight battle between the 750cc side valve Harleys and 500cc ohv parallel twin Triumphs. Riding honours went to Reiman (four), Cal Rayborn (two), with Gary Nixon, Buddy Elmore, Ralph White and Don Burnett all gaining single victories.

In 1970 the AMA brought in European style rules and Dick Mann won on a Honda CB750. Mann repeated his success on a BSA Rocket Three the following year before Don Emde (1972) and Jarno Saarineen (1973) both won on 350 Yamaha two-strokes.

Since then the event has seen a galaxy of stars as victors, including Giacomo Agostini (1974), Johnny Cecotto (1976), Kenny Roberts (1978, 83 and 84) Graeme Crosby (1982), Freddie Spencer (1985) Eddie Lawson (1986), Wayne Rainey (1987) and Kevin Schwantz (1988).

The 1990s saw another major rule change which brought a new look to Daytona. Under the previous rules a machine had only to be suitable under AMA ruling. However, this was amended so that only road-based motorcycles could take part. That included machines built for the World Superbike Series, such as the Ducati v-twins and the entire line of Japanese four-cylinder models from Honda, Kawasaki and Yamaha.

Despite the changes, the Daytona 200 remains *the* race for the manufacturers, riders and, most of all, the thousands of spectators who flock to Florida each spring.

The famous Daytona banking with R. Crawford on a Honda Hawk and J. Lickwar on a Ducati 900SS at full speed in 1996.

Above: The great Kenny Roberts, on a Yamaha, won the '200' three times, in 1978, 1983 and 1984.

Left: The 1970 Daytona winner Dick Mann, on a Honda, is flanked by Gene Romero (left) and Don Castro on Triumphs.

THE WORLD SUPERBIKE

World SuperBike (WSB) is today seen by many as the future for road racing. It was the Americans who really pushed the boat out to convince the FIM that the SuperBike concept was important. After all it was in the US that the premier national championship had been so successfully based on just such bikes. And it is worth remembering that names such as Freddie Spencer, Wayne Rainey, Kevin Schwantz and Eddie Lawson all emerged from this domestic championship.

Early backers for the World SuperBike Championship were the legendary France family of Daytona International Speedway fame who gave the original series' 'salesman', Californian Steve McLauglin, much initial help and guidance.

Their efforts paid off and it was agreed at the FIM's Paris Congress in October 1987 to run the first WSB championship during the following (1988) season.

Ducati launched their first four-valve v-twin at the Milan Show of November 1987. It was an inspired move. The new machine was named the 851 and was offered in both Strada (road) and kit (racing) forms. The factory also built a specially prepared racer for former 500cc world champion Marco Lucchinelli. The first round of the new World Super-Bike Championship was staged at Donington Park, England in early 1988, where Lucchinelli set the racing world on fire with a sensational victory aboard the booming Italian v-twin.

Basically the WSB rules allowed for 750cc fours and 1000cc twins, both with their own weight limits. Later a new rule was introduced which allowed 900cc three cylinder models to compete.

Three main contestants emerged that first year: Ducati with their watercooled, fuel injected, 8-valve v-twin; fellow Italians Bimota with a Yamaha OW01-engined YB4 model and the v-four Honda RC30.

At the year's end it was the combination of American Fred Markel and the Honda RC30 which came out on top against Italy's Davide Tardozzi on the Bimota. Lucchinelli took third, even though he didn't contest all the rounds.

Carl Fogarty followed by Arran Slight on Castrol Honda RC45s during the 1996 World SuperBike series.

Carl Fogarty leading yet another race on his Ducati during the 1994 season; the combination won again in 1995.

Up to then the New Zealand-based Sports Marketing Company had largely funded the World SuperBike project, but only days before the first round in 1989 (again at Donington Park) they pulled out. The event was saved by the Japanese Moto Co, backed by the world's largest advertising agency, Dentsu. The top three in the 1989 season were Fred Markel (still on a Honda v-four), Stephane Mertens (also on a Honda) and Ducati's new signing, former GP star, Frenchman Raymond Roche. But after this Ducati and Kawasaki were to make the WSB theirs.

In 1990 Roche began a trio of titles for Ducati, followed by a double for the American Doug Polen in 1991 and 1992 (with Roche runner-up both years). In 1993 another American, Scott Russell, riding a Muzzy-Kawasaki broke Ducati's grasp on the crown, if only for a single season.

The UK's Carl Fogarty created a stir at the Donington Park round of the 1992 series by soundly beating the works teams on his privately-entered 888 Corsa Ducati. He was signed by the Bologna factory for the 1993 season. Fogarty repaid this trust by winning first the 1994 championship and then the 1995 one for good measure. His main rival, Scott Russell, then quit to join the Grand Prix circuit.

'King' Carl then sensationally signed for Honda for the 1996 season, but even he couldn't bring the title back to Honda; although their RC45 machines finished 2nd and 3rd (Arran Slight and Fogarty respectively). The championship was once again won by a Ducati rider, this time Australian Troy Corser. Fogarty has since signed for Ducati while it looked likely that Corser will move to GPs.

Ducati's success in the WSB has shown everyone that a modern v-twin is still able to mix it with the best in multi-cylinder design. Of course, it's not quite a level playing field, as Ducati had the advantage of the 851, and then, progressively later, the 888, 916 and 955cc against the Japanese 750cc limit as well as a weight advantage, although this has been steadily reduced following Ducati's continued success. Even so the WSB Championship has grown in status each year so that now it challenges the blue ribbon 500cc GP category in popularity with competitors and spectators alike.

ROAD RACERS

Kenny Roberts

(1951-)

The first American to win the 500cc road racing World Championship title, it is little wonder then that racing fans all around the globe gave Kenny Roberts the title of 'King Kenny'.

Born in California on the last day of 1951, he had his first competitive motorcycle race at the tender age of 16. There followed a truly star-studded career which saw him go on to win 33 National victories (making him second in the all-time American winners list), two AMA Grand National Championships, three 500cc World Championships and, after his racing career was over, the position of a world-class racing team manager.

In 1970 he was snapped up by Yamaha-America and responded by becoming AMA Novice Champion the same year, Junior Champion in 1971 and Grand National champ in 1973 and 1974. Equally at home on road circuits or the oval tracks which made up much of the AMA Championships, Roberts rocketed from comparative obscurity to become internationally acclaimed as a true superstar.

If one could name the decisive point in his career it would be 1972, when the young Kenny came under the wing of the Australian Kel Carruthers, the 1969 250cc World Champion. By 1973 Roberts was sweeping everything before him to take his first AMA number one spot. If 1973 was good, 1974 was even better, with another AMA championship and his first appearances in Europe. Not only did he win at the Anglo-American Match Races, but also came near to victory in Italy's Imola 200.

Then came a period where the dirt track

Yamaha was no match for the all-conquering Harley Davidson, so Roberts and Carruthers decided to give Europe their attention: 1978 was supposed to be a learning year, but Kenny amazed everyone by taking the 500cc world championship at the final round, beating no less than Barry Sheene, the 1976 and '77 champion. And if this wasn't enough, he also gained 2nd in the 750cc and 4th in the 250cc championships.

Kenny then went on to become 500cc champion in 1979 and '80. He retired in 1984; but Team Roberts has continued the glory with top riders such as Lawson, Mamola, Rainey and Kocinski.

Mike Hailwood

(1940-1981)

Stanley Michael Bailey Hailwood was born on 2 April 1940, the son of a self-made millionaire motorcycle dealer. Hailwood Senior competed on both two, three and four wheels, before going on to build up the largest grouping of dealerships ever seen in Britain.

Mike Hailwood began his career aboard a 125cc MV Agusta under the watchful eye of his father and Bill Webster, a close friend of factory boss Count Agusta. This

was at Oulton Park, just after his 17th birthday. At the end of the 1957 season Stan packed his son off to South Africa, equipped with an ex-John Surtees 250cc NSU and a 350cc Norton.

It proved an excellent training ground and he came back with not only several wins, but experience enough to score an incredible trio of British Championships (125, 250 and 350cc) in 1958. Into 1959, and his first Grand Prix win was secured on a 125cc Ducati (his father was the firm's British importer). He also won all four British championship series, a feat he repeated the following year and one which no man before or since has ever equalled.

For 1961 Mike had 125 and 250cc works Hondas, plus a 350cc AJS and 500cc Norton. He gained his first world title, the 250cc, on the Honda four, took the 125 and 250cc TTs and the 500cc on the Norton, averaging over 100 mph (160 kmh) for the six-lap, 226 mile race.

He then signed for MV Agusta and won the 500cc world title four years in a row – 1962 to 1965. Mike rejoined Honda in 1966 and won both 250 and 350cc classes on the new six-cylinder models, equalling this the following year before turning his attention to four wheels.

More than a decade later he returned to bikes with an historic comeback victory on a Ducati. The next year he rode a Suzuki to a final TT victory, in 1979. He retired, but tragically was to die in a road accident in 1981.

Eric Oliver

(1918-1981)

Eric Oliver rode solo bikes before concentrating on sidecar events after the Second World War. He is best remembered for his great sportsmanship, with no real thought for any particular financial rewards.

A tough independent character, he paid great attention to every detail of his racing; studying other teams, practising his starts and racing techniques and not forgetting the mechanical preparation of his highly successful Norton machinery, on which he won countless races and no less than four world titles.

His first racing came in pre-war days and in 1937 he competed in the Isle of Man TT, as he did the following year in both the Senior and Junior events. His best solo performance in the Isle of Man came in 1948, on a MK VIII KTT Velocette, when he finished eighth in the Junior event.

Already a member of the 'Continental Circus' by the time the first World Championships series was staged in 1949, Oliver and his passenger Denis Jenkinson won two of the three rounds with their dohc Manx Norton with Watsonian sidecar. The pairing of Oliver/Jenkinson won two of the three rounds (Switzerland and Belgium) and came fifth in the final round in Italy.

In 1950, this time with Italian Lorenzo Dobelli as ballast, Oliver thwarted a serious challenge from Gilera (who had won the final round in 1949). Dobelli was again the passenger when Oliver gained his third consecutive title in 1951 and might have done so again the following year, but an accident in France, combined with a retirement through a sidecar wheel problem, cost him dearly.

In 1953, with new partner Stan Dibbon, Oliver become champion for the fourth and final time. Although he won the first Sidecar TT since the 1920s in 1954 he finally had to give way to the much faster BMWs. He retired the following year and died in 1981.

Barry Sheene

(1950-)

Barry Sheene did more than any other to make racing more accessible to the public, and financially more rewarding to the rider.

Born in London on 11 September 1950, he was encouraged by his ex-racer father, Frank, who also ran a successful tuning business. Barry's race debut came on a 125cc Bultaco at Brands Hatch in 1968, in which he crashed after the engine seized. His father had close links with the Spanish Bultaco factory and this resulted in works bikes for the following season. Then came the purchase of Stuart Graham's ex-factory Suzuki 125cc twin. With the little Suzuki Sheene almost took the 1971 125cc world title, only failing at the last round in Spain when he was beaten by

works Derbi rider Angel Nieto. In 1972 he switched to Yamaha machines, but without real success. But when he returned to Suzuki, this time as an official rider, things changed. At first he rode the 500 twin and later the 180 mph (290 kmh) 750cc three-cylinder. And it was on one of the latter machines that he suffered a horrific accident at Daytona in March 1975. However, he made an amazing recovery and was racing again a mere five weeks later!

Into 1976 and armed with a works RG500 four he won five of the ten round world championship series to take the title. Actually, it was even more convincing than it would appear as he didn't ride or finish in four rounds and finished runner-up at the other. In retaining his crown the following year Barry recorded six victories.

In 1978 (second) and 1979 (third) he fought some tremendous battles with the American Kenny Roberts. Roberts won both the 1978 and 79 titles, and Sheene began to consider a switch to four wheels. But after testing and racing, including a Surtees F1 and a BMW saloon he decided to stick with bikes. This time it was using standard production Yamaha machinery backed by the Akai electrical company.

Barry soon found out that privateer machinery was no match for works tackle and he struggled; but eventually at the end of 1981 Yamaha gave Sheene a contract and he responded by winning the final round in Sweden to finish 4th in the championship table. Then in 1982 came another serious accident whilst practising for the British GP at Silverstone. And whilst Sheene once again recovered, this was really the end of the big time. He finally retired during 1984, going to live in Australia.

Giacomo Agostini

(1942-)

Born on 16 June 1942 at Lovere, Brescia, Giacomo Agostini holds the record for the rider who has scored more world championship victories than any other, a staggering 15 in total.

'Ago' began his competitive career in 1961, riding a 175cc Morini Settebello ohv single. Road racing came a year later, when he competed at Cesenatico on the same machine. Following a string of impressive victories, Agostini plucked up enough courage to book an interview with factory boss, Alfonso Morini, to ask if he could be considered for a works ride. When the answer was 'yes', he was so taken aback that he promptly knocked a typewriter off a desk in the Commendore's office!

Morini's faith was soon shown to have been justified when 'Ago' lapped joint fastest during official practice for the 250cc Italian GP at Monza in September 1963; he proved this was no fluke by leading the race at one stage.

The 1964 West German GP was his first race outside Italy. At Solitude he finished fourth behind the Yamahas of Phil Read and Mike Duff and Jim Redman's Honda, ahead of his former team captain Tarquinio Provini's Benelli 4. By July of that year Agostini had already ended Provini's three-year reign as Italian 250cc champion, breaking many of his lap records on the way. All this made a deep impression on Count Agusta, with the result that for 1965 Agostini was an MV rider.

His first GP win came at the Nürburgring, riding one of the new 350cc MV triples. He finished the year runner-up in both the 350 and 500cc championships. The following year he gained his first world crown – in the 500cc class – the first of no less than seven consecutive titles in the blue ribbon class. From 1968 he notched up seven straight championships in the 350cc category, the last, in 1974 riding a Yamaha. His final title came in 1975; he gained this last championship, while riding a Yamaha 4 to take back 'his', 500cc crown from Phil Read.

In 1974 'Ago' rode a 750cc Yamaha two-stroke to victory at both Daytona and Imola, proving that in F750 as well as GPs he was a true champion.

Eddie Lawson

(1958-)

Like Kenny Roberts, an American graduate of the dirt tracks, Eddie Lawson was born in 1958 and from an early age was very much a motorcycle star in the making. He first sprung to fame by winning the 250cc race in 1979 on a Yamaha.

His wins in the US Superbike Championship in 1981 and 1982 were commemorated by the much-prized Eddie Lawson Kawasaki Z1100R replica. Coming at such an early stage in his career this is a lasting testament to the impact he made in American domestic racing during the early 1980s.

Succeeding the 'King' Kenny Roberts as the number-one rider at Team Marlboro Yamaha was probably the hardest act in racing to follow. But Lawson's great drive and talent saw him through. His record stands for itself, winning the all-important 500cc world championship in 1984, 1986 and 1988. His fourth Grand Prix crown in 1989 for Rothmans-Honda made Lawson the only rider to win the world 500cc title in consecutive season on different machinery.

He signed for the Italian Cagiva team in 1990 for one of the biggest fees ever seen in bike sport. The Californian's win for the Italian factory at the Hungarian 500cc GP in 1991 was the team's first GP victory in 10 years. Factory boss Claudio Castiglioni was so pleased that he promptly gave Lawson a Ferrari Testarossa.

Eddie Lawson retired from GP motorcycle racing at the end of 1992, to pursue a new career in American Indy Lights' cars.

John Surtees

(1934-)

Born on 11 February 1934, John Surtees' first motorcycle race came about as a 14-year-old when his father Jack asked him to be his sidecar passenger. The pairing actually won the event but were subsequently disqualified because of John's age.

His first solo victory came at 17, at the tree-lined Aberdare Park circuit in South Wales. He was riding a 499cc Vincent Grey Flash which the young Surtees had built whilst serving his apprenticeship at the company's Stevenage factory.

After winning the British championships on a single cylinder Manx Norton, John Surtees was signed by the Italian MV Agusta factory to race its machine during the 1956 season.

His first competitive outing on one of the Italian 'fire-engines' came at Crystal Palace in early April. He then proceeded to win the first three rounds of the 500cc World Championships, and even though he suffered a fall at the next round in Germany at the Solitude circuit, fracturing his arm, he had already amassed enough points to carry off the title. Although he could only finish third behind the Gilera pairing of Libero Liberati and Bob McIntyre in the 1957 500cc title race he had the honour of giving MV its first-ever victory with the smaller four-cylinder at the Belgian GP in 1956.

Then came a golden trio of double 350/500cc title years, when Surtees won just about everything in 1958, 59 and 60. Having nothing else to prove in the two-wheel world, John Surtees moved to four wheels and the rest is history.

Dirt Bikes

SCRAMBLING ORIGINS

The sport of scrambling (now known as motocross) began in England on the 29 March 1924, when the Camberley Club decided to modify the rules of its popular Southern Scott Trial by deleting the gymkhana section and concentrating on a timed trial section. Some 80 competitors assembled for the start of what was to prove an historic event. The winner was to be the rider who recorded the fastest time over two heats. Thus the new sport was born.

For the next few years scrambling developed with its own set of regulations, although it was still very much a mixture of existing motorcycle sports and did not become clearly defined until after the war. But what really established the sport was when it crossed the channel to Europe, preceded by the fame of several British riders. The first internationally-organised event was staged in France during 1939, at Romanville, on the outskirts of Paris, just before the outbreak of war.

One of the very first scrambling events was the *Motorcycling* sponsored 'Grand National'. This is the time trial of March 1926.

Left: Belgian rider F. Thomas jumps the 'Bomb Hole' during the 1949 Moto Cross des Nations at Brands Hatch. His mount is a 500cc FN.

Above: Jeff Smith (BSA) was the World 500cc Motocross champion in 1964 and 1965.

MOTOCROSS

The annual Motocross des Nations was inaugurated in 1947, and the first five years saw a titanic struggle for supremacy between Belgium and Britain, with the score three-two in the latter's favour.

In 1952, the FIM established the European 500cc Championship series. In 1957, this was developed into the World Championship. In the same year, and for the two following years, there was in addition a 250cc European Cup and in 1959 this too was granted the prestige of a European Championship. It was not until 1962 that the smaller capacity machines – which until then had played a supporting role in events organised around the impressive 500cc machinery – were elevated to take their place in the world series.

As already mentioned, Great Britain and Belgium were the initial pace setters, then came France, Holland, Denmark, Sweden and Switzerland. Later still Italy and Austria took up the sport, followed by Germany, Russia, Hungary, Poland, Spain, Finland and, finally, the United States of America and Japan.

During the 1940s and 1950s the large capacity four-stroke reigned supreme, usually with an ohc or ohv engine. From Britain came the BSA Gold Star, Matchless G80CS, Ariel HS, Norton Manx, Triumph Trophy and Velocette Scrambler. Belgium provided FN for its riders, whilst Sweden offered the Crescent, Lito, Monark and Lindstrom. The leading riders during these early days included Brian Stonebridge, Geoff Ward, Les Archer, Auguste Mingels, Bill Nillson, Rene Baeten, Sten Lundin, Jeff Smith and the Rickman brothers, Don and Derek.

In Britain at that time the only motocross course with any real pretensions to permanency was Hawkstone Park, the scene of the British Moto Cross Grand Prix and several successful Moto Cross des Nations meetings. Other notable sites included Shrubland Park, Suffolk, which was situated in a delightful country park at Claydon near Ipswich. At Brands Hatch, Kent, the motocross circuit lacked real hills and in any case had to play second fiddle to the road racing circuit. The only other notable British venue at that time was in Surrey, at Pirbright Common, a ☞

stone's throw from the scene of the original Southern Scott of 1924. But this was Army land and its use was severely restricted.

This contrasted sharply with Continental Europe where most motocross meetings were staged on permanent circuits with turnstiles, grandstands and all the rest of the trappings associated with professional sport. Ingenious course planning enabled organisers (notably in France) to make the very best use of their facilities, with the track often doubling back on itself several times, plunging through tunnels and climbing across flyover crossings to provide maximum spectator value in a minimum of acreage.

As for machine development, this, like everything else, came in stages. In 1959 Don Rickman had led the British team to victory in the Moto Cross des Nations at Namur, Belgium. There were six other nations besides Britain and the hosts, Belgium, at the event: Sweden, France, Denmark, Holland, Switzerland and Italy also took part.

The winning team consisted of Rickman (Metisse), Dave Curtiss (Matchless), Les Archer (Norton) and the BSA factory entered trio of John Draper, John Burton and Jeff Smith.

Don Rickman not only won his heat, but also the day's final to put the brother Rickman's Metisse firmly to the forefront of international motocross, a feat he was to repeat the following year when he led the British team to victory in the 1960 Moto Cross des Nations at Cassell, northern France.

So what was a Metisse? In French the word meant a mongrel bitch. Basically, the Rickman bike had started life as a mixture of what they considered were the best features from more than one machine – a BSA Gold Star frame, a set of Norton forks and a Triumph engine. Later a purpose-built chassis was designed, which together with fibreglass bodywork was not only good technically, but had visual appeal too.

By 1963, the Metisses had become so popular that series production began, not just with Triumph engines, but with several others, including Matchless and, later, Spanish Bultaco engines.

Above: World Champion Graham Noyce in action on a works 500cc Honda in 1979.

Below: The British and Swedish teams assemble for the 1958 Moto Cross des Nations. The British team were, from left to right, Don and Derek Rickman, Brian Martin, Ron Langston, Dave Curtis and Johnny Draper.

LATER DEVELOPMENTS IN MOTOCROSS

As motorcycle technology developed, so did the complexion of the sport, particularly with the rapid progress of lightweight two-stroke powered machines, first with 125 and 250cc engines from the late 1950s onwards. Helped by the introduction of the Coupe d'Europe, the early contenders in the smaller classes included DOT, Maico Monark, Jawa, Greeves and Husqvarna.

The Czeck rider Jaromir Cizek on a Jawa was the first holder of the cup, followed in 1959 by Swedish Husqvarna star Rolf Tibblin. In each case the Englishman Brian Stonebridge was runner-up on a Greeves. Sadly he was then fatally injured in a car accident. But Greeves still had Stonebridge's young protege, Dave Bickers. Bickers stormed through to annex not one, but two European titles in 1960 and again in 1961.

With the advent of world status in 1962, the competition became ever hotter and Husqvarna, in the shape of lone runner Torsten Hallman, took on the massed ranks of CZ, who had signed the quartet of Bickers, Tibblin, Joel Robert and Roger de Coster.

The next move came with the introduction in the middle of the decade by CZ and Greeves of 360cc versions of the lightweight, effectively killing off the old heavyweight thumper. But BSA responded by developing a larger-engined version of their C15 four-stroke, which took Jeff Smith to the 500cc world title in 1964 and 1965.

But after this it was two-stroke domination all the way, with not only the Europeans in the shape of Bultaco, Maico and Husqvarna, but the Japanese getting into the act too, headed by Suzuki. In the 1970s four Japanese manufacturers were locked in a battle for dirt racing supremacy. There were fat contracts for the riders and the sport boomed as never before.

Instrumental in this state of affair was the vast American market which had taken the sport to its heart – a position which has not changed over the last two decades. The only difference is that the Japanese manufacturers totally dominate the sport: the European factories have either withdrawn from the fray or are a pale shadow of their former selves.

The colourful Italian motocross rider Diego Bosis, who is a member of the 1997 Fantic works trials team.

ONE DAY TRIALS FEET-UP ACTION

Amongst the vast number of different kinds of motorcycle sport, trials riding is the most popular. It is one of the few types of bike sport in which the rider and his machine are required only to overcome natural obstacles – beating the clock plays no part at all in trials riding.

Because of the skill factor, many see trials as the two wheel sport. To succeed demands perfect balance, instant reflexes, determination and physical strength. They are all needed in abundance to overcome the hazards which present themselves in a rock strewn gully, a forest path, an almost vertical climb, or a rushing stream. The history of trials is entirely British and the first events were organised in the early part of the century. The two most famous trials events are the Scottish and the Scott, the latter held in Yorkshire.

After the Second World War virtually all the major British factories – Ariel, AMC (AJS and Matchless), BSA, Norton, Royal Enfield and Triumph – entered factory trials teams in an attempt to win not only the Scottish and the Scott, but later the British Trials Championship.

A European Championship was established in 1965 and was won by Gustav Franke (Zündapp), who beat the likes of Sammy Miller (Bultaco) and Don Smith (Greeves). But both the British riders went on to become champions in their own right later in the decade. The distinction of being the first world champion, after the series achieved world status in 1975, goes to Yorkshireman Martin Lampkin. There were 14 rounds, the best eight performances from each rider counting towards the title.

As far as machinery goes, up to the mid 1960s it was very much British, such as AJS, BSA, Greeves and Triumph. Then came the Spanish 'Armada' led by Bultaco. In the 1970s many Italian bike manufacturers built trials irons, including Fantic and SWM. But, as in other motorcycle sports, the Japanese finally took over.

INTERNATIONAL SIX DAYS TRIAL

Above: Swedish rider Rolf Tiblin and his mount, a 250cc Husqvarna, at the 1961 ISDT in Wales.

Right: George Rowley on a 498cc AJS at a checkpoint during the 1931 ISDT in Italy. He was a member of the British Trophy squad.

In December 1897 the Automobile Club of Great Britain and Ireland was founded to look after the interests of the early motorist. No distinction was made at that time between four-, three – and two-wheel vehicles. In the 'Emancipation' Run to Brighton in 1897 the only British-made vehicle to complete the course was a tricycle.

These early motorists were a sporting bunch and in 1900 the ACGBI ran the 'Great 1000 Miles Trial'. Among its entrants were a pair of quadricycles, two motor tricycles and a tricycle with a trailer. A couple of French Werner motorcycles were also entered but didn't start. By 1903 the development of the motorcycle was such that 93 members of the motorcycle branch of the parent body set up the Auto Cycle Union. In the very first year of its existence, the ACU organized a 1000-mile (1,600 km) trial which became an annual event as the ACU Six Days' Reliability Trial. The object of the event was to demonstrate the advantages of one machine over another. In 1913 it was decided to incorporate the FICM rules, and thus the first International Touring Trial began.

This event in 1913 is generally regarded as the first International Six Days' Trial and the ancestor to not only this famous event, but also of its ultimate successor, the International Six Days' Enduro (ISDE).

The organisation of the 1913 event, held under ACU direction, was in the hands of the Westmorland and Cumberland County Motor Cycle Club. The only national teams were from Britain and France, the former providing the winning trio of W.G. Gibb, Billy Little and Charlie Collier. The 1914 event would have been the first full International, but was cancelled due to the outbreak of war, so the next event did not take place until 1920. Based in France, Switzerland took the coveted Trophy – the same country going on to win again for the next two years.

The 1920s was a period of technical development and progress and there was a parallel growth in the size and presige of the ISDT. The 1929 event was, uniquely, staged as the International Six Days Trial-Munich-Geneva and was generally regarded as the greatest motorcycle reliability trial ever held.

The 1930s was to see Great Britain, Germany and Italy as the dominating countries as regards the Trophy contest. The 1939 event was marred by what was to become known as the Salzburg Incident. Back in March 1938, Hitler had marched into Austria, which then became a German province. This fact obviously confused much of the foreign press who could not make up its mind in 1939 whether Salzburg, the headquarters of the ISDT that year, was in Austria or Germany. And so it came to pass that German and British competitors were to sit side-by-side in the sun at Salzburg in late August 1939. The trial got underway and for the first few days everything went to plan, but by midweek rumours

abounded about the political situation, to the extent that many foreign riders, including the British, left for home before the final day. The German Trophy team won, but this did not matter, since the results were declared void by the FIM in 1946.

The first post-war ISDT was held in Czechoslovakia in 1947. The host country won both the Trophy and the Vase contests.

Then came a run of British successes, the last in 1953. For the rest of the 1950s the Czechs, plus East and West Germany took the spoils. In 1960 Austria staged the famous marathon and was victorious in the Trophy, with Italy taking the Vase.

Much of the 1960s belonged to the all-conquering East Germans. Using their MZ two-strokes to full advantage they won no less than six Trophy contests in that decade. In a similar way, the 1970s was the era of the Czechs astride their purposeful Jawa machines. These, like the MZ's, were two-stroke singles in various capacities.

The only other Trophy winners during this period were West Germany (1975 and 76) and Italy (1979). Following their victory in 1979, the

Italians then went on four more Trophy victories in 1980, 1981, 1986 and 1989.

However, times were changing. There was less media interest than in previous years and the machines themselves had moved from well-prepared standard roadsters with knobbly tyres to virtually full-blown motocross racers with the minimum of equipment to make them legal for the road.

The last ISDT was held in Brioude in central France in 1980. From then on it became the International Six Days Enduro and the decline of the event gathered pace. Gone were the great days when the world looked on as virtually every motorcycling nation battled for honours on domestically-built machines which the general public were familiar with.

A glance at motorcycle press reports today shows quite clearly the specialist nature of the new Six Days' no longer appeals to many motorcyclists. It is of marginal interest to the vast majority, a far cry from the first 50 years when victory in either the Trophy or the Vase was of vital interest to both the countries and manufacturers taking part.

Left: Czech Jawas dominated much of the 1970s ISDT with success in both the Trophy and Vase contests.

The Speedway World Championships. Hans Nielson on a Jawa during the 1980s.

SPEEDWAY TRACK RACING

Speedway racing can trace its origins back to the American dirt tracks of the early 1900s. Records and photographs prove that the sport was in existence as early as 1902, when tracks were unusually large, often of half a mile, or even a full mile.

Razor-sharp competition existed between various marques, including Cleveland, Excelsior, Indian and Harley-Davidson. Professional riders were retained by these and other manufacturers and race meetings were regular attractions at the massive state fairs which were a feature of the period. As for the tracks, no attempt was made to surface them, hence the term 'dirt track racing'.

At these meetings the art of broadsliding was invented, but it was really the Australians who refined the sport. And this was in no small part due the extended visit during 1925-26 of several American riders 'down under'. It was soon discovered that by laying cinders for track surfaces, with a loose topping, provided a totally new riding method – pouring power via the rear wheel enabling the bike to slide through the bends in one controlled drift.

The next stage in the evolution of the sport came when speedway arrived in England in 1928, with the first meeting staged in Epping Forest, just north of London. This was soon followed by tracks in several major cities including London (Crystal Palace), Edinburgh and Wolverhampton.

Other early features of the British speedway scene included several major competitions, the best known being the renowned Golden Helmet. There was also the novelty of women riders, who, although banned in 1929, created quite a sensation in the short period they competed. This time also saw the beginning of international participation in countries such as Denmark and South Africa.

The next step was the creation of a league system in much the same way as soccer clubs, with track teams riding against each other. In fact, after the Second World War speedway became Britain's second largest spectator sport, with the early 1950s witnessing vast crowds.

The ultimate prize in speedway is the World Championship, first staged in 1936 and the Test Matches between different countries. Even today, speedway remains a popular sport in many countries around the world, with its unique blend of noise, excitement and spectacular flood-

GRASSTRACK RACING

Some of the very first competitive events for motorcycles took place on grass. Between the wars, interest in grasstrack racing snowballed to such as extent that a permanent stadium was built in Britain at Brands Hatch, Kent.

Soon a specialised machine emerged, constructed especially for the sport, rather than one merely adapted from a road model. Development continued on a parallel course with speedway models until the late 1950s and early 1960s, when JAP-powered machines ruled the roost, ridden by aces such as Alf Hagon and Don Goddon.

Anyone who has ever been a spectator at a grasstrack meeting will know the shattering noise echoing back from the hedgerow or trees as riders race along the top straight, the thick dust clouds which roll over the crowd and the pervading incense of alcohol fuel and racing oils mingling in the air.

Since the mid-1970s the old JAP singles have given way to the more sophisticated four-valvers from Jawa, Weslake and Godden. Whilst the basic concept of frame design has remained largely the same, several subtle changes have improved handling considerably. Brakes are not permitted for international events, but a single brake, front or rear, may be

Below: Grasstrack racing is a fast and furious sport, both for the riders and the spectators.

ICE RACING

In the eyes of the world, ice racing is a minority sport for mysterious masked riders from the Eastern extremes of Europe. In truth, the sport has a huge following right across mainland Europe and there are events in most of western Europe, the old Soviet block countries and in Scandanavia.

Although the sport is largely dominated by Russian, Swedish, Austrian, German and Dutch riders also feature strongly.

Most of the machines used are Czechoslovakian Jawa's with the single cylinder 500cc four-valve motor which is so common in speedway. Apart from flat handlebars, by far the most distinguishing feature is the fearsome-looking spikes which protrude from the front and rear tyres. In theory this means the rider merely banks the bike right over as in road racing, and so a sideways slide is not necessary, but in practice, when four riders are let loose on the ice, anything goes!

Usually tracks are kept frozen by an underground system. Distinctive features of ice racing include the almost flat stance of the rider whilst negotiating a corner, the plumes of ice chips which they generate and the surprising speed of the action.

BEACH RACING

What better music is there to any motorcycle enthusiast's ear than the sound of over 500 machines firing up in unison during a Le Mans-style start? Where does this type of event take place: the USA, Australia or the Far East? No, Le Touquet in France and Weston-Super-Mare in England.

Both have grown into vast events attracting thousands of spectators. The French event was staged first, during the 1970s. Even with its success, when the British first ran a Beach Enduro at Weston in 1983 everyone concerned with the organisation underestimated its terrific appeal and found themselves simply overwhelmed both with entries and spectators. The whole atmosphere was akin to Douglas during TT week.

The idea of staging the event was conceived by four off-road buffs, headed by Dave Smith of Birmingham. Weston-Super-Mare was selected because of its beach and tidal system: the sea does not come in fully, so there was no fear of being caught with the tide coming in halfway through the race.

The most amazing aspect of a Beach Enduro is the wide range of machinery and riding skills of those taking part. Motocross, enduro, trail, even the odd trials bike, solo, sidecar and quads, plus, of course, specialised sand racing bikes can all be spotted.

Club riders rub shoulders with the stars. For example, that first event back in 1983 attracted amongst others Geraint Jones, the doyen of the British Enduro scene, the 1981 World 250cc Moto Cross Champion, Neil Hudson; Declan Eccles, many times British Sand Racing Champion and the 1983 Sidecar Motocross Champions, Terry Goode and Gary Withers.

The circuit itself was three gruelling miles in length and incorporated a series of man-made obstacles. There was also a mile-long straight which enabled the faster competitors to top 100 mph (160 kmh).

That first year attracted 500 entries and an amazing 35,000 spectators. This has now grown to over 800 entries (which means that most competitors have to qualify to take part in Sunday's race) and the number of spectators has almost doubled. All this makes it one of the most popular events of any type in the motorcycling calendar worldwide.

In October 1996, Rob Meek, riding a TRM Honda CR250, created history by racking up a record fourth victory in the event.

The first ever beach racing in the UK was in 1983 at Weston Super Mare, in the west of England. The competitors charge down the main straight at around 100 mph (160 kmh).

AMERICAN DIRT TRACK

At first glance, American dirt track competition and speedway racing would seem to be very similar, but in reality the only true parallel between the two is that in each case the action is on dirt ovals. Racing programmes are staged differently, riding styles differ dramatically and the only similarities between dirt tracker and a speedway bike are the use of two wheels and a pair of handlebars.

Early in the 20th century as motorcycles became sophisticated enough for use in competition, board track racing became popular in the States. Tracks were constructed suitable for racing cars and bikes and the spectators took it to their hearts with massed attendances. But there was a problem, board tracks were expensive to build and maintain and were difficult, if not impossible, to relocate.

So by the late 1920s the board tracks had all but disappeared and suddenly horse tracks throughout the vast American heartlands were

GREEN LANES RIDING

Green Lane riding is perhaps the only really challenging form of non-competitive motorcycling left in these days of reliable bikes, super sticky tyres and blanket speed limits. Those enthusiasts who either do not want to, or cannot risk riding in some form of competitive sport but are bored with dodging homicidal drivers on the public highway, can still enjoy another sort of freedom.

Whilst the marketing men of the large motorcycle companies have successfully fostered the notion that a super-trick enduro iron is essential equipment before you turn a wheel on mud, this is not so. Whilst nobody would use a Honda Fireblade or Suzuki GSXR1100, there is a surprisingly wide range of bikes which can venture down green lanes, especially with a change to more suitable tyres. To enthusiasts of 30 or 40 years ago green lane riding was not a separate pastime but an integral part of motorcycling pleasure. A typical British big single such as BSA B33 or Royal Enfield Bullet was little different from the production trials iron of the time and the use of a block tread on the front wheel gave you a machine you could safely do some gentle off-road work with.

Join a trail riding club, and you will be amazed at just what fun you can have. There are approximately 5,000 miles (8,000 km) of legal vehicular right of ways in England and Wales alone. Make use of it whilst it is still there, but treat it with respect – increased legislation and the efforts of political pressure groups seem destined to ban the motorcyclist from the countryside.

reverberating to the exciting sounds of big Harley-Davidson and Indian v-twin engines.

Initially, dirt track and speedway were equally popular, but dirt track was to emerge at the end of the Second World War as *the* American bike sport. Establishment of the AMA (American Motorcycle Association) in 1924 began the trend to standardised rules, and in 1946 a national dirt track championship began. A British Norton ridden by Chet Dykgraff was the first holder, and this certainly stung the domestic factories into action, particularly Harley-Davidson.

In dirt track cornering is achieved by means of broadsliding and throttle control and probably the greatest dirt racing, champions were 'Smokey Joe' Leonard and Bart Markel. Other famous names of the American oval scene have been Gary Nixon, Dick Mann, Carroll Resweber, Kenny Roberts and Jay Springsteen.

Barry Briggs

Called 'The Old Man of the Shale', Barry Briggs MBE dominated the sport of speedway for some two decades like no man before or since. Briggs was born in New Zealand on 30 December 1934 and, bored with his life in a Christchurch advertising agency, set his heart on emulating his boyhood hero Ronnie Moore, who had travelled from New Zealand to England and found track fame with Wimbledon in 1950.

Briggs followed Moore to Wimbledon two years later and at first his true riding abilities were masked by over-enthusiasm which saw the Kiwi youngster suffer several heavy falls. In fact his crashes became so regular in his early outings that a number of senior riders attempted to get Briggs banned! But he rode through this and quickly began to show real talent and a mastery of the shale tracks.

Moore won the World Championship in 1954 and Barry Briggs qualified for the first time, finishing an impressive 5th overall. From then until 1971 he didn't miss another world final and was the model of consistency. His record

read: 1955: 3rd; 1956: 7th; 1957: 1st; 1958: 1st; 1959: 3rd; 1960: 6th; 1961: 4th; 1962: 2nd; 1963: 3rd; 1964: 1st; 1965: 4th; 1966: 1st; 1967: 5th; 1968: 2nd; 1969: 2nd; 1970: 7th.

At a night at Wembley in 1972, Briggs looked set for a record-equalling fifth title victory, but after an impressive winning first outing, he was taken out by a pair of over-enthusiastic Russians, suffering a serious hand injury which excluded him for the rest of the meeting and saw him lose a finger.

That injury, in part, made it no real surprise, when in 1973 he announced his retirement. But although it seemed he had finally quit he was to make a return in 1975 and again in 1976, before finally hanging up his leathers, this time for good.

Sammy Miller

Acknowledged as the world's greatest-ever trials rider, Belfast-born Sammy Miller has also been a true ambassador for his sport. And even though it is now the feet-up trials game for which he is remembered, he could well have been a champion on the tarmac too.

Belfast dealer Terry Hill provided Sammy with the 247cc NSU Sportmax on which he gained his initial road racing successes in northern Ireland. Then came factory rides with FB Mondial, Ducati and CZ, and he also tried his hands at grass track and scrambling. But he was racing alongside a works trials ride with the Ariel company and eventually a decision had to be made, and trials won over racing.

Armed with a 499cc Ariel HT5 with the now-famous registration of GOV132, Sammy won the British Experts three times, the Scottish Six Days twice, and the Scott three times. The list of national events was endless, and several were taken five, six or even seven years in a row.

When Ariel lost interest, the Rickman brothers approached Sammy with a view to his switching to Spanish-made Bultacos, of which Rickman were then the British importers. He signed up and not only rode, but developed the 250 Sherpa into a winner first time out at the 1965 Colmore Trial.

Miller and Bultaco then went on to win the British Championship during that first season, and also made history by winning the equally prestigious Scottish Six Days. Such was the impact that before the year was out Bultaco machines made up a third of all entries in British trials events.

Sammy went on to amass a total of no less than 11 British titles in as many years (including his Ariel achievements), before he retired in 1970. He continued to work for the Spanish factory, before opening his own dealership in Hampshire. Finally, he created the motorcycle museum which bears his name, and which is proclaimed as world's largest private motorcycle collection.

Jöel Robert

To many Jöel Robert was the greatest motocross rider of all time. He was also a showman, someone you either loved or hated. He was born on 11 November 1943 in Belgium, the son of a grasstrack racer. And he followed his father into that branch of the sport, but his temper led to trouble – after assaulting an official the fiery youngster was banned from grasstrack for life. As a result, he switched his attentions to motocross, at the age of 16, making progress which can only be described as meteoric. Only four years later, at the age of 20, he became the youngest ever 250cc World Motocross Champion. All this was achieved with Robert leading the kind of night-life that few others could keep pace with.

His first championship came in 1964, aboard a Czechoslovakian CZ, which was a single cylinder two-stroke with twin exhaust ports, the latter to relieve cylinder distortion. Then in 1965 Victor Arbekov won on a CZ, followed in 1966 and 1967 by the Husqvarna-mounted Swede Torsten Hallman. Robert regained his world crown in 1968 and repeated the success the following year – both times with CZ.

At the end of 1969 he signed for Suzuki and went on to clinch three more 250cc titles (1970, 1971 and 1972). After Robert's fifth consecutive world title it was beginning to look as if the sport's governing body, the FIM, would have to consider having two world championships – one for Robert and one for everyone else!

But technical development never stands still and 1973 saw Yamaha oust Suzuki as top bike in the 250cc title slakes, thanks in no small part to its reed valve engine and monoshock frame. Suzuki's task wasn't made any easier by Robert's stated wish to 'only ride, not develop' a machine

Jöel Robert didn't really have anything left to prove: he had been there and done it, so the Belgian superstar bowed out, his name being carried forward by a clothing firm for future motocross riders to proudly wear.

Jeff Smith

Dual world champion on BSA singles in the 1964 and 1965 500cc World Motocross Championships, Jeff Smith was once described as 'The Rock of Gibraltar itself'. This was a testimony of the dependable and solid style which he displayed right through a career which spanned 19 years from 1953 through to 1971.

Although reared in the urban sprawl of Birmingham, Jeffrey Vincent Smith was born in Colne, Lancashire, and even though he was only three years old when his parents moved south to Birmingham, 'Smithy' was always proud to display the Red Rose of Lancashire on his crash helmet throughout his riding career.

Right from the off the young Smith displayed the kind of skills of which champions are made, winning a gold medal at the age of 17, in the ISDT of 1951 held in Italy; his mount then being a 500T Norton.

His first bike, a 1929 Triumph in 1947 had provided the basics in riding craft. Then at 16 his father bought him a BSA Bantam, which, complete with 'L' plates, enabled him to legally enter trials. In fact much of his early experience was as a trials rider, rather than as dirt racer. But even when he was a BSA motocross star, Jeff still maintained his trials interest.

His first Grand Prix victory came at the 1954 Dutch motocross Grand Prix, where he rode a 499cc BSA Gold Star to victory. Between that first GP win and his first world title in 1964 came a career which saw so many awards it would take a book to list them all. But virtually all were achieved on BSA machinery. Throughout two seasons (1956/57) he was a serving soldier in the British Army, but he still managed to win the British Experts twice, the Moto Cross de Nations twice, a gold in the ISDT and the ACU Scrambles Star.

The Victor motocrosser was a development of the 343cc B40 roadster and first appeared in 1963 as an enlarged 420cc B40 – Smith rode it to finish third in his first attempt at the 500cc world title. With the capacity raised to 440cc, the title went to the Birmingham pairing and the feat was repeated in 1965.

After BSA closed Jeff went to work for the Canadian Bombardier company.

PARIS-DAKAR RALLY

The famous Paris-Dakar Rally was first staged for motorcycles in 1979 and was won by Cyril Neveu riding a modified Yamaha XT500 trail bike. However, BMW was the first factory to really exploit the incredible 6,200-mile (9,975-km) event which runs from Europe (with headquarters in Paris) to Dakar in Senegal, West Africa.

Billed as 'The World's Toughest Race' – and it probably is – competitors first converge at Granada in the south of Spain for a 125-mile (200-km) special stage in the Sierra Nevada mountains. They then set sail for Morocco and things begin to get very serious indeed.

Ahead of the competitors lies two weeks of biking torture, as they face first the challenges of the Atlas mountains and then the Sahara desert, one of the most inhospitable and dangerous places on Earth. Daytime temperatures soar way over 100 degrees Centigrade, but it can freeze at night. Sandstorms can blow up out of nowhere, scouring the face and obliterating the route. The Paris-Dakar is truly the ultimate test for both man and machine.

Special stages, four of which are more than 360 miles (580 km) long, decide the winners in the three categories – bikes, cars and trucks. As there is only one rest day, its very much the survival of the fittest as the sand dunes and the tight rocky paths through remote villages take their

toll. Navigation is a major problem for many of the less well-prepared contestants, who aren't armed with the expensive Global Positioning System satelite navigation aid. Just to complete the trip is is no mean achievement.

BMW were victorious in 1981 and 1983-85. But after this record of four wins, and a poor result in the 1986 event, the factory announced its retirement from the Rally.

Herbert Auriol is the only man to have won the Paris-Dakar on two and four wheels. A former French trials champion, Auriol was victorous in the 1981 event on a BMW GS800 and in the 83 event on a BMW 980. He also won the 1992 Dakar car section in a Mitsubishi.

Former World Moto Cross Champion Gaston Rahier of Belgium won the 1984 and 85 Dakars on 1000cc BMWs. More recently Cagiva and Yamaha have disputed the leading positions with riders such as Edi Orioli and Stephane Peterhansel rising to the challenge.

Perhaps the most technically interesting bikes ever used in the event were a pair of experimental 400cc Honda EXP-2 single cylinder-engined devices which (in 1995) employed ARC (Active Radical Combustion) – a chemical self-ignition system related to the combustion system of the German V2 rocket of the Second World War!

THE ENDURO—NEW FORMULA

The last of the International Six Days Trials (ISDT) was held at Briode in central France in 1980. Then in 1981, it became the International Six Days Enduro (ISDE). This was in recognition that the nature of the event had changed quite dramatically and it was no longer appropriate to call it a reliability trial, since road-based bikes were no longer used.

The ISDE is, and has been since its inception, the province of highly specialised machinery only of use in this type of event. Real enduro motorcycles are, in fact, converted motocross machines which are essential to cope with the speed required on special tests.

Off-road racing has come a long way since the multi-purpose machines that were the backbone of the sport in the 1950s. At the time, Britain was sometimes criticized for entering overweight bikes which were really only slightly modified roadsters, but that was really what the original intention of the ISDT was all about – it was this 'man on the bike in the street' relationship which had made the event so popular in the first place.

The development of single-purpose machines in Europe, in particular in Czechoslovakia and Germany, began the process of change in the 1960s and early 1970s. By the middle of the 1970s a new breed of motocross technology from both European and Japanese factories had begun to take over, in the shape of Austrian Puchs and KTMs, German Zündapps, Italian SWMs, and Japanese Yamahas and Suzukis.

Unfortunately, today's enduro bikes are really little more than motocrossers with lights. They are narrow vision hotshots designed specifically for winning the modern enduro, and this has become a series of motocross-type racing called special tests.

Many enthusiasts are left to ponder that the days of the hand-painted Jawas, the Matchless and Ariels twins, the Gold Star BSAs, the Adlers, Gileras and Triumphs are over. It was truly a golden era which had variety, a wealth of ingenuity and, above all, the multitude of different approaches to the problem which made the old reliability trial so fascinating. The modern Enduro, sadly, has failed to recreate that magic, no matter what its value is to the manufacturers who participate.

SIDECAR CROSS

Sidecar Cross was born in Britain during the early 1960s, but rapidly became popular in the majority of northern European countries. Soon spectators began following this specialist form of spectacular and daring motocross with great enthusiasm and the FIM instituted an official European Championship in 1971 for machines up to 750cc, a limit raised to 1000cc in 1976. At first the Norton Commando was the

Far left: Jens Grüner on an MZ 500 negotiates a water splash during the 1987 Six Day GDR Trophy, which his team won.

Left: European Sidecar Cross Champions, Chris Etheridge and Nick Brace of Great Britain.

Below: A 650cc Triumph rider sand racing in Aden (now South Yemen) in 1965.

SAND RACING DAYS

Names like Redcar, Mablethorpe, Druridge Bay (near Newcastle), Bouloy Bay (Jersey) and Wallasey may not instantly ring a bell, but all have one thing in common – the ancient sport of sand racing – stretching back to the origins of motorcycling itself. Almost any type of machine can be used, from any other motorcycle sport – in the past even roadsters have been successfully employed.

The biggest problem for both organisers and competitors alike are the tides, which, as the old saying goes, 'waits for no man'. Even St Andrew's of golfing fame has seen its beach used for sand racing. During the 1920s it was truly a speedman's mecca and thousands would flock from all over Scotland to watch the racing.

The venue was still in use in 1961, when Veteran Scots' racer Archie Robertson won no less than seven of the day's eight races, riding a MK VIII KTT Velocette road racer – both rider and machine squarely in the vintage class!

chosen power unit but this was later succeeded by big bore (usually 850cc) versions of Yamaha's XS650 twin. The most successful outfits of this era employed a British-built Wasp chassis. Other engines included Triumph, Weslake, BSA, Honda and Hedlund, a v-twin from Scandanavia. The man behind the famous Wasp was Robin Rhind-Tutt. Another well-known sidecar cross frame is the EML.

Front suspension on sidecar cross machines usually consists of leading arms pivoting around the base of an hydraulic spring/damper unit, rather like the system used in rear suspension design. In more recent times, there has been a trend towards the adoption of cast alloy wheels, because of their greater rigidity compared to wire wheels.

TECHNICAL DEVELOPMENTS

Honda has taken motocross technology into a new era recently with the launch of the radical 1997 CR250R production motocrosser. The bike sports more than 20 major new and improved features for 1997, but it's the unique trend-setting aluminium twin-spar frame which sets it apart from the competition.

A first for motocross, the chassis is 2.2 lbs (1 kg) lighter than the previous model's steel frame and boasts dual box-section twin spares and downtubes, plus compact forged pivot plates to achieve an optimum match of light weight, high rigidity and top line handling.

On the highly competitive battlefields of the 250cc motocross class, technical innovation is vital. Over preceeding years there had been several developments. These included the latest in two-stroke technology, including reed and power valves, watercooling, map-type digital electronic ignition, five- or six-speed gearboxes, liquid cooling, aluminium swinging arm, single shock rear suspension, disc brakes, upside forks and plastic body work – the list is almost endless.

Concentrating upon the 1997 model CR250, the Composite Racing Valve (CRV) 249cc (66.4 x 72 mm) two-stroke single was redesigned with a modified port and combustion chamber, flat-top piston, new expansion chamber, and an all-new Power Jet Control (PJC) carburettor with a solenoid-controlled power jet providing an additional 2 bhp of top-end, a more linear torque curve, and quicker throttle response at all rpms. A stronger drive chain, a new single-unit radiator and computer-designed rear sprocket have also helped enhance performance and reduce maintenance.

Like its smaller CR125R brother, the CR250R, was given a map-type digital electronic ignition for more accurate ignition timing and a more rugged new steel water pump gear.

For 1997, the CR250 was equipped with a massive 47 mm inverted front fork featuring Teflon coated stanction tubes for smoother operation to cope better with the towering jumps, pounding washboard, and tight, bumpy corners which abound in modern-day motocross.

At the rear the swing-arm is controlled by an integrated remote reservoir damper which with the revised swing-arm provides no less than 320 mm of suspension stroke and added ground clearance.

Remember, this is just one model in one manufacturer's motocross range – the dirt racing world is one of constant evolution.

Above: Schoolboy motocross is big on both sides of the Atlantic. Youngsters can begin as young as six years old.

Left: A 1997 Honda CR250, the world's first production motocross bike with an alloy frame.

SCHOOLBOY SPORT

Over the past few years, schoolboy participation in all forms of motorcycle sport has grown at a tremendous pace. Today, even road racing is benefiting from this trend. For example, in Britain there has been a SuperTeen national race series since 1991, and from 1994 a series for the members of the newly-formed Junior Racing Association.

But it is motocross which has seen the most benefit so far, with a seemingly never-ending stream of talent progressing from the ranks of the schoolboy sport to adult racing, on both sides of the Atlantic.

Schoolboy motocross had its origins in the United States back in the late 1960s and early 1970s. The sight of a loaded motorhome and a couple of motocross bikes on the back soon became a familiar one with Stateside dirt racers.

This great tide of young talent made such an impact that it was not long before it spread to Britain and by the mid-1970s it was a thriving industry. Almost as many schoolboy motocross machines are sold as adult versions.

Currently, ages range from six to 17 years, with classes for 50cc automatic (in both small and big wheel versions), 60cc Junior, Inter 80cc, Inter Open 100cc and Senior and Expert 125cc classes.

On the organizational front, the very success of the schoolboy motocross fraternity has led to a number of official bodies being founded in Britain. Currently there are three main ones: the ACU (Auto Cycle Union), BSMA (British Schoolboy Motocross Association) and the YSMA (Youth Motorcycle Sporting Association). All three run their own national championship, which makes things rather confusing. Nevertheless, the fact remains that the system has been responsible for producing a number of world champions, including men such as Dave Thorpe and Graham Noyce.

Classics and Retros

CLASSIC BOOM

There has always been a fascination with classic motorcycle models amongst enthusiasts. However, in the course of the last 20 years, the historic motorcycle market has witnessed a complete transformation. Prices have spiralled stratospherically and then plummeted equally dramatically. What had once been the preserve of specialist engineers and amateurs lovingly rebuilding the dream bikes of their youth has developed into both a cult and an internal market in which investment potential has often been a greater motivation than a genuine love of and passion for motorcycles.

During the latter part of the 1970s, interest in British machines of the 1940s, 50s and 60s flourished. At that time machines were available at reasonable cost and the generations that had been in their twenties during these periods found themselves in the fortunate position where they had the money to spare to indulge in their need to recapture the dreams of their youth.

The British publishing house EMAP had the foresight to judge this burgeoning trend to perfection, and in March 1978 they launched the world's first magazine catering for his new breed, called *Classic Bike*. Its first editor was Peter Watson and there were articles on Side-valves machines, Vintage Racing, Ducati Singles, Dustbin Fairings, Edward Turner, and War Department motorcycles. The first issue also tested a Model 7 (500 cc) Norton Dominator. Published monthly, the magazine celebrated its 200th issue in September 1996 and is one of the world's top selling two-wheel monthlies.

Through demand for classic machinery and increased press coverage, values of classic machines rose steadily throughout the early 1980s, before finding a level in the middle of that decade. In hindsight, this was probably the golden era of the classic motorcycle, with the market in a healthy state, but with prices still relatively low, except for genuinely rare and exotic models.

As the 1980s drew to a close, the dealers and speculators who were active in the historic car scene began to move into bikes and this inevitably unbalanced the previous stable market platform. There was a surge in values generally, although the greatest rises were confined to the prestige models, notably Vincents, Brough Superiors and Italian MV Agustas, which in the autumn of 1989 were changing hands for £25,000 ($40,000) upwards, with Broughs commanding even more.

Quite simply the market moved rapidly away from its enthusiast base to an investment-oriented one. The day of the bank vault motorcycle had arrived. In Britain, for example, hundreds of motorcycles, notably British and Italian were being exported to Japan, where the yen-rich could afford to pay often double the price that could be realised in Britain. Often these machines ended up being sold in Tokyo antique shops. The classic craze was sweeping Japan to such an extent that not only were genuine classic bikes becoming much sought after, but there was also a booming business developing for modern-day classic styling exercises. These included models such as Yamaha's SRX600 and Honda's XBR500 being dressed up to look like a Manx Norton, AJS 7R, MV Agusta 750S, or a Ducati Desmo single.

However, every boom has its bust. And in the autumn of 1990, certain factors were leading the classic motorcycle market into decline. The worldwide recession felt in countries such as the United States, Great Britain and Japan resulted in many potential buyers becoming extremely wary and those who had speculated in many cases found that they had overstretched themselves.

As happened in the classic car world, this period saw a glut of machines being unloaded onto a depressed market, and the result was a giant fall in prices. In the 12 months from September 1990 to September 1991, Vincents and MV Agustas, lost on average £10,000/$15,000 in value, with similar losses repeated for Broughs and much of the other exotic machinery that had witnessed such dramatic rises during the boom years.

Whilst this was doubtless unfortunate for those gentleman who had had their fingers burnt in their rush to make money, its effects for the normal motorcycle enthusiast were welcome. There was a flood of bikes on the market at affordable prices once again – the large numbers of popular classics available meant that any potential buyers could be selective in their ultimate choice. By 1992-93 a full return to the enthusiast-driven market had been achieved, with prices generally stabilising. The golden rule should be to buy a bike for love, not greed.

Left: An Italian classic, Moto Guzzi built a range of horizontal 4-stroke singles, including this 250cc Airone of the early 1950's

Right: Triumph 750 Bonneville. This is a limited edition Jubilee model from 1977.

One of the stately Stevenage-made HRD-Vincent 499cc Comet singles from the early 1950s.

One of the more positive consequences of the price explosion of the late 1980s had been the emergence of a market for the hitherto neglected sections of two-wheelers: classic scooters, light-weight motorcycles, mopeds and autocycles. All these have increased in popularity, due to their wealth of technical interest and general affordability, particularly when compared to the established machinery which had been seen as worthy of collection, restoration and riding at the end of the 1970s.

Another growth area has been in Italian and Japanese models, thanks largely to the teenagers of the 1960s and 1970s now having the funds and the will to recapture their youth on the machines that they rode, or had always longed to ride.

Consequently, the classic movement is now at its most diverse. It is again essentially enthusiast-led and the appeal now covers a tremendous range of marques, models, age groups and income brackets. This does not mean the monetary factor is no longer important – an historic motorcycle is, to a degree, always going to be an investment, in as much as it will always have some monetary value. But for those interested in investment value alone, it's worth remembering the market fluctuations of the previous decade.

Experience suggests that the staple 'classic' diet of British four-stroke singles and twins of the 1940s through to the end of the 1960s is the safest choice, having undergone limited fluctuations in price in either direction. This is for a number of reasons. Foremost is the fact that so many have survived. Another factor is that parts are generally available at a reasonable cost which in turn makes restoration more attractive and ensures future running. There are also a number of specialist clubs,

THE CURRENT CLASSIC MARKET

Above: A 1957 Norton International overhead cam Model 30 490cc, one of the last 'Inters' ever made.

Right: Berthold Haller with one of the now rare British 1927 DOT 350cc, with London-built JAP engine.

Opposite: Classic British between-the-wars ohc single, the 1934 348cc Velocette KSS.

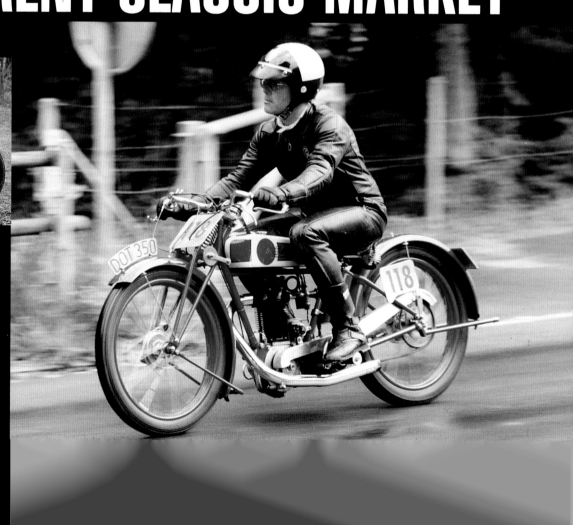

catering for all the major marques which are ready to advise members whatever their level of commitment.

Pre-Second World War machines, including pioneer, veteran and vintage machines enjoy a more stable market base, probably as a result of their comparative specialisation, although this may limit their appeal compared with the more broad-stream area of post-Second World War bikes.

Japanese machines are still largely cheap and readily available, although spares, particularly cycle parts, can be difficult to find, and are often considerably more expensive than similar components for British machinery.

Other even more specialised bikes such as Italian, German, American models and the like are often considerably more expensive than Japanese machines, both to buy in the first place and to keep serviceable, due to the usually higher costs of spares. This is particularly relevant from the used parts situation. How many Ducatis, Harley-Davidsons, Indians or BMWs do you find in a breaker's yard?

In 1994, *Miller's Classic Motorcycles Price Guide* was first published and is now produced annually. Just as with *Classic Bike*, *Miller's Classic Motorcycles Price Guide* has quickly built up a strong and loyal readership, acting as it does as a unique annual guide to classic and collector's motorcycles, covering an extensive range from veteran and vintage to post-war classics. Besides providing a price guide, it also reflects just what marques and models have been offered for sale in Great Britain during the previous year. The book includes a comprehensive listing of auctioneers and dealers who provide information including the likes of Brooks, Sotheby's, Verralls, Atlantic Motorcycles and The Italian Vintage Co as well as recording important private transactions. There are also appendices including a Directory of Museums, a Directory of Clubs, Bibliography, Glossary and other information. The 1996 edition has sections on Racing; Specials and Café Racers, Sidecars, Mopeds, Scooters, Mini Motorcycles, Restoration Projects and Motorcycle Memorabilia.

AUTOJUMBLES

Autojumbles are very much a way of life for many classic bike owners and restorers. Old bikes, just like new bikes, need parts to keep them running in good order. Unlike the latest tackle, however, getting the part you need is not simply a task of walking into your local dealer and placing your order. Quite often you have to spend a great deal of time and energy looking, but for 99 per cent of enthusiasts that is part of the joy of the ownership of a beloved classic.

This is where autojumbles come in and can often prove invaluable. At many shows for old-timer bikes the biggest display (and some would say the most interesting) is the autojumble section. You may have to spend many happy hours looking and it's best to

Triumph T140E-S, a 750cc twin with electric start, produced by the now defunct Meriden worker co-operative in the late 1970s and early 1980s.

arrive early to find what you need. Even if you go away empty handed, you are sure to have met up with a fellow enthusiast and with luck, picked up some useful tips on the grapevine.

At autojumbles you will see anything from what appears to be simply old junk, to a complete bike simply needing restoration. Then there are the basket cases (not people, but an assortment of bits which should be from one bike, but quite often are not), to a vast array of engine and cycle parts for almost all the popular models.

Sometimes the wierdest and rarest things will turn up. Autojumbles can be like an antique shop without expensive prices. If you are lucky you can still turn up valuable items for next to nothing.

Below: An assortment of Velocette bikes and bits of bikes at an autojumble stall greets the classic enthusiast.

Above: A 1923 Harley-Davidson at an American classic show.

SHOWS

There is also now a classic motorcycle show circuit. One of the earliest was the *Classic Bike*-sponsored Belle Vue and Stafford extravaganzas in the early 1980s. Later came the Bristol Classic Bike Show. All these events still flourish today.

But the biggest classic motorcycle showcase in Europe is that held twice annually in Holland. The Utrecht 'Old Timer's' show and auto fair is usually staged in early March and mid-August. The exhibition is held in a modern complex in the centre of town and attracts enthusiasts from across the world.

There are a host of other shows, fairs and autojumbles in other locations on both sides of the Atlantic where classic bike fans can feast their eyes, spend their money and talk bikes to their hearts' content.

THE RESTORATION PASSION

In classic motorcycling the subject of restoration is vitally important. In fact many purchase a classic bike for just that purpose. For them the actual restoration is as much a part of the enjoyment as eventually riding the finished machine.

For the beginner the first question is: where to start? The answer depends upon whether you already own the bike, or need to buy one. If it is the latter, you will first need to decide which make and model you require. Obviously this is not just about what you would like, but also what you can afford. This latter area is all-important, as without sufficient funds no-one, no matter how enthusiastic, will be able to see through the demands of a full restoration. In fact, before you do anything, you must put your financial position in order. This includes setting a limit on how much you intend spending.

Right from the beginning, it is best to face up to the fact that motorcycle restoration and repair requires time, patience, equipment, knowledge and last, but not least, money. As a general rule of thumb, take your estimate of time and cost and then add on at least half those amounts again.

The next consideration is ability. This will determine what you can do yourself and just how much will need to be farmed out to others. Again, don't be too optimistic.

Tools and equipment are also vital. In an ideal world, everyone would like a full set of factory tools and a fully-equipped workshop. For most, the reality is somewhat different. But make sure your workplace is clean, warm, well-organised and secure.

You will then need to draw up a workplan. This single requirement is all-important to achieving a successful restoration. Without a workplan, you will find the task a nerve-racking experience, which may even bring you to the point where you lose patience with the project altogether and sell the incomplete machine in sheer frustration.

Before starting on a restoration it is a good idea to research the spare parts availability and costs for your particular make and model. Dealers, autojumbles and private advertisements are three tried and tested ways of obtaining bits. There is also the possibility of using secondhand components for some tasks.

Data-workshop manuals, parts books, magazines and books are all useful sources of information and joining an owner's club can help you make useful contacts. At the outset, the task of restoration may seem a daunting one for a novice, but nothing compares to the sense of pride and achievement felt when you have finally seen the project through and your very own classic stands before you in all its shining glory.

The famous American Barber Museum restoration shop with work being carried out on a Triumph unit twin.

Left: Des Orman, riding a 1923 7700cc BSA sidecar, leads brother Geoff Orman, riding a 1928 500 BSA, on a Pioneer Run in 1983.

Below: Triumph 499cc on Banbury Run during the 1980s.

THE PIONEER RUN

The most prestigious event in the world for veteran motorcycles, (those built before 31 December 1914), is the annual Pioneer Run from Tattenham Corner on Epsom Downs to the seaside location of Madeira Drive, Brighton. This has been the eagerly awaited herald of spring for many motorcycle enthusiasts since 1930 and is organised by the equally long-running Sunbeam Motor Cycle Club.

The club was formed in 1924, having Frederick Pinhard as Secretary and prime mover. Originally for owners of Sunbeam motorcycles, membership was soon opened to other marques, even cars, as Pinhard's flair for organisation attracted the leading riders of the day to the club. Pinhard was one of the first to have the vision to see the need to preserve machines from the earliest days of the sport. The benchmark taken by Pinhard to set the transition of the motorcycle from the halting efforts of the pioneer constructors to a reliable practical transport was set as the end of 1914.

At first the machines used in the Run were not vetted in any fashion. But soon it became apparent that the credibility of the event was likely to be in question if certain guidelines were not adhered to. Accordingly, in 1938, the Pioneer Register was introduced to establish the eligibility of machines entered. A dating committee, with an extensive archive at its disposal was established to assess each application and issue a certificate when satisfied that the machine was a genuine 'pioneer'. Notwithstanding the rigorous vetting procedures, which have resulted in a number of doubtful machines being rejected, interest is such that numbers on the Register have grown from the original 60 to well over 1,000 machines today.

Within the broad classification of veteran, the Sunbeam Club recognises three classes. The first, for machines prior to 1905, includes the true primitives. Many and varied are the mechanical layouts of these early devices, with some sharing dual eligibility for the VCC (Vintage Car Club) London to Brighton run, particularly the three-wheelers.

Next comes the Class Two, for 1905 until the end of 1909, with names such as Douglas, P&C, Triumph and Indian in evidence. This class also includes the first sidecars. Finally, Class Three is for machines dating from 1910 until the end of 1914.

A Sunday in late March is usually the setting for the early morning start from Epsom. It's a mecca for any lover of the best in veteran motorcycling – try to be there if you can.

PARADES

Parading is a way of sampling race action without actually taking part in a race, but still having a great time with your classic bike.

Britain's leading classic racing organisation, the CRMC (Classic Racing Motorcycle Club) stages a number of parades alongside their normal race-day programmes. To parade, you still have to enter the meeting, pay the entry fee, go through the pre-race scrutineering process and park alongside the real racers; but no competition licence is required. It's ideal if your racing days are over for whatever reason, or if you just want to try your bike out without actually competing in a race. You will be allocated a number, and under CRMC rules you must display a small 'P' on each number background.

A huge variety of bikes take part in parades. These can be anything from a carefully prepared standard sports roadster through to a pukka ex-Grand Prix bike. Unlike racing, many types of machine can be circulating at the same time, although riders are usually despatched from the starting grid in small groups. Sessions start and finish in the same way as 'real' races.

You also have the same opportunity as actual racers for at least one pre-parade practice session. Even though you will not be racing for real, attention to preparation, machine condition, riding gear, tyres and the like are still of vital importance. You will also need to proceed in a safe manner once out on the track, and because of the huge differences in machine performances and riding skills encountered in parades, it is important to still use a 'racers brain'.

Above: Sammy Miller parading a 1939 500cc four-cylinder, water-cooled super-charged AJS.

A pre-1965 500cc Triumph Mettise being put to good use in a Classic Scramble event.

PRE-'65 MOTOCROSS & TRIALS

At the Classic Scramble, staged as part of the Post TT international race meeting at Mallory Park, Leicestershire, on Sunday, 9 June 1996, over 120 competitors took part in a series of dirt bike races. Famous names from the world of off-road racing included the likes of Terry Challinor, Brian Nadin, John Giles, Arthur Browning, Mick Andrews, Chris Horsfield Ken Sedgley and Jim Aim. The machines they rode were a varied and impressive reminder of just what motocross meant three decades and more ago. Amongst the massed ranks of thundering Triumph Mettises, Cheney BSAs, Tribsas, BSA Gold Stars and Victors came a sprinkling of 2-strokes including CZ Twin Port, Husqvarna, Cotton, Greeves and Dot machines. The entire sidecar field was made up of Norton Wasp outfits with either 850 or 920cc engines.

All this was a vivid reminder of an age gone by when a competition Gold Star BSA scrambler was the bike to beat, when riders wore ex-fire-man's boots, a rugby jersey or something similar and fun was fun, although the competition was fierce. Classic scrambling, like classic racing, enables competitors and spectators alike to re-live those glorious day from long ago.

Much the same is true of Classic Pre'65 trials. Here too machines and riders are able to recapture a bygone era. Once again the vast percentage of bikes are of British origin and with the pre-1965 cut-off, four-strokes are very much in vogue.

CLASSIC RACING

Above: Jon Schults riding a 1972 Harley Davidson XRTT 750 v-twin at Daytona in 1996.

Along with the great upsurge of interest in vintage and classic road bikes has come a parallel growth in the sporting side of older bikes, most notably in racing. Today, classic and vintage racing is an integral part of the road racing scene on a worldwide basis.

In the past, when a competition machine became outdated it was simply pensioned off, but since the beginning of the 1980s this trend has been reversed and many thousands of previously unwanted racers have been put back in service. At first it was simply the original bikes being re-raced, often by their original riders, but with the rises in values towards the end of the 1980s many bikes started to change hand for super-inflated prices. They became too valuable to risk on the track.

During the early 1990s a new breed of classic racer and machinery appeared in the sport. Many of the bikes raced were either replicas of originals (the Seeley G50 for example) or cheaper bikes, such as BSA unit singles and Triumph unit twins. There has also been the rise of the Forgotten Era class, the intention of which is to allow bikes previously outlawed by classic rules (such as post-1968 two-strokes and post-1972 four-strokes). This has proved so successful the CRMC (Classic Racing Motorcycle Club) have now decided to allow some of these machines (notably early TZ Yamahas and RG500 Suzukis) into their meetings, albeit in a class of their own.

Besides specialist meetings for classic-only and vintage-only racers, many other events are staged for these types of racers. One of the best examples is the famous Mallory Park Post TT meeting, held annually each June at the well-known Leicestershire circuit.

In September 1996 Oliver's Mount, Scarborough, was the venue for probably the biggest ever gathering of 'pastmasters' in Great Britain. *Motorcycle Sport and Leisure* described the assembled machines as 'The crowd-pulling oldies'. The gathering marked the famous North Yorkshire circuit's 50th anniversary. Over 60,000 enthusiasts made the journey – they had come to see the finest racers from yesteryear, including the likes of Giacomo Agostini, Barry Sheene, Mick Grant, Phil Read, Jim Redman and many more. And the machines they rode were just as exciting – the 250 Honda-6, the 500 MV-3, the 750 Heron Suzuki, the 750 Kawasaki-3 and the 350 AJS three-valver. Even modern greats like Joey Dunlop and Carl Fogarty got into the act.

Another very special event held in 1996 was Forza Italia. This, too,

Right: Famous names from the past gather with a trio of ex works BMW twins at Salzburg, Austria in the summer of 1983. On thebike at left is Jock West with Georg Meier on pillion; they were one-two in the 1939 TT. On their left is Walter Zeller.

Ex-world champion and founder member of IHRO (International Historic Racing Organization), New Zealander Hugh Anderson, on a Matchless G50, is seen here competing in an Austrian historic event.

was truly international and attracted riders from the UK, United States, Holland, Spain, Switzerland, France, Italy, Germany, Sweden and even Mexico! Races included ones for singles, BEARS (British, European, American Racing Series), scooters, twins and even one for Ducati single cylinder machines.

There was also a series of races for members of IHRO (International Historic Racing Organization). This is a group of enthusiasts who aim to recreate the spirit and atmosphere of the 'Continental Circus' of Grand Prix racing of the 1960s and early 1970s, with selected international meetings throughout Europe during the summer months.

IHRO insist on only machines of the type which raced at Grand Prix events in the period: the fact that a machine is old does not automatically qualify it as suitable for competition with IHRO. The organization is very strict about which modifications they will allow; except in the case of safety features, everything has to be strictly period modifications only. All of their machines race with drum brakes on the front and rear wheels and must be of period appearance with regard to fairings, seats and other details. The IHRO also only race with open exhausts, so that spectators can hear, as well as see, the past glories of yesteryear. Their races have attracted many former world champions, including Hugh Anderson and Phil Read.

The IHRO classes include 350 and 500cc machines and in 1996 they held their first historic race for Formula 750 bikes. It is hoped that this event will become a pilot for an international series in future years. The basis will be a four-stroke only race for machines which competed in world championship Formula 750 races in the early Seventies.

The classic race scene continues to grow and grow, providing riders and spectators the chance to re-live the excitement, glories and sounds of what would otherwise be a receding memory for some and an unknown experience for younger followers of the sport.

RETROS
THE NOSTALGIA BUSINESS

Motorcycle manufacturers are seldom slow to cash in on a trend. In the late 1980s, the Italian Moto Guzzi factory played the nostalgia card and introduced the world's first true 'retro' bike, the 1000S. This drew on the long-gone, but much loved, 750S3 model of the early 1970s.

As Kawasaki and its Zephyr range of retro-machines was soon to do, Guzzi provided potential customers with the many advantages offered by the technical improvements which had occurred since the original bikes had bowed out.

In the case of the 1000S, these were limited to engine improvements first seen on the Le Mans III in the early 1980s, a larger 948cc engine capacity, revised lighting and electrics, quieter mufflers, and very little else. In many ways the 1000S was a far closer imitation of its earlier brother than were the Zephyr's (or for that matter any of the later retros). Guzzi offered their retro with a choice of wire or cast wheels, either naked or with a small fairing. The final batch was built in 1993.

Meanwhile, the first Zephyr was a specially-produced American-only 550 four in 1990. The instant success of this model led to the 550 going on sale in Europe the following year, closely followed by a 750 in 1991 and an 1100 which came out the following year.

To cash in on the retro craze Honda recreated the CB750 (Nighthawk in the USA) in 1991. This 'back-to-basics' street bike epitomized the almost timeless qualities that made Honda famous in the big bike league. The 'new' CB750 has an engine based on the 1984 CBX 750 with dohc, rather than the sohc of the original 1969 CB750 four. Then in 1992 Honda went a stage further to create their CB1000 Big One. This employed a liquid-cooled engine based on the one currently fitted to the CBR1000 sports/tourer.

Not to be outdone, Yamaha then joined in with the XJR1200, using the air-cooled engines from their long-running FJ1200, itself derived from the earlier FJ1100 of the mid-1980s. The same company also offers the 600 and 900 Division models, but these are not strictly retros, although they appeal to a similar customer base, with their affordable price and back-to-basics approach.

But what of that fourth member of Japan's big tour biking elite, Suzuki? Well, they bided their time, but when they did enter the retro market they did so in style, with two machines. The first came in time for the 1995 season, in the shape of the GSF 600 Bandit.

The 600 Bandit was a total knockout, the press enthused and the public voted with their wallets. Many agreed that this was the best bike of 1995, irrespective of class. For a Japanese bike it had real character. It was a quick-steering, well balanced back-lanes beast that would scratch, wheelie or pack the miles in with no problem. Even the pillion seat was pretty good. It also cost considerably less than the opposition.

Motor Cycle News proclaimed it as being among the top five bikes of modern times (the others were the Honda C90, Honda CX500, Honda CBR600 and Suzuki GSXR 750). MCN said: 'Of thousands of bikes on the roads, only a handful stand out as red-hot winners. They're the bikes that have got it all.'

Suzuki achieved the seemingly impossible – an excellent bike at a knock-down price. It used an engine borrowed from the GSX600 retuned for improved mid-range power which allows the Bandit to be hurried along far more quickly than you'd think possible. It's still keen to rev, but stirring the excellent gearbox is easy and it's surprising what sort of sports bikes the Bandit can keep in its sights.

The frame is only a basic steel tube cradle affair, but works well and unlike the other Japanese retros the Bandit has the more modern single shock rear suspension. This improves both handling and comfort over the period twin shockers. Suzuki claim a power output of 76.4 bhp at 10,500 rpm from the 599cc four-cylinder dohc oil/air-cooled motor. There are four-valves per cylinder and a six-speed gearbox.

Not content with producing the top middleweight retro, Suzuki made another inspired move a year later, when in early 1996 it launched

Honda CB1000

The Honda CB 1000 Big One encapsulates the essence of the retro – essentially modern technology married to old time values.

Above: The worlds first true retro was the Moto Guzzi 1000S of 1989.

Right: The author testing one of Honda's 'new' CB750 four cylinder models in 1995.

the GSF 1200 Bandit, which boasted the same sharp handling and aggressive looks. But unlike its revvy smaller brother, the 1200 packed a heavyweight punch. Coupled with a lithe chassis and a dry weight of just 211 kg (465lb) – 10 kg (22 lb) less than Yamaha's XJR, 24 kgs (53 lb) less than Honda's CB1000 and a whopping 41 kg (90 lb) less than Kawasaki's 1100 Zephyr – the bigger Bandit has a serious power-to-

Below: Racing version of Yamaha's X5R 1200 retro on display at the Tokyo Show, 1995.

Below right: Best of the big retros is the Suzuki GFS 1200 Bandit. Launched in 1996, it offers stomping performance with a bargain basement price tag.

weight ratio advantage over the opposition And not only was it faster and endowed with better handling, it was cheaper too.

Suzuki can claim real heritage too, the engine being based around the power plant of the company's top muscle bike, the revered GSX-R1100. Suzuki engineers achieved an excellent job of repeating the 600 formula so that the two bikes share almost identical proportions. It's not until you let out the clutch that you feel any real difference, but when you do it's quite breathtaking. Whereas the 600 needs revs, the 1200 has instant grunt – simply open the throttle and take off. The 1157cc four developed 100 bhp with almost 70 ft/lb of torque at 4,000 rpm. As one British magazine commented: 'The only old-fashioned thing about this bike is its steel frame.'

THE EUROPEAN RETROS

It hasn't only been the Japanese companies which have exploited the retro craze. Several European factories have also seen the potential of combining classic styling with the latest in motorcycle technology. Triumph, Ducati and Laverda have all produced creditable offerings to tempt enthusiasts. In many ways, today's purchaser has an unrivalled choice of variety and quality available in the showrooms.

Thanks solely to the efforts of John Bloor, that great British name, Triumph, has been reborn, not just as a nostalgic badge, but as a company aiming to again rival the best in the world. Of all the modern Triumphs, the 900 triples are the ones that ooze a character all their own. And of all the 900 triples, the Trident is by far the best. It's not trying to be a sportsbike, so it doesn't matter that the top heavy layout and soft suspension limit cornering potential. It's not trying to be a tourer, so the lack of a fairing doesn't matter. It's just a well-balanced, capable, everyday machine with enough go from that lovely three-cylinder dohc

Moto Guzzi V10

engine to provide ample pleasure for most people, most of the time. There's also a 750cc version, but this lacks the low-down power of the bigger Trident.

Triumph also produces the Thunderbird 900. This was originally introduced with the American market in mind, but it quickly found favour in Europe, too. Its ultra-retro looks and respectable performance struck a chord with many riders who wanted a traditional 'classic' Triumph with all the historic associations the marque carries with it, but also a machine with a modern specification.

Although maybe not quite a retro, but certainly very close, is Ducati's Monster series, which has been one of the sales successes of the 1990s. Just what an impact the M900 made when it was launched back in 1993 is best illustrated by the following extract from a Bristish magazine in April 1994: 'Twice in succession, Ducati has created the most talked about bikes of the year. Right now the number 916 is on everyone's lips, usually while they're wondering when it will arrive. And last year people were muttering the same question about the Monster, desperate even to see one of the radically-styled machines!'

The motor is the same as that used in the 900SS, which means a capacity of 904cc, 73bhp and air/oil cooling. Other technical details include a pair of 38mm Japanese Mikuni carbs, a six-speed gearbox, 41mm inverted front-forks, triple disc brakes and a dry weight of 184 kg (405 lb). It also features single shock rear suspension.

A 583cc '600' arrived in 1994 with much less power (53 bhp) and several cost-cutting exercises, including a single disc front brake, no oil

The outrageous, amazingly styled retro Moto Guzzi V10 Centauro 1000cc v-twin.

cooler, a mechanical clutch and plastic instead of carbon fibre side panels. A 750 (748cc) version followed in 1996.

Also new for 1996 was the Laverda Ghost, which is similar in size and purpose to the Monster, with its steel trellis chassis, inverted forks and single rear shock. What is different is the 668cc dohc parallel twin engine with six-speeds, four-valves per cylinder and fuel injection.

But even if the original Ghost didn't quite match the Monster on looks, the new-for-1997 Ghost Strike certainly did, with its striking yellow/black paint job, alloy beam frame borrowed from the company's 668 sportster, and mini fairing.

So who makes the most outrageous retro yet? Moto Guzzi, of course, with the amazingly styled V10 Centauro. If Harley-Davidson hadn't already registered the name, the Centauro should have been called Fat Bob. It's the type of visual art that has one either loving or hating the beast. It looks as if it were to have an accident, even a ten-ton truck would come off worse! The engine is untypical for a retro, a four-valve fuel-injected Daytona, with Carillo rods and Nikasil bores. This produces a handy 92 bhp and a solid torque curve.

In a few short years the retro scene has grown from what was almost an experimental niche market into a high-profile major section of the industry's output.

the Customising
Cult

DAYTONA BIKE WEEK

Around 200,000 plus bikers visit the annual Daytona Beach Bike Week every spring in sunny Florida, but how many actually get around to watching the racing is debatable. Nevertheless, the competition held at the nearby International Speedway circuit, home of the famous 200-miler, and a host of other events (including motocross), is enthralling and intense.

But most visitors are more interested in strutting their stuff along Main Street, which reverberates to big-bore v-twins on open pipes. You would probably think you were visiting a convention for Hells Angels rather than something to do with motorcycle sport.

Heavy looking dudes wearing shades stand beer gut-to-bear gut, shoulder to tattooed shoulder on every last inch of the sidewalk. You'd think that the townsfolk would be getting worried – motorcycling mythology says the whole bad-assed pack are like this, but reality is something rather different.

As in most countries, the large majority of the American bikers are more akin to law-abiding angels. Lines of patiently-queing bikers seem to sit in stationary traffic all day. In the United States most motorcyclists act just like their four wheel cousins in heavy traffic.

For many Daytona-bound 'riders' the journey down to Florida is achieved in air-conditioned luxury as they trailer their 'Hogs' (Harley-Davidsons) south to the sun. Forget the movies, forget imported US TV, and most all, forget *The Wild One*. The truth is that although they may look wild, the vast majority of American bikers are a well-behaved and courteous bunch.

In fact, it's mostly its all about show. But what a show it is – the weirder the better. Obviously there are many who just ride a normal bike, wear a helmet and get on with it. But during Daytona Bike Week you get to see just about everything. As one journalist reported: 'Daytona posing ain't just a matter of cruising down Main street a few times. You gotta do it all day.' The same source said: 'They come to pose, not to ride, in their week off from the real estate office or the law firm, or wherever they work.'.

Then there's the 'them and us syndrome'. There is nothing, repeat *nothing*, quite so condescending as the look a Harley rider gives a non-Harley rider when the two pull up together at a red light.

Thousands upon thousands of American bikers visit the annual Daytona Beach Bike Week every spring in sunny Florida.

It may sound unbelieveable, but many people spend the whole week just queuing to get on to the same stretch of Main Street because they know that that's where they'll always have an audience.

As a spectator you will see almost everything: Harleys of all shades and hues, bejewelled customs next to the most awful rat bike, bikes with massive V-8 car motors grafted in, vintage Indians, old British bikes such as Triumphs, Nortons and Ariels, even oddballs such as Vincent v-twins and Velocette singles, plus countless one-off specials of every size and description.

There's also plenty of bare flesh on parade, but after a while it all becomes tiring and it's time to unwind in one of the many bars in downtown Daytona's seething centre.

The main problem is that Daytona is in the wrong place for a motorcycle jamboree. Florida maybe the 'sunshine state'. but it is also flat, bends are infrequent, and, above all, there is a host of oppressive rules, all taken very seriously by the vast majority who turn up.

Can you imagine an Isle of Man TT week where only a small percentage of biker visitors actually bother to watch the various sporting events? Well, this just about sums up Daytona Week, which is a shame because there's so much going on.

Besides the well-known 200-miler (now basically a Superbike race) there's the 100-miler (250cc), Supertwins (Ducatis and the odd Brittain, mainly). The support races include events run by AHMA (American Historic Motorcycle Association), a BMW-sponsored BMW twins race, a Harley-Davidson event for the company's 883 model, and a host of others, including Pre-1939, Pre-1951, Classic 60s and the Premier for 500 and side valve 750s.

Supercross is staged at the Speedway too, but the dirt track is held at the Municipal Stadium on the edge of Daytona's urban sprawl. It is a shame then that so many don't take advantage of all this action spread over seven days each year.

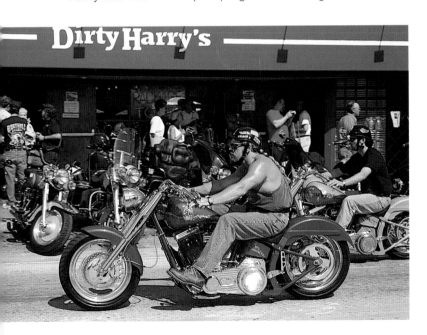

Opposite and left: During Daytona Bike Week, bikers cruise main street and the beach, mainly on customized Harleys.

THE BIRTH OF THE CHOPPER

Traditionally, Stateside bikes were built and styled for long distance touring and comfort; mudguards were deeply valenced, there were wide section 'balloon' tyres and broad saddles. Handlebars were equally massive, and windshields, saddlebags and crash bars were very much part of the standard specification. The rider's feet rested not on pegs, as was the European practice, but long, wide boards instead.

During the early post-war period it was discovered that by junking all the unnecessary paraphernalia and substituting lighter components for the major bits, the Harley or Indian enthusiast could reduce his bike's overall weight by as much as 50 kg (110 lb). Small solo seats from a flat track racer, a tiny peanut tank, straight-thru pipes and often a total absence of front mudguarding and narrower 'bars transformed the big 'hog' image into something more akin to imported European machinery. These early v-twins were nicknamed 'bobbed-jobs'; the term for slicing back bulk and unwanted equipment. Later the term 'chopping' was borrowed from the hot-rod fraternity.

Once established, the chopped motorcycle quickly developed further and further from convention. The chopper was still, basically a bobbed-job and the extensive use of chrome plate and garish paint designs were a legacy of the hot-rod days of 1950s. Soon high-rise 'ape hangers', back rests named 'sissy-bars' and extended front forks, hard tail or soft-tail (denoting if the frame was rigid or sprung) and a host of other more minor alterations became part of the chopper's armoury.

Bike artist Dave Mann depicted the chopper as a long, lean warhorse; a motorcycle which looked aggressive even when stationary. And it was Mann who largely created the chopper on canvas, for others to create into reality out on the street.

Actually getting a 'Dave Mann look' was not always possible. Few owner-builders had the expertise (let alone the facilities) to extend a front end or give a frame additional rake. So a new custom cottage industry was born, producing everything for the custom freak from King and Queen seats through to peanut tanks and even complete bikes and, sometimes, trikes!

By the mid-1970s customizing had become a multi-million dollar business, with the chopper an accepted feature of the bike world. And so it has remained today.

A fully 'chopped' Honda four. To many the custom cruiser style of biking is their whole way of life.

The chopper lifestyle is epitomised by Hells Angels and other motorcycle gangs. Here are members of the Tennessee chapter of the Rampagers.

THE CHOPPER LIFESTYLE

To many, the custom cruiser style of biking is their whole way of life and a whole cult has built up around it. The accent is on freedom. To many, the film *Easy Rider* (1969), with its chopped Harley-Davidsons and breathtaking American landscapes, contemporary soundtrack and two of the most superbly customised machines ever seen on the big screen, caused a whole generation to become converts, almost overnight, to a new sub-culture.

The film fed fantasies depicting the customised cruiser life as one in which the sun always shone, the air was clean and the highways stretched on for as far as the eye could see – a straight arrow of asphalt unfolding into the distance.

It's probably true that most of the followers of the custom cult either own or aspire to own a Hog – Harley-speak for one of the much revered Milwaukee, Wisconsin-built v-twins. As Harley-Davidson expert David K. Wright wrote: 'You don't just show up a Harley. You arrive.' It's all a matter of presence. Owning a Harley, or for that matter any custom bike, is very much a statement. You crave to be noticed, you are an individual, you want to live your life differently from Joe Public.

Harleys don't remain standard for very long after they've left the factory. Each is personalised with either parts from the factory's giant customising catalogue, or just as likely items from one of countless specialist aftermarket goodies are added. Then there's the little matter of customising the owner and his lady with jewelery, clothing and even tattoes – known as 'skin art'

But probably the biggest business of them all all is Bike art, where fuel tanks become the focus of attention once the air brush artist has finished his work.

Harley-Davidson freely admits that its clothing and accessories list makes almost as much money as its bike manufacturing arm. Everything from designer sunglasses, expensive Rolex watches, art trinkets, top quality clothing and much, much more. For some people, the machine itself is almost incidental.

Harley-Davidson Electra Glide v-twin, the ultimate 'off-the-peg' American custom cruiser for over a quarter of a century.

HARLEY-DAVIDSON

Harley-Davidson is all that remains of a once great and vibrant American motorcycle industry. The United States can rightly be regarded as one of the true pioneering nations in the birth of the motorcycle, both for street and competition use.

The first Harley was a 3hp side valve, single, the Grey Ghost, built in 1903 when pattern maker Arthur Davidson teamed up with draughtsman William Harley to build their first bike, with Davidson's brother Walter also lending a hand.

However, it was not until 1907, when working from little more than a small wooden hut, that Harley-Davidson was incorporated as a company and moved into more substantial premises. From then on progress was rapid in the extreme. By the time the USA entered the First World War in 1917, HD was building an astonishing 17,000 motorcycles a year.

The Wisconsin company's first v-twin, a 800cc 45-degree model, had been launched in 1909 and started a trend which still exists today. During the war, some 20,000 v-twins were supplied to the Allied forces, most with sidecars, many seeing military service in Europe.

Post-war, main production centred on 1000 and 1200cc v-twins, but the company suffered in decreased sales from an abundance of cheap cars, led by the Model T Ford.

In racing, Harley-Davidson was soon challenging Indian for the top spot and, like their rivals, made successful trips to Europe in search of race victories. Joe Petrali was Harley's number one rider for much of the 1920s and 1930s. During the early 1940s Harley-Davidson built mainly military bikes once again.

AMF (American Machine & Foundry) took over the company at the end of the 1960s and around the same time the XR 750 racer made its bow. This replaced the venerable KR-side valver which had done sterling service since the 1940s, both on tarmac and dirt. The XR found fame in the next decade, thanks to men such as Rayborn, Brelsford and Springsteen.

A management buy-out occurred in the early 1980s and with it came the 'new nostalgia', a trend-setting idea inspired by Willie G. Davidson, in which H-D's v-twin street bikes were very much the motorcycle to seen on, as indeed they still are. During the late 1980s and early 1990s Harley-Davidson continued to boom as never before.

As this book was being compiled, the company had no less than 18 different models available on the British market alone, including the Sportster 883, the XL1200cc Sportster Custom, the FXDL Dyna Low Rider, the FXSTS Springer Softail, the FLSTF Fat Boy, the FLUR Road King (based on the long-running Electra Glide) and the FLSTCN Heritage Softail Special. All use variations of the famous v-twin engine in various sizes ranging from 883 to 1340cc. Harley-Davidson really is No. 1 in the US of A today.

ELECTRA GLIDE

Harley call the Glide the King of the Highway, and that exactly what the rider feels like, sitting astride all that American chrome plate, glitter and excess. As you cruise down the road onlookers drop what they are doing and stare, other road users stare: in fact everyone stares!

The Glide's' natural competition is Honda's Gold Wing, but although in theory they are in direct competition, under the skin things the two are wildly different.

The 'Wing' is like a super-sophisticated hi-tech Flash Gordon, whilst the 'Glide' is a totally brash all-up-front Dolly Parton. The Japanese bike is technically-superior to the American bike, but it doesn't have *that* name on the tank, which is what counts with many people. As a journalist once put it: 'I don't know about you, but give me a piece of history to a piece of plastic any day.'

When Harley-Davidson first stuck telescopic front forks on their big tourer they named it the Hydra Glide. Next came rear suspension and the title Duo Glide. And when they finally got around to finding a starter motor with enough energy to crank up the massive v-twin engine, they called the model the Electra Glide. These days there are three models in the Glide range. All come with the latest 1340 cc engine. This is generally smooth and reliable enough, but it's strangled by emissions and noise legislation regulations.

The base model is the FLHT. This makes do without the fuel injection of the pricier models, but still offers the authentic Glide experience of, well, Gliding along. There's also less chrome plate and fewer accessories.

Next comes the Electra Glide Classic. Fuel injection helps clean up the big twin's cold starting and low speed running. Then there's the massive top box, with armchair-style back rest for the pillion, more lights, a seriously-loud stereo and lots of other goodies. But the absolute tops in Glide-life is the Ultra Classic. This adds yet more goodies and weight (now up to whopping 765 lb/347 kg).

'Trade up to a Harley' read one of the company's advertisements and that motto effectively sums up the bike and the culture that has grown up around it.

A Harley v-twin engine showing where the engraving artist has been at work – another aspect of customising.

THE HONDA GL1000 GOLD WING

THE GOLD WING HONDA'S HONCHO

Following on from their mould-breaking CB750 superbike, Honda stunned the motorcycling fraternity at the Cologne Show in Germany in October 1974, when it launched the incredible Gold Wing.

The period prior to the launch was rife with rumours concerning the bike's features, which included a flat four 1000cc engine with shaft drive and watercooling, yet nobody in the motorcycling world seemed quite prepared for the reality.

The 'Wing' was, perhaps naturally, compared to the Harley-Davidson Electra Glide, but in truth it was a quantum leap ahead of the American machine. Like the Harley, the proportions of the Gold Wing were large, and since then it has evolved in stages, so that today it is powered by a 1500cc six cylinder engine.

That first bike, back in 1975, was probably the origin of the term 'two wheeled car'. Many people saw this as a term of derision and consequently bought other bikes, but almost 400,000 (a large proportion of them in the USA) took it as a compliment and purchased a Gold Wing.

The Wing is renowned for its dummy petrol tank which houses the electrics, tool tray and fuel filler cap. The fuel supply is actually carried under the seat, thus lowering the centre of gravity.

The prototype Gold wing was a flat six, single overhead cam 1470cc monster, but its relatively low state of tune meant a modest 80bhp, but due to a comparatively light weight of 484lb (220kg) it was capable of a 12 second standing quarter mile with a terminal speed of 130 mph (200 kmh).

This original prototype had much in common (except the engine!) with other designs of the time, demonstrated by its CB750-type frame and engine mountings, whilst its shaft final drive bore a striking resemblance to a BMW. However, only one example was built and although test riders enthused over its smoothness and excellent torque, it was finally defeated by the poor riding position, due to the sheer length of the flat six engine, and so the machine was consigned to obscurity.

When Toshio Nozue replaced Soichiro Irmajim as project leader, Honda had already decided that a flat four would be the most practical layout. Hence Nozue's concept of a grand tourer prototype that was a flat four, watercooled, belt driven dohc, 999cc engined bike with four carburettors and a power output of 80bhp, a five-speed gearbox and a host of other good ideas assembled into one motorcycle for the first time. Honda believed that their machine was the first with watercooling but they were wrong: Scott and a host of others had been there before.

Nor was it the first bike to carry the fuel beneath the seat, but it was the first to use the AC generator as a contra-rotating fly wheel to counteract the inherent torque reaction of the inline crankshaft.

After receiving favourable results from its test programme at Honda's Tochigi facility, the first bikes finally reached the showrooms in 1975 as the GL1000, and so the Gold Wing was born.

Even in early 1974, Honda had foreseen a fully-equipped touring version, almost an early version Interstate, which combined Krauser panniers with a Windjammer fairing. Ironically, the latter became very

popular with 'Wing' owners, many of whom also replaced the stock shock absorbers with other makes such as Koni or S & W. So one could say that these owner-modified examples were the humble beginnings of the Interstate (the Gold Wing Deluxe in UK) and the Aspencade. Honda having chosen to uprate the engine, first to 1100 (1085cc/75 x 61.4mm) in 1981, followed by 1200 (1182cc/75.5 x 66mm) for the 1984 season.

Not satisfied with simply bumping up the engine capacity, Honda engineers then went for the ultimate solution: a 1500 six cylinder machine. Launched in the autumn of 1987, this 1520cc (71 x 64mm) monster produced 100bhp at 5,200 rpm, had a maximum speed of 125 mph (200 kmh) and weighed in at a muscle-wrenching 798 lb (362 kg).

Gold Wing production is carried out not in Japan, but the in USA, and it is in this latter market that the vast majority of 'Wings' are sold. The machine is ideally suited to the vast distances and restrictive speed limits which are so much a part of the American touring rider's way of life.

Opposite: A tanatalising advertisement for the original 1975 999cc GL1000 Gold Wing.

Above: The Honda Gold Wing 1100 De Luxe of 1982, with an engine size upped to 1085cc. In 1984 the engine size was increased again to 1182cc.

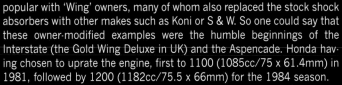

Left: 1987 saw the launch of the even more massive 1520cc six

Sturgis Main Street, South Dakota – the Sturgis Rally is the really big happening in the Stateside biking calendar.

THE STURGIS RALLY

Should you have the time and the money available, you should maybe head on down the road one August to Sturgis, South Dakota, especially if you like to meet fellow soulmates and see lots of two (and three!) wheelers. No doubt about it, Sturgis has to be one of the better places to go motorcycling if your penchant is a laid-back, easy riding lifestyle.

Even compared with Daytona, for the custom cruiser biker Sturgis is the really big happening in the Stateside biking calendar: great country, great riding, great atmosphere. There's usually plenty of good weather and an ideal camping environment.

Under the grand title of The Black Hills Rally and Race Week, Sturgis shuts down a section of its Main Street to all traffic except motorcycles. The town may not exactly love the idea of thousands of motorcycles and riders showing up each year, but it is still a wonderfully friendly place to be in. The rally is a casual affair where old friends are greeted, new friends made, and tall tales are told.

If you want to find out what's the latest style in customising your bike, this is the place. If you want to see what's coming down in parts and accessories for your machine, this is the place. And if you need a new tattoo or a T-shirt, or want to lay down some bucks for a trick piece of leather goods, this is the place. The local shopping centre for bikers is the Main Street corner descriptively referred to as the 'Pit'.

If you're one of those guys or gals who have not wandered on down to Sturgis before, it's in the middle of the territory where frontier history was made. The city of Deadwood, the real Deadwood where Calamity Jane and Wild Bill Hickok hung out, is just a short stretch from Sturgis. You'd be hard pressed to come across a Sturgis biker who didn't make a pass through Deadwood, taking in the scenic route from Sturgis through the twisty road via Boulder Canyon. This is a road to be mightly aware of, as it has claimed the lives of far too many bikers – mostly caused by simply going too quickly.

Talking about Sturgis isn't the best way to tell the story. Its something to experience, more a gathering of bikers that's a laid-back meet up with old friends and the chance to gain new ones and, best of all, to talk and ride bikes. If you haven't been there, it's something to put high on your list of things to do. Just like Daytona, there's only one Sturgis!

CELLULOID DREAMS OF REBELLION

The American Dream biker, at least on the big screen, has often be portrayed as a beer-swilling, leather-clad rebel of whom society is so afraid that daughters are locked behind bolted doors and the shutters drawn when they come into town.

Stanley Kramer's shock-horror *The Wild One*, ostensibly a fictionalised account of the infamous Hollisher episode of 1947, saw Marlon Brando and Lee Marvin strut their stuff across the screen clad in black leathers. Marvin played Chino alongside and in confrontation with the Triumph Thunderbird-mounted Brando.

Made in black and white, *The Wild One* was banned in Britain until the late 1960s by British film censors fearful of the effect it might have on what was a fast-developing youth culture, but many got to see it anyway, by way of a loophole in the law which allowed motorcycle clubs to give private viewings. Viewed today it seems pretty harmless stuff compared to some of the foul language and horrific violence of the 1990s American film industry.

But if *The Wild One* created the biker in a leather jacket brigade, it was the 1969 road movie *Easy Rider* which largely manufactured the laid-back, easy-going custom cruiser style known from then on in as the chopper. *Easy Rider*, much to chagrin of the establishment, really did create a whole new lifestyle, with its hippy drug culture mixed with the 'bad biker' theme.

Overnight almost, new-age bikers were quickly transforming their mounts into choppers by way of 'ape-hangers' and 'sissy bars', whilst the more adventurous lengthened forks and fitted peanut tanks. Many a good bike suddenly became transformed into an entirely new animal, unfortunately often with clumsily-fitted, cheaply-made accessories.

Film star and biker Steve McQueen attempted to redress the bad boy image with his film *On Any Sunday* (1971), which really was a tribute to motorcycling, with its fine action photography and open air panoramas and today is seen as a classic in its own right.

Top: Ground breaking biker movie, *Easy Rider* (1969), with Dennis Hopper, Peter Fonda and (riding pillion) Jack Nicholson.

Above: Marlon Brando in the *The Wild One* (1953), the first time Hollywood explored the myths surrounding biker gangs.

JAPANESE CUSTOMS – THE NEW BREED

Yamaha's XV535 has done more to lift the Japanese industry's fortunes in the battle of the custom cruisers than any other machine. For years the Japanese tried to take on Harley-Davidson and lost. But with the XV535, it built a bike that people wanted to buy. Its secret lay in its unique qualities of lightness, cheapness (to purchase), adequate performance, amazing reliability, good finish and the fact that it looks twice as expensive as it really is. It also handled a whole lot better than earlier Jap cruisers.

But what XV535 did most was to create a whole new market which, once it had attracted buyers, meant these same customers would then most likely move up to a bigger machine – one that was hopefully Japanese.

Yamaha's entry-level custom first appeared in the UK during 1988 and its sohc v-twin develops 47 bhp allowing the XV535 to despatch the quarter mile in a creditable 14.8 seconds and reach a top speed of 101 mph (160 kmh). Specification is completed by a choice of flat or pull-

Kawasaki's VN800 is probably as near a Harley-Davidson as it is possible to get.

Left: Following the Kawasaki 1000/ 1100 VL Eliminator comes a smaller more affordable version. The 600 Eliminator is powered by a detuned ZZR four cylinder engine.

Bottom left: Suzuki's excellent value 1997 VZ800 v-twin custom is not only affordable but good too.

rear brake with a four piston caliper ensure it stops a whole lot quicker than its American competitors.

For 1997 there was a new star. It was long, it was low and it had the mean and moody attitude of a heavy duty cruiser combined with the easy handling of a middleweight and an affordable price tag: it was the XVS650 Drag Star.

The extra-long stretched chassis had been designed to provide an ultra-low seat height which allowed you to get both feet down with ease. And for that authentic cruiser look, the Drag Star's Monocross rear suspension featured a rigid-style swinging arm that enhanced the bike's clean and simple form. Its aircooled 650cc v-twin engine was tuned for low- to mid-range torque for laid-back cruising and featured a new exposed shaft drive system.

A challenger to Yamaha's Drag Star is the Suzuki VZ800, which uses a watercooled 805cc engine from the earlier VX800 street bike. Called the Marauder, the Suzuki's biggest advantage is price and a proven engine design.

Kawasaki also offer an 800 series custom, the VN 800, plus a whole range of others stretching from the tiny EL250 parallel twin through to the truly massive VN1500 v-twin, which weighs in at no less than 644 lb (292 kg).

But of course market leaders Honda had to have the last laugh and this came at the end of the 1996 when the company unveiled what they claimed was the 'Ultimate Custom Motorcycle.' This was the awesome F6C. With parallel twins, v-twins, and V4 engines already featuring in its existing custom range, the 682lb (309kg) F6C (Flat Six Custom) uses a modified version of the imposing 1520cc six-cylinder motor from Honda's grand touring GL1500 Gold Wing.

With six 28mm carburettors and reprofiled cams, the engine has been re-tuned to provide higher performance and extra mid-range punch. Its six-into-six exhaust has three pipes enclosed in a single silencer-like casing each side to produce an evocative exhaust note.

Other features include a maintenance-free hydraulic clutch, 546-watt alternator to power accessories, shaft final drive, inverted 45mm front forks, large section radial tyres (a 17-inch front, 16-inch rear), cast alloy wheels, 20 litre tank, rear backrest and a two-piece seat with detachable rear section.

At last it seems as if the Japanese have managed what they had previously found so elusive in the custom niche of the market – quality engineering and style in the same package.

back bars, shaft final drive, front disc and rear drum brake and a dry weight of 401 lb (182kg).

The easy-to-ride XV535 introduced many newcomers to biking and was also responsible for returning quite a few others after years away from the saddle. And then Yamaha decided it was time to take the process a stage further. The result was the Royal Star. As *Motor Cycle News* said: 'It takes on America's Harley-Davidson on its own territory – and wins! There's finally a bike good enough to claim Harley's cruiser crown. The Royal Star has all the style and charm of a full-dress Hog, but none of its vices.'

When in mid-1996 public demand forced Yamaha to bring the model to the UK, the V-4 sold out instantly. The 1300cc engine, with air-cooled styling (although actually using liquid cooling), kicks out heaps of torque, peaking at just 3,500 revs – and it makes a great noise too.

Rubber mounting calms the vibes many customs suffer from and meaty twin disc front brakes with four piston calipers and a single disc

the Super Bikes

ORIGINS – THE 1970S

The 1970s began with Honda very largely at the helm of the motorcycling world, thanks to one machine, the CB750 four which had stunned the world when it first appeared. Although it was revolutionary for a street-bike, there was nothing really new about the across-the-frame layout of the CB750's slightly undersized 736cc engine. For years the Italians had been winning races with exactly the same format, as indeed had Honda themselves with their own variations on the theme.

But the CB750 broke new ground in being the world's first mass-produced four-cylinder motorcycle. It made its bow in public at the Tokyo Show in October 1968 and was launched in America, where Honda had been selling bikes for almost a decade, in January of 1969. The price was set at little more than the newly released BSA/Triumph triples and was seen to be competitive for such a sophisticated machine.

Given the general conservatism in the world's motorcycle industry, Honda had taken a brave step indeed. And it worked; cementing as it did their position as world leader in the industry, a position they have retained ever since.

The CB750 was powered by a single overhead cam 736.5cc engine with full unit construction, including the five-speed transmission and multi-plate clutch. Of course the machine was not perfect, but it did create a new word – Superbike – and both Honda and others were to soon exploit the concept to the full. Maximum power output of the CB750 was 67 bhp at 8,000 rpm, giving a top speed of 115 mph (185 kmh).

At first Honda's Japanese rivals attempted to compete with two-stroke models such as Kawasaki's fearsome 500H1 (Mach 111) three-cylinder, Suzuki's GT750 triple and Yamaha's YR3 twin. But none of these really offered a creditable challenge.

It was Kawasaki who made the next move, one which was to play as important a role for the company as the CB750 had for Honda. Launched in 1973, the newcomer, named the Z1, rewrote biking parameters and established Kawasaki as builders of large capacity high performance muscle bikes.

The Z1 sported a mighty 903cc aircooled dohc four-cylinder motor, work on which had begun back in 1967. This was before any of its three-cylinder two-strokes had even entered production; the aim being to provide Kawasaki with a big-bore four-stroke replacement for the then current W-series parallel twin. Peak power was 82 bhp at 8,500 rpm, giving a maximum speed of 130 mph (210 kmh).

During its four year production run, the Z1 (later updated as Z900) not only sold in large numbers all around the world, but set new records for speed and acceleration wherever it went. For example, at Daytona Week in March 1973 a trio of Z1s claimed no less than 45 American and world speed and endurance records. Like the CB750, the Z1 sported a disc front brake, electric starter, five-speed gearbox and full instrumentation.

The remaining pair of Japanese makers were much slower to rise to the challenge. Suzuki introduced their four-cylinder dohc GS750 in 1977, whilst Yamaha brought out the three-cylinder dohc XS750 a year later.

By the end of the decade all four Japanese marques had even bigger and faster models on the market. Honda offered a dohc 750 (introduced in 1976) and CB900 and followed up that with the 1979 six-cylinder CBX. Yamaha's response was its XS850 triple and XS1100 four.

By 1977 Kawasaki had increased its four to 1015cc, creating the Z1000. But, like Honda even this wasn't enough, so in 1978 it produced the Z1300; a liquid-cooled 294 kg (653 lb) shaft-driven monster, which was only beaten for bulk by Honda's Gold Wing and Harley-Davidson's Electra Glide.

At the end of 1977 Suzuki had also joined the 'muscle-muscle' class with their GS1000 – a machine seen by many as the best handling of all the oriental models of that time. But it was not just the Japanese who designed and built superbikes in the Seventies: the European manufacturers knew that they had to enter the market too.

Italy's first big bike of the modern era: the 1972 Moto Guzzi V7 Sport. Lino Tonti transformed what had previously been considered an overweight tourer into a sleek sportster.

Left: The trend setting Japanese Honda CB750 (736cc), single overhead camshaft, four-cylinder of 1969. It was the bike that created the Superbike tag.

Above: The 1976 Laverda Jota three cylinder was the first production street bike to exceed 140 mph (225 kmh).

THE EUROPEAN RESPONSE

BMW's long awaited replacement for its Earles-fork boxer twins made its public bow at the Cologne show in September 1969. There were in fact three new bikes: the R50/5, R60/5 and R75/5. In the context of this chapter it is the larger model which is of importance here. The engine was still a horizontally-opposed pushrod twin with shaft final drive. What was new were features such as electric start, direction indicators, five-speeds, and telescopic front forks, but the model still only offered drum brakes on both wheels.

In October 1973 BMW made its next move, with the R90S sportster. The choice of the Paris Show was no doubt deliberate, for it was there, 50 years earlier, that BMW had presented its very first motorcycle, the R32, to the public.

In its styling – by Hans Muth – the R90S represented a milestone in the company's history, featuring as it did a dual 'racing' style saddle, fairing cowl, twin hydraulic front disc brakes and an exquisite airbrush custom paint job for the body work which ensured that no two machines were ever the same.

The biennial Cologne Show in September 1976 heralded the stroke 7 series, including a new concept for BMW (and it must be said the industry as a whole) – the fully-faired R100RS. To achieve the optimum shape, BMW had hired the famous Pininfarina wind tunnel in Italy.

And it was to Italy that many looked during the 1970s – both for styling flair and for speed, as suddenly the likes of Ducati, Laverda, Moto Guzzi and MV Agusta produced a glittering array of superbike exotica.

Ducati had entered the superbike stakes by way of the Fabio Taglioni-designed 750GT which debuted in the summer of 1970 and entered production the following year. This featured a 90-degree ohc v-twin engine with integral five-speed transmission. Its layout ensured a long wheel-base, but even so handling was a major bonus, as was the flexibility of the engine. The 750SS sportster was the first production bike with triple disc brakes in late 1973.

An 864 cc version (known as the 860) debuted in winning fashion at the 1973 Barcelona 24 hour race, and the bike entered production late

the following year, quickly followed by the classic 900SS. Mike Hailwood's famous 1978 TT victory led to the Hailwood Replica of 1979.

Laverda had entered the fray in 1969 with a 743.9cc sohc vertical twin, itself derived from the earlier 650 of 1966. In 1971, the famous 750 SFC was put on sale. Like the later Ducati 750SS, the SFC was a truly hand-built model with the express task of flying the factory's colours on the racing circuits. But it was the 3C and later Jota, with their three-cylinder dohc 1000cc-class engines, which really created Laverda's reputation.

A brochure for the Jota boasted it to be 'a legend in the lifetime'. And it certainly was, with a maximum speed of over 140 mph (225 kmh) and a whole crop of race victories to prove it. The bike was the brainchild of British importer Roger Slater. First deliveries arrived in January 1976. Later an even larger model, the 1200 Mirage appeared, but it was the Jota which everyone fell in love with and remembers today.

MV Agusta built small batches of their exclusive four-cylinder models during the decade; notably the 750S, 750 America and finally the 850 Monza. They were a rare sight then, and are much sought after today.

The Moto Guzzi V7 was Italy's first big bike of the modern era and the legendary Mandello del Lario marque offered a host of models during the 1970s with 750, 850 and 1000-class engines. Their most revered machines were the V-7 Sport (1972-74) and Le Mans 1 (1976-77).

HOME BREWED SPECIALS

Much as the mogels of the motorcycle industry might wish to deny it, but many of the most interesting and innovative machines have been the products of small engineering workshops or even of single-minded enthusiasts constructing their own home-built specials in a garage or garden shed.

Long before the 1970s there had already been a considerable number of one-off or limited-run hand-built bikes which had been constructed and ridden over the decades and won a place in the history books. Graphic examples include George Brough's inter-war period creations, Fred Marsh's home-built 500 four of the 1950s, the Wooler four, Friedl Münch's Mammoth, which first appeared in the mid-1960s, and countless more.

Even during the 1970s many enthusiasts still built their own machines, despite the unprecedented range of exotic machinery that was readily available on the market.

To pick out only a few of these rarities seems unfair, but highlights from this period include the best specials from Great Britain, France, Holland and the USA.

Two of the most interesting British-creations were the Motodd-Laverda and the Quasar. The latter was truly strange – was it a motorcycle or a car? Well actually, it was a combination of the two. Its power source was a Reliant four-cylinder 700cc ohv car engine; the one-off frame gave a feet-forward riding stance and the rider was semi-enclosed.

The Motodd employed the Laverda three-cylinder Jota engine in a special set of cycle parts and was the work of Phil Todd; a Croydon-based Laverda specialist.

From Holland came the Tabia. This machine made use of a Honda four-cylinder car engine and the Hultink-NSU (Hulinsu). It was a Dutch alternative to the Münch Mammoth.

The French contributed the Motobecane-backed MOC-Benelli six-cylinder endurance racer, whilst the Americans had several home-brewed turbo-charged Kawasaki fours, with either Z1 or Z1000 motors. The best examples put out an amazing 170 bhp!

Above: Lord Hesketh with his ill-fated Hesketh 1000cc v-twin Superbike of the early 1980s.

Right: Style and speed, the 1985 Harris Kawasaki GPZ900R. This bike was based around a British chasis and a Japanese engine.

(Italy 1946 –)

Ducati's dominant position in the world of superbike racing in the 1990s is miles apart from its 1930s beginnings as a radio manufacturer. The great days of the company really began in 1954 when Ducati's management signed up engineer Fabio Taglioni and the start of a legend was born. Taglioni, or 'Dr T' as he is known, was not only a talented designer, but also a racing enthusiast. The following year saw Taglioni's first design for his new employers, the 100 Gran Sport, a machine which was to be the beginning of a lineage of ohc singles culminating with the 450 model in 1969.

Next came a 125cc single in both valve spring and Desmo form. The latter won the first race it contested, the 1956 Swedish Grand Prix.

By 1958 Ducati not only had a new range of sports roadsters headed by the 175 Sport and 200 Elite, but also finished the year in second spot in the world championships, after a season-long battle with MV Agusta. In 1959 a youthful Mike Hailwood won his first-ever Grand Prix on a Ducati (the 125cc Ulster).

The 1960s saw the introduction of the famous 250 Mach 1. However, the company was in trouble and the government bought out the Vatican's remaining shares by the end of the decade.

The 1970s saw the arrival of the famous v-twin models, the first bring the 750 GT in 1971. Victory in the Imola 200 (1972) brought considerable prestige, as did Mike Hailwood's triumphant return to the Isle of Man TT in 1978. During the early 1980s the factory won no fewer than four world Formula 2 titles, the rider on each occasion being Englishman Tony Rutter.

A significant business partnership began in 1983 when Ducati began supplying engines to Cagiva. Two years later Cagiva – owned by the Castiglioni family – acquired the Ducati business. It is now jointly owned by the Castiglioni's and an American banking group.

(Italy 1948 –)

The first Laverda appeared in 1948, after it had taken its builder Francesco Laverda a year to design and construct the prototype. Initially, the concept was for his own personal use. It was only when enthusiastic friends in the north-eastern town of Breganze saw the machine that the famous lineage was born. The first model had a 75cc ohv single cylinder engine.

The descendants of this model continued through the 1950s, including a highly successful racing version. These were regular class winners in both the Milano-Taranto and Giro d'Italia long distance road events.

In the 1960s came a small four-stroke scooter and Laverda's first twin. This latter model was powered by a 200cc four-stroke unit construction engine but was designed more for touring than for sport. The annual International Motor Cycle Show at Earl's Court, London, was the setting for the launch of the Laverda 650 Twin (1966). This was to lead to the marque's most revered model, the 750 SFC. Altogether nearly 18,500 big twins were manufactured over the next decade or so.

A prototype of the three-cylinder 998cc dohc model appeared in 1970 and was to herald a decade of success, culminating in the 140mph (225 kmh) Jota sportster. It wasn't just a sales hit, but also, like the SFC, a winner on the track. A major success was the prestigious British Avon Production Series which was won by Jota-mounted Pete (PK) Davies in 1976. Unfortunately, Laverda also made some costly mistakes, including failures such as the Zündapp-powered 125/175cc two-stroke roadsters the Husqvarna-powered 125/250cc enduro machines.

One of the sensations of the 1981 Milan Show was the new RGS, but even this bike, using the legendary 1000cc triple engine failed to attract sufficient customers to stave off a financial crisis. This came to a head in the late-1980s, after several owners failed to materialise. Laverda was eventually relaunched in the early 1990s with the excellent 650 (668cc) Sport dohc, thanks to the efforts of Francesco Tognon.

Kawasaki 900R

DEVELOPMENTS IN THE
1980s

The 1980s were very much a time when the Japanese motorcycle made great technical advances, whilst Europe largely sat on the sidelines, at least until the very end of the decade. Ducati was the first of the European manufacturers to rise from its long sleep, helped by the takeover in 1985 by Cagiva.

Of the 'big four' Japanese manufacturers, Honda built the most bikes but seemed to lack a coherent game-plan in its big-bike strategy during this period. This is typified by the company's series of V4 designs which took much longer to develop to a successful conclusion than the company had ever anticipated.

The first was the ill-fated touring VF750S, which arrived at the end of 1981. Then came the F sports version for the 1983 model. Unfortunately, this was plagued by camshaft and associated problems.

This prompted Honda to build a racing version with gear, instead of chain driven cams; from this was to come success at last in the shape of the VFR 750 (1985) and the RC30 (1988). But all this took time and this allowed the company's competitors to forge ahead.

Of the other Japanese companies, Kawasaki was the first to get a new generation of big-bore sports bikes onto the market, in the shape of the all-new GPZ900R (Ninja in North America). If the legendary Z1 was a bench-mark machine of the 1970s, then the 900R was equally so when it was first shown to the press in December 1983. It was the world's first liquid-cooled 16-value dohc in-line four-cylinder production motorcycle engine and also the first to combine a lightweight diamond frame, aluminium rear frame section and 16-inch front wheel. And, Kawasaki claimed, it was the first with a fork that delivered truly progressive wheel travel combined with the company's rising rate Uni-Trak rear suspension. The 908cc motor produced almost 114 bhp and was good for nearly 160 mph (258 kmh), a phenomenal speed for the time.

Although Kawasaki went on to build bigger fours based on the 900R, including the 1000RX and ZX10 later in the decade, none made such an impact as this trend-setting original.

Yamaha's contribution was its FZ/FZR series with the unique four-cylinder 20-valve engine with deeply slanted cylinders and, on some models, EXUP (Exhaust Ultimate Power Valve). This latter device was a special variable valve fitted to the exhaust system's collector box, oper-

ated by a computer-controlled servo motor which performed according to engine rpm. The first model was the FZ750, launched at the end of 1984 and went on sale early the following year. In 1987 came the FZR1000 with its 989cc engine developing 135 bhp in 'full power' mode and offering a breathtaking 165 mph (265 kmh) speed potential. There was also the strictly limited production run FZR 750R (OWO1). First offered in 1989, it was really a track bike and as such won countless races over the next few years.

But of all the Japanese manufacturers it was Suzuki who really set the 1980s alight with their mould-breaking GSX-R750 of 1985. As the American *Motor Cyclist* magazine commented in their March 1996 issue: 'Contemporary sports bike history is clearly divisible into two chunks: the Dark Ages, i.e., before the 1985 GSX-R750, and the Renaissance thereafter. Suzuki's 388-pound GSX-R was a rifle shot that echoed over back roads and racetracks worldwide. If you were making motorcycles 10 years ago, you either answered it in kind or were instantly out of the sporty-bike biz.' It wasn't simply that the GSX-R750 was the fastest. It was a complete sportster with superb performance, handling and braking wrapped in a mouthwatering package.

A year later came a larger version, the 1100. The actual capacity was 1052cc and, although largely unchanged from the smaller model, the newcomer was a much more practical street bike. The 1986 GSX-R1100 could reach 165 mph and cover the standing quarter in under 10.8 seconds with a terminal speed of 126 mph (200 kmh).

So what of the Europeans? Only BMW built anything really new in the first half of the 1980s, with their K-Series range. The first of these was the four-cylinder K100; soon nicknamed the 'Flying Brick' due to its engine shape. From this was to appear a whole range of modular types including the K100RS sports/tourer and the three-cylinder 750-class K75 line. There was also higher tech KI with the four-cylinder 987cc engine with four-valves per cylinder. All the K-series had fuel injection.

The big three Italian superbike producers of the 1970s – Ducati, Laverda and Moto Guzzi – all languished during the 1980s. But at least Ducati was making positive moves following the takeover by Cagiva in May 1985. This showed first with the launch of the 750 Paso at the Milan Show later that year. But the really big news came two years later with the launch at the same venue of the 851 (in two versions) in a blaze of publicity. The design was the first Ducati to employ four-valves per cylinder, dohc and fuel injection to the Bologna company's 90-degree v-twin. As such the 851 was the forerunner of today's much admired 916 and fully deserves proper recognition.

BMW K1000RS

The 1984 BMW K100RS was a 987cc sports/tourer with brick-type engine configuration. There was also a three cylinder K75S model.

(Japan 1962 –)

Kawasaki

Unlike its Japanese rivals, Kawasaki can rightly claim that motorcycling is only a tiny part of its vast industrial empire. When the Second World War ended, Kawasaki found its engineering skills in such demand that only one of its many plants was left standing idle. This, too, soon found a niche by producing engine and gearbox assemblies for the emerging motorcycle industry. One of Kawasaki's customers was Meguro, and it was through this marque that Kawasaki ultimately became a bike builder in its own right.

Meguro was taken over by its bigger cousin in 1961 and the following year, 1962, saw the first model to carry a Kawasaki badge, the 125cc B8, a single cylinder two-stroke. By then Honda, Suzuki and Yamaha were well established at home and abroad. It is probably true that without its considerable financial and industrial strength, Kawasaki would have been unable to rise to its current position as an equal member of the Japanese 'Big Four'.

Along the way it has created some trend-setting machines: the Z1 (1973), the Z1000 (1977), the Z550 (1980), the GPZ 1100 (1983), the GPZ 900R (1984), the ZXR 750 (1989) and the ZZR 1100 (1990).

Kawasaki has also built a number of interesting and innovative competition motorcycles from the 1969 world champion 125 twin (ridden by Dave Simmonds) through to the fearsome 750 H2-R triple two-stroke used by the likes of Yvon Du Hamel at Daytona in the early 1970s. There was also the world championship winning 250 and 350cc KR inline twin two-strokes and a horde of four-strokes for endurance events, Daytona and Superbike racing.

(Italy 1973 –)

bimota

The Bimota marque was born more by accident than design, although for superbike enthusiasts the accident was a singularly happy event.

Massimo Tamburini owned a heating business in the town of Rimini, an area of Italy which had long been a centre motorcycle manufacture. As a hobby, Tamburini modified several local riders' machines to make them not only faster, but also lighter and sharper-handling. Before long his work on a particular machine, the MV Agusta 600 four, had gained the admiration of the Italian biking fraternity.

But it was in 1972 at the Misano race circuit where Tamburini, his friend Giuseppe Morri, and racer Luigi Anelli were testing a specially-framed Honda CB750 that Bimota was born. A journalist who was present wrote a feature about Tamburini's Honda, creating such interest that a commercial organisation was established to meet the consequent influx of orders. The company took its name from the three partners who set it up: Bianchi, Morri and Tamburini.

The new venture began trading on 1 January 1973. In addition to the Honda, Tamburini had just completed a pure racing machine powered by a Yamaha TR2 two-stroke engine. This too was an instant success and in 1975 Johnny Cecotto won the 350cc World Championship on a Bimota-framed TZ Yamaha.

The first Bimota superbike was the Suzuki GS750-engined SB2 (the SB1 was a racer) which debuted at the Bologna Show in January 1977. The next development in the evolution of the Bimota street bike came at the 1977 Milan Show in the shape of the KB1, housing either a Kawasaki 903 or 1015cc dohc four-cylinder motor.

The publicity and sales success led to more superbikes and soon Honda, and later Yamaha, wanted a piece of the action. Bimota received support from the respective companies it worked with. During this period, Bimota introduced several innovations for production roadsters, including variable steering geometry and the space frame.

During the late 1970s and early 1980s Bimota boomed. Then came the crunch. At the 1983 Milan Show it foolishly displayed a prototype of the futuristic Tesi which wasn't ready for sale. The result was no sales and bankruptcy. The company was only saved by government support and the first Ducati-powered product, the 1985 DB1. The success of the DB1 ensured a comeback which continues in the 1990s with Ducati and Yamaha engines, plus Bimota's watercooled 500cc two-stroke street bike.

ROTARIES
A BLIND ALLEY OF THE 1970S

During the late 1960s and early 1970s many observers considered the Wankel Rotary engine to be the ultimate replacement for the conventional reciprocating piston engine

The Wankel had many apparent advantages: low weight per horsepower, excellent toleration of low-grade and unleaded fuels and smooth, vibration-free power delivery. The basic premise was a brilliant notion of mechanical engineering but was to suffer many setbacks in the course of its development, not least the blight of heavy consumption in a fuel-conscious age.

The Wankel engine was the idea of the gifted German engineer, Felix Wankel, who had experimented during the Second World War with rotary disc valves for torpedo engines. Later, in the 1950s, he applied his experience to a simple supercharger-compressor which enabled an NSU moped engine to propel a streamlined motorcycle to a record-breaking 121.9 mph (196.1 kmh), all on 49 cc!

Although generally referred to as a rotary, the Wankel engine is, in fact, a combustion process which takes place in a chamber shaped like a fat-waisted figure of eight. This is an epitochoidal chamber within which a rotor rotates eccentrically. This 'rotary piston' is of triangular shape and is connected to the central power shaft by gearing and supported on eccentric bearings which allow it to rotate whilst keeping its three tips in contact with the epitochoid chamber. Gas sealing strips are provided at the tips of the rotor, a feature which proved to be the design's Achilles' heel in the early days. Only the use of ceramic materials has finally overcome the problem. In fact, the gas sealing problems on its Wankel-engined R080 car were instrumental in NSU's financial collapse at the end of the 1960s.

Despite the fact that there have been several Wankel-engined cars, including several from the Japanese Mazda concern, only four motorcycles have reached production status: the Hercules W2000, the Suzuki RE5, the Norton Rotary and the awesome Van Veen OCR1000.

The German firm Hercules, whose machines were sold under the DKW label in some markets, were the first to offer a Wankel-engined bike for general sale in 1974. This was equipped with a Sachs Single-rotor air-cooled engine of 294cc working chamber displacement, producing 32 bhp at 6,500 rpm.

The Japanese Suzuki RE5 made its appearance hot on the heels of the German model later the same year. Originally Suzuki saw the RE5 as a means of demonstrating its grasp of modern technology. Unfortunately, it was to prove a costly financial failure, due in part to its ungainly looks and its lack of real development. It had been somewhat hurriedly rushed into production and was quietly withdrawn from sale in 1977. Its single rotor engine displaced 497cc and churned out 62 bhp. Despite the equivalence of the engine to a conventional 1000cc, the RE5's performance was not even on par with a 750 of the same era, whilst its fuel consumption averaged less than 30 mpg.

The beautiful and awe-inspiring Dutch-made Van Veen was the next Wankel to go on sale, in 1976. Cost more than anything else limited the appeal of this 100 bhp hand-built twin rotor superbike. The Van Veen OCR1000 is today highly-prized and fetches top money when it appears for sale, in part because of its rarity value alone.

Other companies such as Honda, Kawasaki and even MZ built prototypes, but none reached the production stage. The only other rotary to emerge into the public domain was the Norton and this proved the most successful of the motorcycle rotaries from an engineering viewpoint, although sales were disappointing.

The Norton involvement came via BSA, who had begun to study the concept in the late 1960s. Because of financial troubles with first BSA and later its successor NVT (Norton Villiers Triumph), the whole project took many years to reach fruition.

The first production Norton Wankel was the police-only Interpol II of the early 1980s. The success of this venture led to the Classic Commander and then, during the early 1990s, the F1. But racing was the real forte of Norton's design and thanks to the talented engineer Brian Crighton, the 588 racer won several British Championship titles, the last coming in 1994. But as with the road-going Wankel-powered bikes, racing was also to prove a blind alley, and development of the rotary was not helped by the rule-makers of the sport.

The Van Veen Rotary with OCR1000 twin-rotor engine was heavy, but had staggering acceleration.

The 1983 Towcester Tuning Shop supercharged 1100cc Suzuki Katana, a tyre smoking dragster.

TURBO'S

If the Wankel engine belonged to the 1970s, the Turbo was the big idea of the 1980s, with all the big four Japanese bike builders introducing production models. Honda was first with the CX500 Turbo as the decade dawned, and followed up with the bigger CX650 Turbo; both were powerful machines, but proved commercially to be poor sellers. And so it continued: Yamaha were next with their turbo entry, the XJ650T. This strangely styled, so-called sportster's only claim to fame was a fleeting appearance in one of the James Bond movies of the era, otherwise it was an even bigger flop than were Honda's earlier efforts.

Suzuki's offering was the 672cc XN85. Again sales were disappointing. Its complicated installation really only offered 750 performance, coupled with dreadful fuel consumption.

While the buying public stayed away from the competition's turbo's, they flocked for a time to Kawasaki's version. This might have been because, in appearance, it was like a standard GPZ750 of the time but had much improved acceleration. It was also less complex and faster than any of the other manufacturer's turbo offerings. In its day this 122 bhp missile was capable of destroying virtually anything else on the road. However, the demand didn't last as the new breed of Superbikes appeared, led by machines such as the GSX-R750 Suzuki, the FZ750 Yamaha and the VFR750 Honda, which eclipsed the Kawasaki in virtually every area. Thus the factory built turbo-charged motorcycle died, never to reappear again.

SPECIALIST MANUFACTURERS

From the beginning of the 1970s and the era of the superbike up to the present time, the world's motorcycle manufacturers have poured out a never-ending stream of desirable and often innovative machinery which in previous decades could never have been dreamt of by enthusiasts.

Against this scene it would appear that the position of the limited-production specialist bike-builders and customizers would be badly affected. But, for a variety of reasons, this has not proved the case.

For a start, there have always been those who want to own something truly unique. Then there is the fact that the early Japanese superbikes didn't handle particularly well, while the Italian industry shot itself in the foot by producing some truly superb bikes which had truly awful finishes. And, finally, there was the fact that the major manufacturers always had to keep one eye on the increasingly vociferous 'green' lobby, with the result, as time passed, that many machines have become overloaded with environmental features. The bevel-drive Ducati v-twin is an excellent illustration of this trend during its career which spanned 1971 to1985.

During the 1970s and early 1980s, factory-built superbikes didn't always perform as their manufacturer's had promised and their customers would have liked, either from a strictly performance viewpoint, or from that of handling, braking, or a less-than-perfect ancillary equipment or finish. This in turn created a demand for specialist superbikes, which resolved one or more of the problems outlined above in a single machine.

Among the plethora of names which flourished in this environment, were Dunstall, Gus Kuhn, Seeley, Rickman, Bimota, Egli, Dresda, Münch and Van Veen. Later came yet more specialists, including names such as Moto Martin, Harris, Niko Bakker Magni and Moko.

Several of these specialist manufacturers had interesting backgrounds. For example, Paul Dunstall entered the 1970s renowned as the 'King of the Customisers' and a man more responsible than any other for the café racer boom of the previous decade.

Dunstall had displayed a talent for judging exactly what the market needed, but during the 1970s, despite the appearance of some truly remarkable machinery bearing his name, this magic touch was not always in evidence.

He stuck with Norton for a shade too long and when he finally switched to Japanese hardware the styling was not always right. But even so, the Paul Dunstall Organisation was still a major force in small-batch superbikes and aftermarket goodies. In addition, Dunstall's Suzuki and Kawasaki machines had the extra advantage of being fully approved by the respective marques.

Another famous British specialist builder was Rickman, with their legendary Metisse chassis. Like Dunstall, the Rickman brothers Derek and Don at first used British engines, notably Triumph and Royal Enfield, before switching to Japanese power in the shape of Kawasaki – again with full factory approval.

The Dutch-based Van Veen organisation is famous for two main reasons: firstly for its World Championship-winning 50cc Kreidler racers,

Magni MV Agusta 862 Special

Above: The 1975 Rickman Z900 was based around the famous Kawasaki Z900 engine in the race-bred Metisse chassis.

Right: The 1977 Bimota KB1 prototype on display at the Milan Show. The bike's Kawasaki dohc four cylinder engine was placed in a space frame with monoshock rear suspension.

Left: Former MV Agusta race manager Arturo Magni has created a number of superb specials, including this Magni MV 862 of 1978.

and secondly for the development and limited production during the late 1970s of the fabulous OCR 1000 Wankel-engined superbike described earlier.

The first Münch Mammoth was built for a Frenchman during the mid-1960s. It used a tuned version of the recently released NSU Prinz 1000TT car engine housed in a one-off set of cycle parts, many of which were made by constructor Friedl Münch himself in his small Friedberg Workshop. For the past three decades Münch has built small quantities of his Mammoth superbike using the NSU-based engine, with capacities up to an incredible 1700cc.

Of all the specialists, Bimota is without doubt the most famous and today is regarded in much the same way as Ferrari is in the four-wheel world. It is strange therefore that the marque, which began in 1972, never set out to be a manufacturer at all, but simply to improve the handling properties of machines such as the MV Agusta 600 and Honda CB750 four-cylinder models.

Arturo Magni was the man who for over 25 years did most to ensure success for the MV Agusta race team, even though Count Agusta paid the bills. Then, when MV quit the bike scene, Magni set up in business, at first selling frame kits for MV roadsters before branching into the world of motorcycle manufacture using BMW and Moto Guzzi engines.

The British aristocrat, Lord Hesketh, ran his own Formula 1 car team in the 1970s. He then attempted to produce a limited production super-bike using a 1000cc v-twin engine. Launched in the early Eighties, Hesketh's dream floundered in a financial morass. However, this was not to be the end and limited production of machines was to continue for the exclusive few for many years thereafter.

Kawasaki ZZ-R1100

THE WORLD'S FASTEST PRODUCTION ROADSTER

Above: Introduced in 1990, Kawasaki's ZZ-R1100 ruled the roost until Honda's Super Blackbird arrived in late 1996.

Right: Named after the American Mach 3 spy plane, the 1997 Honda CBR1100XX Super Blackbird makes 164 bhp and a claimed 180mph (290 kmh) top speed.

Since its launch in 1990, Kawasaki's 1052 cc ZZ-R1100 (the ZXII in the States) ruled as the world's fastest production roadster. But in September 1996 all this changed with the arrival of motorcycling's latest sensation: the Honda CBR1100XX Super Blackbird, named after the American Mach 3 spy plane.

The 1990s has witnessed a proliferation of high-powered, big-bore superbikes that promise and deliver breathtaking performance. However, although it has largely dominated the 600 and 900 categories with its CBR and Fireblade respectively, Honda's contribution to this supreme class of litre-plus Super Sports machines had until then been conspicuous by its absence.

Applying lessons learned in the development of its best selling CBR600F and CBR900RR Fireblade, Honda's design team set out to develop an open-class Super Sports machine that didn't just focus on developing the highest output or the fastest terminal speed at the expense of other factors.

Aerodynamics meant that the fairing was wind-tunnel tested to achieve a small frontal area and one of the lowest effective drag coefficients in motorcycling, whilst still maintaining a high level of wind protection and rider comfort.

The fairing aerodynamics also brought about a new piggy-back styled headlamp that positioned the high beam unit directly over and behind the low beam. The fairing incorporated an isolated air intake to ensure ample quantities of cool, fresh air reaching the carburettors under all conditions. Additionally, two intake ducts visible in the nose of the fairing had nothing at all to do with the engine's air intake, but instead direct cooling air to the oil cooler positioned under the steering head.

The Super Blackbird's engine displaces 1137cc, with 79 x 58 mm short-stroke dimensions. Running on an 11:1 compression ratio, the liquid cooled 16-valve dohc four-cylinder engine breathes through a quartet of slanted flat-slide CV-type 42 mm carburettors.

Important features of the engine are its compact size, a cylinder block which is canted forward some 20 degrees farther from the engine powering the Honda CBR 1000F sports/tourer, a new dual-shaft balancer system and a 3D map-type ignition system. This latter item is a high-accuracy system featuring sensors that monitor throttle angle and engine speed for precise response, optimal performance and acceleration, and smoother transitions throughout the rev range. There are also new slim-tipped spark plugs to provide superior performance.

The Blackbird's engine features Honda's innovative, spring-loaded, scissors-type primary drive gear, which reduces lash and noise output. The floating clutch cover uses a thick rubber gasket and rubber inserts around its mounting bolts to minimise the transmission of noise from the clutch area.

In the pursuit of making full potential of the superb engine – 164 bhp at 10,000 rpm – the development team chose a dual-spar diamond configuration, triple-box-section aluminium frame. The swinging arm, also in alloy, is of the same material.

Backing this up are a set of 43mm cartridge-type front forks featuring Honda's latest HMAS (Honda Multi Action System). The swinging

arm is supported by the company's Pro-Link rear suspension system.

First introduced on the 1993 CBR1000 and completely revised on the 1996 ST1100 Pan European, Honda's ABS system engages both brakes when either the front or rear brake is applied. At the front, dual combined three-piston calipers bite onto 310 mm dual hydraulically-operated discs, whilst at the rear a 256mm single disc operates with dual combined three-piston calliper; all featuring sintered metal pads. The 17-inch hollow-section triple-spoke cast alloy wheels use radial tyres – 120/70 ZR front and 180/55 ZR rear.

Specification is completed by way of a six-speed gearbox, 22 litre (4.5 gal.) fuel tank, 4-2-1-2 exhaust system with stainless steel mufflers, newly developed 530 'O' ring drive chain and a lightweight integrated instrument console which includes an electronic instruments and fuel gauge (with LED low-fuel indicator) and LCD clock display. Dry weight of the machine is 223 kg (492 lb).

The designer's brief also called for 300 kph (187.5 mph) to enable the Super Blackbird to snatch the ZZ-R1100 crown. At the press launch which was held at the French Paul Record circuit in the late summer of 1996 *Motorcycle International*'s tester Dave Campbell achieved 281 kph (175.6 mph) at just over 10,000 rpm with a strong headwind blowing along the slightly uphill Mistral straight. Given these disadvantages, it seems likely that the 300 kph barrier might well be broken in ideal conditions.

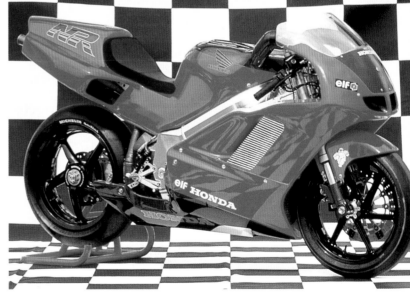

With a price tag of around £35,000/$50,000 Honda's hi-tech oval piston NR750 holds the record for the world's most expensive production street bike.

A NEW CLASS OF TOURING BIKES

For many, touring is what motorcycling is all about. And today the rider wishing to head off into the highways and byways has never had a better choice of purpose-built touring motorcycles. Honda, Kawasaki, Yamaha, BMW, Triumph, Moto Guzzi and Ducati all offer specialised mounts for this purpose. It should also be noted that Suzuki offer a sports-tourer (the GSF 1100F) and Harley-Davidson make a range of Glides which can be successfully employed in the touring role (see page 156).

Market leaders Honda offer the ST1100 Pan European (simply sold in the States as the ST1100). The Americans also get the Pacific Coast, which uses an 800cc 45-degree v-twin engine.

The ST1100 was designed by Honda engineers from the ground up to be a practical, reliable tourer, and it certainly lives up to its brief. The liquid-cooled 16-valve dohc 90-degree v-four is modern engineering at its very best; offering torquey, usable power in a smooth and unstressed fashion. This is coupled to a slick-operating gearbox and largely maintenance-free shaft final drive. A choice of screen heights helps tailor the ST to the individual rider's needs. It is also available with ABS and Honda's Traction Control System (TCS), the latter preventing the rear wheel spinning under power in slippery conditions.

Kawasaki's offering is the long-running 1000 GTR. Launched in the spring of 1986, it was one of the first of a new generation of touring machines for the rider who wanted to travel fast without sacrificing the comfort, convenience and load-carrying capacity of something like either a BMW or Moto Guzzi twin cylinder model. Essentially the GTR was a combination of a detuned 997cc 1000RX engine, with new diamond frame, shaft drive and radial tyres. But compared to more modern machines, it is now beginning to show its age.

Launched in a blaze of publicity in 1993, the GTS 1000 was Yamaha's first bike with hub centre steering, but the model suffered from an identity crisis. The company originally tried to sell it as a sports-tourer – with the accent on sport. As such sales were abysmal. Since switching to a touring tag sales have improved, if only slightly. But with a higher cost and without the benefit of shaft drive, Honda's ST1100 seems to offer much better value.

The German BMW company has always been seen as one of the main

Honda's ST1100 Pan European is a tourer in the truly grand tradition. It has a liquid-cooled 16-valve dohc 90-degree v-four engine.

providers of touring machines, and so it remains today, with both twin and four cylinder models being offered.

The four-cylinder is the K1200LT, which replaced the earlier K1100RT, and still earlier K1000RT, as the German manufacturer's flagship model. The fuel injected 1200cc engine is much smoother than the earlier K-series tourers, whilst the level of equipment is impressive, with ABS as standard. The fairing is one of the most efficient around and the riding position is perfect for all-day two-up touring. Shaft drive and a comprehensive list of optional extras which includes heated handlebar grips and an electrically adjustable windscreen complete the package.

BMW tried to quit making its famous flat twins during the 1980s, but there was such an outcry from owners and potential owners that they had to relent. Then in the early 1990s they introduced a new 1085cc four-valve engine. The first model was the R1100RS, but as a pure tourer this is overshadowed by the new-for-1996 R1100RT, which offers more weather protection, greater luggage capacity and a softer ride. A catalytic converter is available as an option. BMW claim a 127 mph (205 kmh) top speed and 90 bhp for the fuel injected motor.

British touring hopes are carried on a pair of Triumph Trophies – the 1200 and 900. The larger model can reach almost 140 mph (225 kmh), making it one of the fastest touring models available. Both come with a huge twin-headlamp fairing and hard panniers as standard. The larger model is the best for all-day riding with its so-smooth and torquey engine, combined with acceptable fuel economy.

Although many may see the Moto Guzzi California more as a custom cruiser, its real forte is serious touring. The 1064cc ohv v-twin engine can trace its origins back to the V-7 of the mid-1960s, but the advantage of this long pedigree is virtually bullet-proof mechanics. All models now come with electronic fuel injection. This has cleaned up the big twin's low-down running and starting, so it now performs with the best of them. The handling's good, too, with more ground clearance than you'd expect.

Huge panniers and a usefully comprehensive screen are available as options. Other pluses are the comfortable dual seat and the shaft drive. With these the California makes a truly excellent tourer and the overall quality of build is much improved.

At the end of 1996, Ducati stunned the motorcycling world by introducing an all-new touring model, the ST2. Powered by a 944cc liquid-cooled 90-degree engine with two-valves per cylinder, the newcomer looked an impressive piece of kit with its steel trellis frame, inverted forks, triple Brembo Gold line brakes, comprehensive fairing and colour-matched panniers. Although only chain final drive was specified, the ST2 does benefit from the excellent Weber-Marelli fuel injection, similar to that used in the famous 916 superbike.

BMW updated its touring image in 1996 with the launch of the R1100RT. Specification includes a fuel injected, eight-valve, twin cylinder engine, paralever rear suspension and ABS brakes.

Touring is about travelling, and where better to visit than the Italian lakes. The bikes are a pair of Moto Guzzi Spada 1000 v-twins from the late 1980s.

NEW GENERATION OF MINIATURE SUPERBIKES

In general terms a superbike usually means a machine of a least 750cc engine size, but over the last few years a whole series of smaller bikes have appeared on the scene which, judged by the standards of performance, are also worthy of the term.

These are split into three groups: 250cc two-strokes, and 400cc or 600 cc four-strokes. In Japan even 250cc four-cylinder four-strokes of amazing specification are worthy of the being added to the list.

The modern hi-tech quarter-litre two-stroke can be linked back to the original LC (Liquid Cooled) Yamaha of the early 1980s. Other ancestors include the RG Suzuki of 1984, the TZR Yamaha, which first appeared on the Japanese home market in 1986, the KRI (and later KRIS) Kawasaki, the RGV Suzuki (1989) the NSR Honda (1990) and, finally, the RS Aprila (1995). All were liquid-cooled twins with various performance enhancing help from the likes of reed and power valves and fancy ignition systems to optimise power output. The LC, RG and KRI/KRIS were parallel twins, but as with GP racing, the latter bikes – the RGV, NSR and RS – switched to the v-twin layout. All use pump lubrication and six-speed gearboxes.

The next grouping is often referred to as the 'Pocket rocket 400s'. High performance 400s sell by their thousands in Japan, but less so in other countries. Admirers appreciate their lack of bulk, their single-minded sporting character and their excellent power-to-weight ratios. Others question the need for the complication of four cylinders in an engine of only 400cc. And some riders don't like the way these four-strokes have to be revved like two-strokes to extract the most from their engines.

In Britain only Honda, Kawasaki and Yamaha have chosen to officially import their respective Super Sport 400s. Although 'grey imports' mean that the Honda CBR-400 and the Suzuki GSX-R400 can occasionally be seen.

It is generally accepted, certainly if racing results are studied, that the FZR Yamaha is top dog in its class. It was also the first production Yamaha model to feature EXUP and at the time (spring 1987) was 'Japan only'. Unlike the larger FZR models, the 400 has four instead of five-valves per cylinder. There's very little power below 7,000 rpm and it's only above 10,000 that the bike flies.

Above: Laverda 650 Sport out on test with the author in the summer of 1995. The re-born Italian marque uses a 668cc dohc, eight-valve, fuel injecteed parallel twin engine. Top speed is 134 mph (216 kmh).

Opposite: Kawasaki's 'pocket battleship' Ninja ZX-6R features a 16-valve dohc 599cc four cylinder engine which gives amazing levels of performance.

Left: The Yamaha FZR 400 RRSP. Introduced in 1987 remains a major force in the 400cc class, featuring prominently in racing results.

The ZXR 400 Kawasaki is a great looker, but suffers from overhard rear suspension, whilst its engine is not quite in the same class as that of the Yamaha.

This leaves the NC30 Honda, which proved a sales failure in Britain. Too few buyers made it viable for Honda UK to continue imports after 1992. Perhaps this was to be expected, because the tiny V-4 cost over £1,000 more than a CBR600F!

In the remaining category it's the CBR600 which has usually led the annual sales war in what is now one of the most popular classes in motorcycling – the Super Sport 600.

Launched back in 1987 to take on the then class leader, the GPZ Kawasaki, the original CBR (coded F) put out 83 bhp and clocked 140 mph through the timing lights. The GPZ's days at the top were over. Handling was best in its class, as were the brakes. But the all-enclosed body work was not to everyone's taste.

For 1991 came a complete overhaul, the machine now coded M. The bore was increased, the stroke decreased and power was lifted to 99 bhp. More efficient cooling also helped and the rest of machine was beefed up to cope, whilst revised bodywork gave more pleasing lines. Kawasaki's ZZ-R600 out-sold it that year in UK for the only time since the

same firm's glory days with GPZ. But nobody's topped the CBR since.

In 1995 the model enjoyed another significant update (which was necessary to keep ahead of new bikes from the opposition). One of the major new features was the uprated Direct Air Induction System (DAIS), with air intakes positioned under the headlamp, using a two-stage system with two sets of ducts, one positioned further forward than the other. At speeds of less than 12 mph (20 kmh), both sets opened and prevented low-speed blow-back of fuel-air mixture. Over 12 mph the outer ducts closed off. That same year *What Bike?* recorded a 'dazzling 165 mph (265 kmh)', the fastest ever speed for a standard 600, albeit aided by a two-mile run and a slight tailwind.

Then in late 1996, Suzuki decided to enter the race with the GSX-R600, aimed directly at taking the CBR's crown. Suzuki's new machine was a scaled-down version of the GSX-R750 which was launched a year earlier. The new Suzuki delivered almost 110 bhp and weighs 174 kg (384 lb) compared to the CBR's 185 kg (408 lb). On paper it appears the most serious threat to Honda's near stranglehold on this all-important middleweight class. Kawasaki (ZX6) and Yamaha (Thundercat) are also both trying hard to get on fully competitive terms, as are Ducati and Laverda with their twins.

TECHNICAL DEVELOPMENTS
NEW GENERATION TWO-STROKES

Many of tommorrow's superbikes may well be powered by two-stroke rather than four-stroke engines. The first of this new breed is the Bimota 500 V Due, which went on sale in mid-1997.

Why use a two-stroke? The most obvious reason is the excellent ratio between weight and power. The two-stroke engine, and therefore the whole bike, can be made more compact. In fact Bimota's 500 weighs as little as a 250, but packs much more power.

But a good power-to-weight ratio is not enough, so Bimota have attached other features to ensure low fuel consumption and low pollution emissions, which the company says is comparable with a typical four-stroke engine of the mid-1990s.

The internal mechanics of the engine are very simple. The main objectives of the project were from the beginning the smallest possible dimensions and lowest weight. Every piece from the con-rods to the pistons, from the gearing to the crankcase, has been designed by computer and then bench tested with the aim of achieving the best results in terms of weight and reliability.

The traditional downside of the two-stroke is pollution. Bimota parried this by using direct fuel injection – a first on a two-stroke. This means that the 499cc (72 x 61.25mm) 90-degree v-twin not only produces a sensational 110 bhp, but also that this outstanding output is achieved with clean running. Fuel is squirted directly into the cylinder rather than indirectly into the inlet tract as in other injection systems.

This results in only the air that the engine needs flowing through the crankcase, not the excess that the conventional two-stroke requires. The intake and exhaust ducts have been designed with the purpose of providing the engine with both good power and torque at low and mid-range – a flaw in the traditional two-stroke character.

But probably the biggest breakthrough is in the lubrication system. In

a conventional two-stroke, the oil is mixed with the fuel. In the Bimota V Due engine, there is separate lubrication. The oiling goes through some galleries into the crankshaft and on to the cylinders, while the lubriation of the main bearings is achieved by the gearbox oil. In this way it is possible to obtain a remarkable reduction in emissions because the oil consumed is only that despatched to the cylinder and crankshaft. In addition, lubrication is improved since the oil is not being diluted by the fuel.

The electronic fuel injection system ensures that a fuel saving of between 60 per cent to 70 per cent is made over a similar two-stroke engine with conventional carburation.

To aid rider information, details such as engine revolutions, speed and even the gear you are in, are shown digitally. The Bimota V Due also features a *Windows* computer programme, which can be used by the dealer network to optimise servicing.

Above: Bimota's 500 v-twin engine. It features low pollution and high output thanks to its new lubrication system, direct fuel injection and other hi-tech aids.

Left: Bimota's 1997 499cc V Due, a Superbike for the next millennium.

Opposite: Honda's radical NSR500V racer. It has a computer-controlled, rotating exhaust valve which has turned a major engine design problem into a technical plus.

The bike's five-speed gearbox is constructed as a cassette, again assisting maintenance, while the clutch is dry, with multi-plates and is hydraulically-operated.

Styled by Sergio Robbiano, who worked with Massimo Tamburini on designs such as Ducati's 916 and the Cagiva Mito Evolution, Bimota's ultra-modern two-stroke not only looks a million dollars, but its power-to-weight ratio is a staggering 0.76bhp/kg, compared with the 0.68bhp/kg of Suzuki's GSX-R750 – a model which is at the very cutting edge of four-stroke 'Super Sports' technology.

Although Bimota are the first, it seems likely that other new generation two-strokes are likely to appear, with at least three Japanese designs under development. All three are road-legal GP-based machines.

Honda's NSR500V and Yamaha's TZR750 and 500 all ape their racing brothers. Honda employed its stunning lightweight v-twin 500GP racing machine as the basis for its street scorcher, while Yamaha have borrowed heavily from their works Grand Prix machines for their 500 and 750 V-4 bikes.

Both Yamahas will employ fuel injection and separately lubricated top and bottom ends, like Bimota, to maximise fuel economy and slash engine emissions to comply with increasingly strict worldwide pollution laws

Honda's ingenious AR (Active Radical) combustion system turns one of an engine designer's major problems into a technical plus. Engine efficiency is increased when combustion chamber pressure and temperature are raised, but a limit is reached when these cause the fuel/air mixture to explode prematurely. This explosion is produced by active radicals – highly reactive fragmented molecules left over in a cylinder after combustion – which causes the incoming mixture to ignite spontaneously. In conventional engines this causes pinking or knocking.

Honda's solution is to use a computer-controlled rotating exhaust valve, so that the active radicals induce the combustion at the optimum time in the engine's cycle.

With Bimota, Yamaha and Honda on the prowl, the four-stroke's grip on the superbike world may be under threat and the two-stroke looks set to offer a serious challenge.

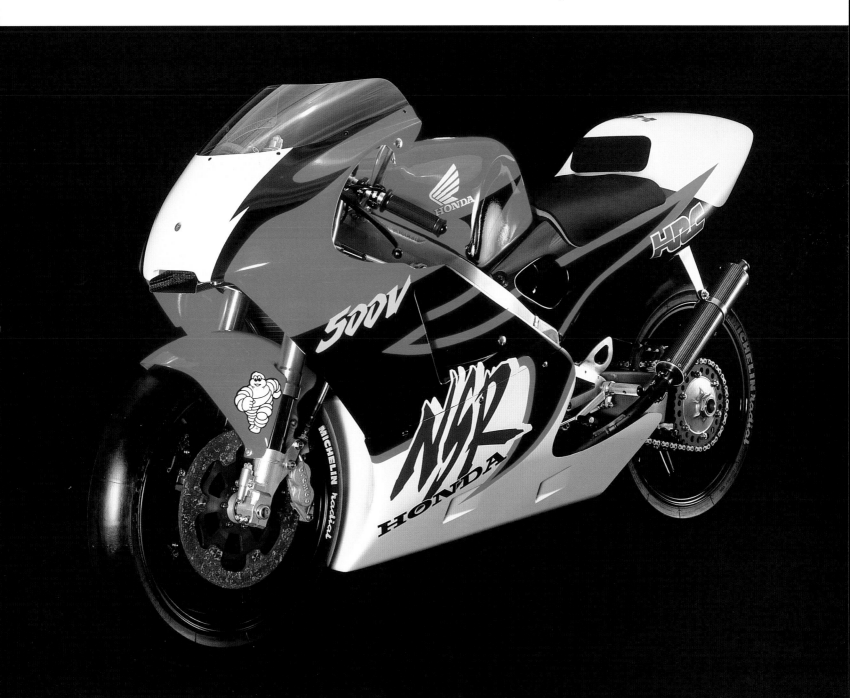

TODAY AND TOMORROW

In the Superbike stakes, the first half of the 1990s was dominated by two machines: Honda's CBR 900RR Fireblade and Ducati's 916. The original CBR 900RR rewrote the rules of Super Sports design, putting all of its Japanese four-cylinder opposition in the shade, with its combination of lightness and searing power.

The liquid-cooled 16-valve dohc across-the-frame 918cc four develops 128 bhp at 10,500 rpm (1997 model figures), giving a maximum speed approaching 170 mph (275 kmh). This, combined to its low 183.5 kg (404 lb) weight, has seen the model lavished with praise, repeatedly earning 'bike of the year' awards from magazines throughout the world. Only its unusual 918cc engine size has limited its use in racing, otherwise the Fireblade might have been even more successful.

Its technical specification is impressive and explains why the positive power-to-weight ratio is so good. Honda's engineers had set out to design a machine with no compromise in the quest for minimum weight.

Flat-topped, ultra-light slipper pistons allow high rigidity and lightweight conrods and crankshaft, to minimise inertia and provide extremely crisp engine response and smooth control. Another weight-saving help is the magnesium cylinder head cover (from 1994 onwards) that is lighter than the original aluminium unit. The Fireblade's 16 valves are worked directly by twin camshafts, resulting in a compact, low-friction valve train that requires adjustment only every 16,000 miles. The bank of four 38 mm diameter flat-slide carbs are assisted by a single-port induction system, which combines with a high-capacity airbox to provide maximum throttle response.

The ignition system is computer-controlled and digitally transistorised, with electronic advance. A cartridge-type liquid-cooled oil cooler ensures lubricant temperatures are kept strictly under control for stable output and maximum engine life.

Honda CBR 900RR Fireblade. Together with Ducati's 916, it set the motorcycling world alight in the 1990s.

The Fireblade's light, yet sophisticated chassis also plays a vital role. The frame, based on twin main spars of extruded aluminium, weighs just 10.5 kg (23 lb). It features a semi-floating rubber engine mount to combat vibration, and supports a high-rigidity aluminium swinging arm designed using in-depth computer analysis and rigorous track testing. The suspension is a combination of an inverted front fork with massive 45mm stanchions and a refined version of Honda's Pro Link system, with a remote reservoir single shock at the rear.

Honda were the first manufacture to use the combination of 16-inch front wheel and 17-inch rear wheel on a road bike, ensuring razor sharp response and sure-footed handling in a single package. Twin 296 mm front disc brakes with four-piston calipers, backed up by a single 220 mm rear disc, haul the Fireblade down from any speed with minimum rider effort.

The rest of the design has had the same amount of attention lavished upon it, helping to explain just why the Fireblade has been such a runaway success story.

From one top seller to another: Ducati's amazing 916. To many, the 916 is not merely a superbike, but *the* superbike. Judged on style and charisma, there is simply nothing in the world to touch it.

Its choice of a Ferrari racing red colour scheme only adds to the overall effect, as does the 'pillar-box' twin-headlamp fairing, hi-level aluminium (Termignoni carbon fibre on SP/SPS) silencers, single-sided swinging arm and a deep-throated, booming exhaust note.

The Kawasaki GPZ1100. In the Eighties this bike would have been considered an out-and-out sportster. However, such is progress that it is now regarded as an all-rounder but a great bike nonetheless.

Not only does the 916 have style in abundance, it also has a pedigree that is virtually unmatched in modern motorcycling. Essentially, it's a pure breed racer, with the bare minimum of equipment necessary to make it road-legal: lights, an electric starter and a number plate holder! In reality it is no less than a production version of similar machines used by the Italian factory to such great success in WSB (World Super Bike) racing – and Ducati have won all but one of the world titles since the beginning of the 1990s.

The 916's predecessor was the 888, and earlier still the 851. All of these bikes share the same basic liquid-cooled dohc eight-valve 90 degree v-twin layout, with Weber-Marelli integrated electronic fuel injection and ignition system.

The type of system used by Ducati is of the 'open loop' variety first employed by Ferrari in their Formula 1 race cars. This features a number of sensors which monitor air temperature and density, coolant temperature, engine revolutions, throttle position and ignition combustion (or detonation). There is no box-like flow meter as used in the Bosch FI system (and employed by BMW), nor a lambda probe (to enhance fuel injection), commonly found on much more expensive car ignition systems.

Ducatis's 916 v-twin. This Italian stallion set new standards in the sports bike arena when it came onto the market in 1994.

INCREASED COMPUTERISATION

In the Weber-Marelli computer memory used by Ducati, a number of maps have been encoded on the basis of the engine's running conditions, combined with information coming from the system's sensors. The computer then plots the optimum ignition advance curve as well as the timing of the injectors. Fuel is supplied by an electric pump and hence squirted directly into the inlet tracks by a single injector for each cylinder (on the original 851 up to 1989, there were two injectors per cylinder, a feature shared by the 916 SP/SPS models) in a phased mode.

Weber's designer Aureliano Lionello converted the system to suit Ducati's engine layout, delivering a programme which can be varied to improve such matters as engine braking, fuel consumption and exhaust emissions. Any changes to an engine's specification – a different camshaft, for instance – will usually require a reprogrammed chip.

The fuel injection also allows a much larger inlet track which can feed fuel dead straight to the inlet valves. Without doubt, Ducati's use of computerised fuel injection and ignition systems has been a major feature as to how the combinations of old world virtues (a 90-degree v-twin engine) and modern technology have come together so successfully.

At the end of 1996 both Honda and Suzuki announced 'Ducati-type' Vees, with the Honda VTR 1000 Firestorm (996cc) and Suzuki TL1000 (also 996cc). Interestingly, only Suzuki chose to use fuel injection; the Honda v-twin sports a pair of 48 mm flat-slide CV carbs instead.

As for Ducati, the 1997 production 916 remains just what it says it is: 916cc (94 x 66 mm), But the SPS (customer racing model) has now grown to 996cc, so who's copying whom?

Certainly as far as the concept is concerned, it's very much a case of Japan following Italy, which in itself marks quite a change. After all, it was the Japanese and Honda who were first with the modern superbike concept, back in 1969 with the CB750 four.

And it's not just Ducati who are moving forward in Europe: Triumph, Moto Guzzi and Laverda are all making positive moves to compete with the Japanese in the big bike league.

Motor Cycle News shouted the headline in October 1996: 'New Brit Superbike Hits The Bullseye!' This marked the public debut of the new T595 sports bike – the most important machine made at the new Triumph factory since their first, the 1200 Trophy, was introduced back in May 1991. The T595 (and the unfaired T509) represented a break from the company's concept of building a modular range of machines, in which all of the different models feature a large percentage of common components.

The first bikes built at the Hinckley, Leicestershire, plant shared almost all their parts, including frames, tanks, running gear and most

The 1997 Suzuki TL1000 was Japan's answer to the Ducati 916. Its 996cc engine closely follows the Italian v-twins progress, but who's copying who?

engine bits. Engine capacities were altered by using three and four-cylinder versions with 55 and 65 mm strokes, resulting in 750 and 900 triples and 1000 and 1200cc fours. This allowed Triumph to cover various niches with minimal cost and to produce all its bikes on the same production lines. But the T595 and 509 share nothing with the older models, and neither, say Triumph, will future models.

Triumph's boss, John Bloor, has much to be proud of. In a few short years he has created a vibrant reborn marque from nothing: all Bloor bought was the name. Bikes such as the T595 prove that he has achieved a brilliant success.

Both the new Triumphs feature a unique oval-section twin-spar chassis and the most advanced fuel injection (Sagem) ever fitted to a motorcycle. And in new across-the-frame three-cylinder engines – T595 955cc and T509 885cc – Triumph employs high-tech casting techniques and materials more advanced than those used by even the Japanese.

The earlier 900 triple was used as a basis for the new engine, but only the original conrods remain. Car makers Lotus were consulted with aspects of the design, particularly gas flow and combustion chamber shape. The T595 produces 128 bhp and the T509, 106 bhp.

For 1997, the reborn British Triumph marque launched the sensational T595, a superbike to compete with anything in the world.

Meanwhile a revitalised Moto Guzzi factory have been busy with new versions of their familiar v-twins. First came the eight-valve Daytona in late 1991, followed two years later by the more conventional two-valve per cylinder 1100 sport. Both have helped Guzzi's profile to take an upward curve and there are more new bikes in the pipeline.

Laverda is another famous name from the early days of the superbike, with the likes of the long-gone, much admired Jota. But Laverda can take heart as new owner Francesco Tognon (who bought the ashes of the company from the liquidator in 1993, in much the same way as John Bloor acquired Triumph) has already marketed the 668 sportster, and is launching a new liquid-cooled 750 twin in mid-1997. There are also plans for a new triple by 1999, currently envisaged as being in both 900cc racing and 1000cc street forms.

The future for motorcycling, and the superbike in particular, looks extremely exciting as the next millenium approaches.

index

Numbers in italics refer to illustrations

A

Abe Star 67
Aberdale 51
ABS brakes 178, *178*
accessories 76, 154, 157, 178
Ace 19
Active Radical Combustion (ARC)
    system 131, 183
ACU 1000 Miles Reliability Trial
    15, 19
Adler 13, 132
    MB250 51
advertising *17, 43, 46, 67, 68,*
    71, 73, 79, 83, 94, *159*
aerodynamic designs 102, 176
    see also machine design
Aermacchi 44, 45, 49, 53, 105
    Ala Verde 53
    Chimera 45
after-sales service 43
    see also dealer networks
Agostini, Giacomo 104, *105,*
    105, 112, 117, *117,* 146
Agusta, Domenico 102, *103*
    see also MV Agusta
Aim, Jim 145
air cooling systems 10, 13, 14, 15,
    16, 109, 148, 151, 163, 165,
    172
air filtration systems 72
air intakes 176
AJS 15, 24, 27, 31, 32, 49, 61,
    71, 82, *82,* 83, *122,* 146
    Porcupine 102
    see also AMC
Aksland, Skip *129*
alloy engines 72
Alberti, Fausto 24
Allen, Johnny 58
aluminium frames 134, 135, 151,
    169
Amal carburettors 43
AMC 23, 31, 41, 71, 82-3, *82,* 121
    G3L 15
    see also Matchless
AMC gearboxes 82
America 11, 19, 21, 26, 32, 37,
    38-41, 43, 49, 57, 58, 63, 67,
    79, 81, 86, 100, 106, 110, 112,
    119, 121, 124, 128-9, 135,
    153-4, 156-7, 160-1, 165, 166
American Historic Motorcycle
    Association (AHMA) 153
American Machine & Foundry see
    AMF
American Motorcycle Association
    (AMA) 52, 112, 129
AMF Harley-Davidson 53, 156
    see also Aermacchi
Amm, Ray 59, 93
Anderson, Hugh 104, 147, *147*
Andrews, Mick 145
Anelli, Luigi 171
Anglo-American Transatlantic Trophy
    Race 100, *100*
Antionescu, Lessman 15
Anzani 32
Aprila 111, *111*
Archer, Les 119, 120
Ardie 37
Ariel 24, 35, 35, 41, 41, 50, 51,
    61, 121, 132
    HS 119
    Huntmaster 15
    Leader 15, 51, *51*
    Red Hunter 15, 27, 35, 61
    Square Four 15, 27, *27,* 79
    W-NG 41
armaments manufacturers 14, 15,
    23, 24
armed machines 21, 38, 39, *39*
Asahi 41, 63, 67
Associated Motor Cycles see AMC
Atlas engines 83
auctions 140
Auriol, Herbert 131
Austin engines 29
Austin Sevens 64
Australia 19, 43
Austria 15, 17, 35, 119, 122, 126,
    132
Austrian Grand Prix 105
Austro-Hungary 13, 17
Auto Cycle Club (ACC) 91
Auto Cycle Union (ACU) 19, 111,
    122, 135
Auto Union 26
autocycles 23
autojumbles 140-1, *141*
Automobile Association (AA) 50, 122
Avon components 53

B

badge engineering 82
badges and emblems 15, 19, 23,
    29, 30, 31, 52-3, 55, 64-5,
    79, 168, 171
    see also colour schemes
Baeten, Rene 119
Bakker, Niko 174
Baldwin, Oliver 32
Ballington, Kork 106
Bambini sidecars 50
Bandirola, Carlo 103
Baragwanath, E C E 'Ted' 29, 94
Barber Museum 142
Barcelona 24 hour Race 166
Bateman, Frank 93
battery/coil ignition 16, 74
Baumm, Gustav 59
Bayerische Flugzeug Werke (BFW) 23
Bayerische Motoren Werke see BMW
beach racing 127
Beaumont, Roger 89
Bekamo 26
Belgium 13, 14, 37, 119, *119,* 120,
    131
Belgium Grand Prix 53, 95, 96, 103
Bell, Artie 99
Belle Vue classic bike shows 141
belt drives 7, 12, 159
Benelli 24, 35, 37, 44, 49, 79, 99,
    104, 166
    Devil 79
Bennett, Alex 29
Berlin Shows 35
Berliner Corporation 49
bespoke machines
    see customised machines
Bettmann, Siegfried 10
Bianchi, Edoardo 12, 13, 44, 171
    Edoardo Bianchi & Co. 12, 12, 35,
    37, 100
Bickers, Dave 121
Bickford, Oscar 94
bicycles 7,8, 9, 10, 11, 12, 13, 14,
    15, 64
bike art 154
    see also colour schemes
Billand, Rolf 96
Bimota 114, 171, 174, 175
    500 V Due 182-3, *182*
    KB1 175
Bison 23
Black Hills Rally and Race Weeks 160
Blacknell 50
Blackpool shows 82
Bloor, John 79, 150, 187
BMCRC 19
BMW 13, 23, 23, 26, 32, 35, 37,
    38, 43, 46, 49, 50, 57, 58,
    93, 96, 109, 146, 153
    980 131
    Flink 52
    GS800 131
Helios 52
    K series 169-70, 170, 178
    R series 39, 39, 52, 56, 56,
    74, 166, 178
    Super Rocket 60, *61*
BMW engines 23, 52, 175
board tracks 128
'bobbed-jobs' 154
Böhn, Hermann 58
Bol d'Or 24 hour race 108-9, *109*
Bollée Voiturette 17
Borgo pistons 83
Bosch magnetos 13
Bosis, Diego 121
Boulogne Speed Trial 32
Bouton, Georges 16
Brace, Nick 133
braced wheels 58
Braithwaite, Pat 83
braking systems 13, 14, 45, 56,
    72, 81, 106, 109, 124, 134,
    151, 163, 165, 166, 177, 178
Brampton Biflex forks 29
Branchi 96
Brando, Marlon 161, *161*
Brands Hatch circuit 83, 100, 119,
    119, 124
Brelsford, 156
Brembo Gold brakes 178
Bridgestone 68, 72
Briggs, Barry 130, 130
Bristol Classic Bike Shows 141
Britain 7, 10, *21,* 26, 27, 32-3, 37-
    41, 50-3, 57, 59-61, 71, 79, 80-
    3, 85-6, 94-5, 102-3, 106, 110-
    12, 119-20, 124, 127, 132-3,
    135, 137, 143, 166, 174-5, 178
    see also Isle of Man TT races
British Schoolboy Motocross
    Association (BSMA) 135
British Moto Cross Grand Prix
    119
British Trials Championship 121
broadsliding techniques 124, 129
Brockhouse 82
Brockhouse, John 19, 49
Brooklands circuit 14, 18, 19, 19,
    27, 32, 35, 58, 76, 79, 94, 94,
    96
Brooks 140
Brough 24, 26, 29
    Dream 29
    Superior 24, 28, 29, 29, 32,
    32, 33, 35, 137
Brough, George 29, 29, 166
Brough, William 29
Brown, Bob 104
Brown, George 52, 110
Browning, Arthur 145
Brussels Shows 56
Bryants 50
BSA 14, 15, 17, 24, 27, 41, 43, 43,
    50, 57, 71, 74, 75, 79, 82, 99,
    100, 120, 143, 146, 172
    500 143
    A series 60, 61, 79
    B series 51, 129
    Bantam 51, 65, 76, 79
    Blue Star 27
    C15 79, 121
    D1 51
    Empire Star 27
    Gold Star 27, 60, 61, 61, 76,
    79, 80, 81, 119, 119, 132, 145
    Lightning 76, 81
    M20 39, 41
    Road Rocket 60
    Rocket Gold Star 60, 76
    Rocket Three 89, 89, 109, 112
    Round Tank 79
    Shooting Star 60
    Sloper 79
    Spitfire 76
    Victor 145
BSA engines 133
Bultaco 55, 55, 105, 121
Tralla 55
Bultaco engines 120
Bulto, Francisco Xavier 55
Burgess-BSA 76
Burman gearboxes 52, 82
Burnett, Don 112
Burns, Robert 58
Burton, John 120
Butler, Edward 7, 7
Butler's Petrol-Cycle 7, 7

C

C-364 (Soviet Union) 75
Cabton 41
café racers 76, 79, 80-1, *81*
Cagiva 53, 106, 110, 129, 131,
    168, 170
    Canyon 129
Camathias, Florian 52
Camberley Club 119
Campbell, Dave 177
Campbell, Malcolm 112
camshafts 15, 72, 89, 163
Canada 43
Capriolo 44, 45, 49
car industry 21, 27, 46, 50, 63,
    156, 172
carbon fibre materials 106
carburettors 7, 8, 43, 83, 99, 135,
    151, 163, 176, 186
Carillo 151
Carruthers, Ken 79, 104
cast alloy wheels 133
Castle forks 29
Castro, Don 113
Castrol Honda RC45c 114
catalytic convertors 178
Cavanna, Luigi 59
Cecotto, Johnny 112, 171
Ceska Zbrovka see CZ
Challinor, Terry 145
chassis see frames
Chater-Lea 50
chemical ignition systems 131
Cheney BSA 145
Chevrolet engines 110
choice:
    of machine 111
choppers 154, 154
Christenson, Tom 110
cinema films 77, 80, 153, 154,
    161, 161
Cizek, Jaromir 121
Clark, H 60
Clark, R O 14
Clarke, Freddie 27
Classic Bike 137, 141
classic bike shows 141, 141
classic bikes 137-47, 137-47
    see also retros
classic races 146-7, 146-7
Classic Racing Mororcycle Club
    (CRMC) 144, 146
Classic Scrambles 145, 145
Clement engines 29
Clement-Garrard 10
Cleveland 124
clothing 76, 80, 81, 106, 111, 145,
    154
clubman machines and races 60,
    61, 76, 79, 80-1, 81, 94, 127
clubs 111, 112
    for classic bikes 138, 140
clutch systems 14, 38, 56, 151, 163,
    165, 176
    substitutes for 7
Clymer, Floyd 19
Collier, Charlie 15, 18, 19, 31, 82,
    91, 94, 122
Collier, Harry (junior) 15, 31, 91
Collier, Henry 15
Collins, Russ 110
Cologne Shows 158, 166
colour schemes 15, 23, 56, 83, 151,
    154, 166, 178, 185
    see also badges and emblems
Colt engines 15
Columbia motorcycle see Pope, Albert
combustion chambers 134
comfort see safety and comfort
commuter bikes 51, *51*
    see also lightweight machines
computer aided design 182
computer controls 169, 182, 183,
    186
conservation see restoration and con-
    servation
construction materials 30, 50, 76,
    81, 106, 133, 134, 135, 148,
    151, 169, 176, 178
Cook, W E 'Wee-Wee' 19
cooling systems:
    air 10, 13, 14, 15, 16, 109,
    151, 163, 172
    liquid 134, 148, 163, 165,
    169, 169, 178, 178, 180
    oil 109, 148, 151, 176
    water 7, 10 ,15, 37, 102,
    109, 114, 135, 148
Cooper, John 100
Corgi scooters 40
Corsa Ducati 115
Corser, Troy 115
Cottle, Marjorie 28
cotton 24, 41, 99, 145
Coupe d'Europe 121
CR Speed Shop 76
Craig, Joe 29, 93, 99
crank handles
    see also starting systems
crankcases 15, 16, 99
crankshafts 15, 16, 56, 72, 86
crash helmets 57, 81, 93, 111
    see also clothing
    safety and comfort
Crawford, R 112
Crescent 119
Crighton, Brian 172
Cripps, Stafford 43
Crosby, Graeme 112
Crosley 37
Cruiser 68
Crystal Palace speedway 124
Curtis, Dave 120, 120
Curtiss 11
Curtiss, Glenn 112
Cushman scooters 40, 41
customised machines 76, 153-63,
    153-63, 166, 174
Cycle World 72
cylinders 9, 14, 169
    see also specific number of
cylinders
CZ 24, 75, 121, 145
Czechoslovakia 24, 121, 122, 132
Czepel 75

D

Daimler, Gottlieb 7, 7, 8, 13
Dale, 79
damping devices 56, 134, 163
    see also shock absorbers
Daniel, Harold 29
Darracq, Alexandre 9
Davidson, Arthur 156
Davidson, Douglas H 32, 94
Davidson, Willie G 156
Davies, Howard Raymond 31, 52, 93
Daymar 10
Dayrell, F 10
Daytona 200 112, 112-13, 153
Daytona Beach 21, 32, 89, 89, 110,
    112, 146
Daytona Beach Bike Weeks 153,
    153, 165
Daytona engines 151
Daytona International Speedway
    112, 114, 153
de Coster, Roger 121
de Dion, Albert 16
de Dion engines 12, 15, 29
de Dion Bouton 9, 16

de Dion Bouton engines 10, 16
de la Hay, 94
de Rosier, Jake 19, 94
De Tomaso 79
dealer networks 24, 49
    after-sales service 43
    see also sales
Degans, Dave 76
Degner, Ernst 65, 99, 99, 104
del Lario, Mandello 166
Dell'Orto carburettors 83
Denly, Albert 32
Denmark 119, 120, 124
Denney, T W 96
Dentsu 115
Derbi 54, 105, 106
    Super 54
Derny, 17
desert crossings 23, 131
    see also endurance racing
desert warfare 39
design patents 7, 75
    see also machine design
diamond frames 169, 175
Diamont 13
diaphragm clutch systems 56
Dickie, Tom 108
Dickinson, Marty 52
Direct Air Induction System (DAIS)
    181
direction indicators 68, 72, 166
dirt bikes 119-35, 119-35
dirt-track meetings 67, 124-5,
    124-5, 128-9, 129
disc brakes 45, 106, 109, 134,
    151, 163, 165, 166, 177
dispatch riders 15, 38, 39, 41, 99
    see also military machines
diversification 15, 26, 44, 64, 65
Dixon, Freddie 29, 32, 96, 96, 110
DKW 13, 24, 29, 29, 30-1, 30,
    35, 37, 74, 75, 99, 172
    RT series 46, 51, 65, 75
    SM 30
DKW engines 30
Dolphin, J R V 40
dolphin fairing 81
Donington Park Circuit 114, 115
Doohan, Mick 106, 107
DOT 121, 128, 145
Douglas 24, 35, 37, 41, 49, 50,
    96, 96, 143
    350 37
Dourdon races 17
Dow, Eddie 76
DRs see dispatch riders
D-RAD 26
drag racing see sprinting
Draper, John 120, 120
Dresda Autos 76, 109, 174
drive chains 24, 109, 134, 176,
    177
Driver, Paddy 104
driving techniques 124, 126, 129
drum brakes 163, 166
Drusiani, 45
du Hamel, Yvon 100, 171
Du Pont, E Paul 19, 21, 26
Ducati 49, 55, 109, 112, 115,
    115, 147, 170, 174
    175 Cruiser 45, 45
    750 Paso 166, 170
    851 114, 160
    860 166
    900SS 112, 166
    916 184, 185, 185, 186,
    186
    Cucciolo 44
    Mike Hailwood Replica 166,
    169
    M900 151
    Mach 1 83, 83
    Monster series 151
    Sports 45
    ST 178
Duebel, Max 52

Duff, Mike 104
Duke, Geoff 60, 79, 93, 93, 99,
    102, 102
Duncan, H O 8-9
Dunelt 23, 50
Dunlop, Joey 93, 99, 146
Dunlop, John Boyd 7
Dunstall, Paul 76, 81, 174
Dürkopp 13
Dutch TT races 53, 54, 95, 96,
    103, 105
Dykgraff, Chet 129

E
Eadie cycles 10
Earles forks 56, 166
Earls Court shows 29, 83
East German Grand Prix 75
East Germany see Germany
East Midlands Racing Association
    (EMRA) 111
Easy Rider (film) 154, 161, 161
Eccles, Declan 127
economic problems 9, 19, 21,
    26-7, 31, 43, 46, 49, 60, 63,
    67, 71, 79, 80, 82-3
Edera 59
Egli 109, 174
eight-cylinder machines 35, 181
electric ignition 45, 68, 72, 134,
    165, 166
electrical systems 43, 72, 106, 109,
    148, 163
Elmore, Buddy 112
EMAP 137
EML sidecar chassis 133
emblems see badges and
    emblems
Emde, Don 112
Enders, Klaus 52
endurance racing 9, 14, 19, 23,
    24, 72, 89, 95, 100-1, 101,
    108-9, 109, 122-3, 122-3,
    131, 131, 166
    see also reliability trials, speed
    records and trials
Enfield drive hubs 29
engine construction 7, 8
engine speed 7, 8, 9, 9, 10, 15,
    16, 28, 29, 51, 52, 56, 72,
    86, 99, 112, 156-9, 162-3,
    165-6, 168-9, 173, 175-8,
    180-1, 183-5
    see also speed records and
    trials
engines 10, 13
    see also specific makes and
    types
England see Britain
environmental issues 174, 182, 182
Epping Forest speedway 124
Etheridge, Chris 133
European 250cc Championship 119
European Championship 95, 121
    see also specific races
European International Cup Race 17
European Sidecar Cross
    Championship 132-3, 133
evaporating carburettors 7
Excelsior (UK) 10, 40, 49
Excelsior (USA) 21, 37, 124
Excelsior engines 40
exhaust systems 8, 53, 76, 99, 106,
    177
Exhaust Ultimate Power Valves (EUPV)
    169
expansion chamber exhausts 99
exports 19, 43, 43, 64, 68, 71, 72,
    79, 79, 89
Express 13

F
Fabrique Nationale d'Armes de Guerre
    see FN
factory involvement:
    in road racing 109

Fafnair engines 13
Fantic 121, 121
fatalities 93, 101, 103, 121
Fath, Helmut 96, 96
FB Mondial 44, 45, 101, 101, 102
Featherbed frames 60, 61, 76
Federation Internationale des Clubs
    Motorcyclistes
    (FICM) 17, 19, 32, 95
Federation Internationale Motorcycliste
    (FIM) 19, 52, 58, 96, 100, 102,
    104, 114, 119, 122, 133
Fernihough, Eric 29, 32, 33
Ferrari 45
Ferri, Remolo 58
Fiat 26
Fifty-Nine Club 81
Finland 75, 119
First World War see World War I
fish-tail silencers 80, 94
five-cylinder machines 9
five-speed gearboxes 83, 134, 159,
    165, 166, 183
float-feed carburettors 7
floating disc brakes 109
the 'Flying Brick' 169-70
the 'Flying Fish' 59
the 'Flying Flea' 40, 51
the 'Flying Hammock' 59
FN 13, 14, 14, 37, 37, 108, 119,
    119
FN engines 13
Fogerty, Carl 114, 115, 115, 146
fold-up machines 79
Fonda, Peter 161
foot controls 81, 83
Ford, Henry 21, 21
Ford Model T 21, 21, 156
forks and stays 9, 12, 14, 15,
    29, 49, 54, 56, 60, 74, 81,
    83, 134, 151, 157, 163, 166,
    169, 176, 178
Forza Italia 146-7
Foster, Bob 53
four-cylinder machines 10, 13, 14,
    15, 29, 31, 79, 99, 104, 109,
    112, 124, 148, 165, 166, 169,
    181
Fournier, Maurice 16
four-speed gearboxes 37, 39, 89
four-stroke engines 7, 7, 24, 35, 45,
    52, 53, 64, 102, 105, 106, 114,
    115, 119, 121, 126, 137, 178,
    180
Fowler, Rem 15, 29, 91
frames 7, 8, 11, 15, 19, 29, 30, 60,
    61, 74, 134, 148, 150, 151,
    158-9, 166, 169, 175, 178
France 8-9, 10, 15, 16, 17, 17, 41,
    108-9, 119, 120, 122, 127, 131,
    132, 166
France family 114
Francis-Barnett 15, 24, 31, 51, 71,
    82
Francisci, Bruno 101
Franco, General 54
Franke, Gustav 121
Frankfurt Shows 46
Franklin, Charles B 19, 21
Frazer Nash 50
Free, Rollie 52
French Grand Prix 79
Frera 100
Frith, Freddie 29, 53, 102, 102
front brakes 56, 163, 165
front suspension 133
fuel consumption 14, 172
fuel injection 114, 151, 157, 170,
    178, 181, 182, 186, 187
fuel systems 11, 182
fuel tanks 9, 14, 29, 56, 76, 81,
    159, 163, 177
Fuji 67
Fujisawa, Takeo 68
funding see sponsorship

G
Galbusera 35
Gardner, Wayne 106
Garelli 44, 100, 106
    Mosquito 44
Garrard 50
Gas Den 68
gearboxes 7, 14, 15, 23, 29, 37, 38,
    39, 52, 56, 74, 76, 82, 83, 89,
    104, 134, 148, 151, 159, 177,
    178, 180, 183
General Motors 13
George, Sydney 19
German Grand Prix 29, 95, 95
Germany 7, 8-9, 10 ,13, 19, 23,
    26-7, 30-1, 35, 37, 38-41, 46,
    49, 50, 52, 57, 58, 63, 71, 75,
    95, 96, 99, 102, 110, 119, 122,
    126, 132, 178
Ghersi, Pietro 93
Gibb, W G 122
Gilera 33, 33, 35, 44, 49, 93, 93,
    96, 97, 99, 100, 101, 102, 132
    Gigante 37
    Rondine 31
Gilera, Giuseppe 31
Gilera, Luigi 31
Giles, John 145
Giliet-Herstal 108
Giro d'Italia 100-1, 101
girder forks 15
Gladiator cycles 9
glass-fibre materials 50, 81
Global Positioning System (GPS)
    131
Godden 124
Goddon, Don 124
Godfrey, O C 19, 93
Godier and Genoud racing team
    109
Golden Helmet competition 124
Goode, Terry 127
Goodman, Eugene 53
Goodman, Percy 53
Graham, Les 102
Grand Prix races 15, 72, 95, 95,
    102-17, 102-17
    see also specific races
Grant, Mick 146
Grasetti, 79
grasstrack racing 124, 125
Great 1000 Miles Trial 122
Green Lane riding 129
Greeves 51, 121, 145
Grant, Mick 146
Grüner, Jens 133
Guthrie, Jimmy 29, 93
Guzzi, Carlo 24, 29
    see also Moto Guzzi

H
Hagon, Alf 110, 124
Hahn, Carl 99
Hailwood, Mike 89, 93, 93, 99, 99,
    103, 104, 116, 116, 166, 169
Haller, Berthold 138
Hallman, Torsten 121
handlebars 7, 9
Handley, Walter 93
Harley, William 156
Harley-Davidson 11, 11, 21, 24,
    32, 37, 38, 39, 48, 53, 63,
    67, 74, 75, 94, 104-5, 105,
    112, 124, 129, 129, 153,
    153, 154, 156-7, 156-7
    Café Racer 81
    Duo Glide 49, 157
    Electra Glide 156-7, 156,
    158
    Grey Ghost 156
    Hydra Glide 49, 157
    XR series 100, 146, 156
Harley-Davidson engines 156,
    157, 157
Harris 174
Harris Kawasaki GPZ900R 166

Hawker 23
Hawkstone Park 119
headlamps 176, 178
Hedlund engines 133
Hedstrom, Carl Oscar 19
Heinkel 46
Hele, Doug 89
Hele-Shaw, Doctor 91
Hell's Angels 153, 154
helmets see crash helmets
Hendee, George M 19
Henderson 21
Henne, Ernst 33, 58
Henry, Ernest 15
Hercules 172
Heron Suzuki 750 146
Herstal 14
Herz, Wilhelm 58
Hesketh, Lord 166, 175
highway codes 24, 45
Hildebrand & Wolfmüller 8-9, 8-
    9, 10, 13
Hillebrand, Fritz 52
Hislop, Steve 93
Hispano-Villiers engines 54
Hobbs, John 110, 110
Hocking, Gary 102, 103
Hodaka Ace 72
'Hogs' see Harley-Davidson
Holden, Henry Capel Lofft 10
Holland 53, 110, 119, 120, 126,
    141, 166, 174-5
    see also Dutch TT races
Hollaus, Ruppert 102
Holley, George M 11
Honda 63, 64, 68, 93, 100, 103,
    104, 105, 105, 109, 109, 113,
    115, 120, 154, 168, 172, 176,
    178
    6 146
    Aspencade 156
    C90 148
    C100 Super Cub 68, 68, 72
    CB72 72, 72
    CB77 72
    CB92 72, 72
    CB450 Black Bomber 85-6,
    85-6
    CB750 Superbike 86, 108,
    112, 149, 165, 165, 175
    CB790 148
    CB1000 Big One 148, 148,
    150
    CBR400 180
    CBR600 148
    CBR900RR Fireblade 129,
    176, 184-5, 184
    CBR1100XX Super Blackbird
    176-7, 177
    CBX750 148
    CR series 127, 134, 135
    CX series 148, 172, 173
    D model 64
    E model 64
    EXP-2 131
    F6C 163
    GL1000 Gold Wing 157,
    158-9, 158-9, 163
    Hawk 112
    Interstate 159
    MV-3 146
    NC30 181
    Nighthawk see CB750
    NR750 177
    NSR500 107
    NSR500V 182, 183
    Pacific Coast 178
    Racer 69
    RC series 109, 114, 114,
    115
    ST1100 Pan European 177,
    178, 178
    Super Hawk 72, 86
    VF series 169, 173
    VTR1000 Firestorm 186,
    187

XBR500 137
Honda, Soichiro 64, 71, 86, 86
Honda engines 133, 166
Honda Technical Research Institute 64
Hopper, Dennis 161
Hopwood, Bert 89
Horex 24, 49
horizontal engines 8, 23, 23, 24, 29, 39, 53, 102
Horsfield, Chris 145
Horsman, 94
Hosk 67
hot tube ignition 7, 8, 9
HRD 24, 26, 49, 52, 138
    see also Vincent
Hudson, Neil 127
Hultink-NSU 166
Humphries, Ernie 52
Hungary 75, 119
Husqvarna 121, 122, 145
hydraulic clutch systems 163

I

ice racing 126
ignition systems 7, 8, 9, 12, 17, 74, 131, 134, 176, 180, 184
IMC 67
IMN Rocket 45, 79
import tariffs and controls 19, 54
imports 19, 43, 49, 54, 63, 180
    engines 10, 24, 29, 63
Imperial 26
India 71
Indian 11, 11, 19, 19, 26, 32, 37, 38, 39, 49, 63, 93, 94, 100, 112, 124, 129, 143, 154
    Big Chief 19, 21, 21
    Brave 19
    Chief 19, 21, 49
    Scout 19, 21, 48, 49
    Warrior 49
information sources 140, 142
inlet over exhaust (ioe) engines 10, 11, 12, 15, 21, 31, 32
instruction see training schools
instrumentation 43, 72, 76, 83, 165, 177
internal combustion engines 31, 63
    first use of 7, 7
International Cup Races 91
International Historic Racing Organization (IHRO) 147, 147
International Six Days' Enduro (ISDE) 122, 123, 132, 133
International Six days Trial-Munich-Geneva 122
International Six days trials (ISDI) 19, 31, 35, 56, 122-3, 122-3, 132
Intyre, Bob 104
Irish North West 200 Race 99
Irmajim, Solchiro 159
Irving, Phil 52
Isle of Man TT races 11, 14, 15, 19, 24, 29, 31, 52, 60, 61, 63, 65, 69, 83, 89, 91, 91, 93, 93, 96, 96, 99, 103, 104, 166
Iso 44
Italian Grand Prix 95
The Italian Vintage Co. 140
Italy 12, 24, 29, 31, 33, 37, 39, 40, 41, 44-5, 49, 53, 57, 59, 71, 79, 83, 95, 100-1, 102, 114, 120, 121, 122, 123, 132, 166, 168, 170, 171
Itoh, 93
Ivanitsky, S 75
Ivy, Bill 104

J

'jam pot' suspension 15
James 15, 24, 31, 37, 40, 41, 51, 71, 82
JAP engines 10, 10, 18, 19, 26,
29, 32, 52, 124, 138
Japan 41, 49, 63-5, 62-3, 66, 67, 71, 72, 72-3, 83, 85-6, 85-6, 104, 119, 121, 132, 162-3, 165, 168-9, 171, 173, 178, 180
Japanese Moto Co. 115
Japauyo racing team 109
Jaubert, Jean-Claude 109
Jawa 24, 54, 74, 75, 75, 121, 122, 123, 124, 124, 126, 132
Jeeps 39
Jefferies, Allan 60
Jenkinson, Denis 102
Johnson, W E (junior) 'Bill' 43, 79
Jones, Geraint 127
Jonghi 108
Judd 94
Junior Racing Association 135

K

Kaaden, Walter 99, 99
Kawakami, Genichi 65
Kawasaki 68, 105, 109, 109, 110, 112, 115, 166, 171, 174
    3 146
    1000GTR 178
    1000/1100VL 163
    50041 165
    GPZ900R 166, 169, 169, 171, 181
    GPZ1100 171
    KRI 180
    Le Mans 108-9, 148, 161
    Ninja ZX-6R 169, 169, 181, 181
    VN series 163, 163
    Z series 165, 169, 171, 175
    Zephyr 148, 150
    ZX series 109, 169, 169, 171, 181, 181
    ZZ-R1100 171, 176, 176, 181
Kelecom, Paul 14
Kettenkrad 37, 37
kit cars 114, 175
Klamfoth, Dick 112
knee grips 56
'kneelers' 59, 96
the 'Knucklehead' 49
Koni shock absorbers 159
König 96 -
Krauser 96, 106
Krauser panniers 159
Kreidler 105, 174
Kretz, Ed 21, 112
Krupp 23
KTM 132
Kubelwagen 39
Kuhn, Gus 174
Kurier engines 52

L

Lacey, Bill 32, 94
Lambretta scooters 44, 44, 49, 58, 76
Lampkin, Martin 121
Langen, Eugen 7, 13
Langston, Ron 120
language problems 43
Lario races 95
Lashmar, D C 60
Laurin-Klement 13, 17, 17
Laverda 109, 151, 166, 168, 170, 186
    3C 166
    650 Sport 181
    750SFC 166
    1200 Mirage 166
    Ghost 151
    Ghost Strike 151
    Jota 166
Lawrence, Thomas Edward (of Arabia)
29
Lawson, Eddie 106, 112, 114, 117
LC formula racing 111
LCD displays 177
Le Vack, Bert 29, 32-3, 94, 96
The Leather Boys (film) 80
LED displays 177
Lefevre, Gustave 108
legal problems 9
Leonard, 'Smokey Joe' 129
Levis engines 24
licences:
    for racing 111
licencing agreements 9, 24, 54, 55, 64, 67
Lickwar, J 112
lightweight machines 14, 15, 24, 29, 40, 44-5, 45, 50, 51, 51, 65, 71, 72, 73, 79, 80-1, 82-3, 82, 102, 104, 121, 134, 135, 150, 158, 180, 182
    ultra-lightweights 103
    see also machine weight scooters
Lilac 68, 68, 72
    MF39 68
Lindstrom 119
Liner 68
Lionello, Aureliano 186
liquid cooling systems 134, 148, 163, 165, 169, 169, 178, 178, 180
Lito 119
Little, Billy 122
long distance races see endurance trials
loop scavenge systems 31
lubrication systems 13, 72, 83, 109, 180, 182, 182
Lucas 43
Lucchinelli, Marco 106, 114
Lundin, Sten 119
Lyta fuel tanks 76

M

M21 (Soviet Union) 74
M72 (Soviet Union) 74
M75 (Soviet Union) 75
McCormack, Denis 79
machine design 35, 46, 71, 102, 134, 165, 176, 177, 182, 183, 185, 187
    see also customised machines
machine weight 7, 14, 15, 72, 132, 150, 151, 154, 157, 162, 177, 185
    see also lightweight machines scooters
machines:
    choice of 111
McIntyre, Bob 59, 93, 93
McLauglin, Steve 114
McMinnies, W G 94
McQueen, Steve 161
magneto ignition 12, 13
Magni, Arturo 174, 175, 175
Maico 121
maintenance and servicing 134, 178, 182
Maison Sarolen 14
Mallory Park circuit 89, 100, 111
Mallory Park Post TT Meeting 145, 146
Manchester Eagle Club 60
Mang, Anton 106
Mann, Dave 154
Mann, Dick 100, 112, 113, 129
Markel, Bart 129
market competition 16, 21, 43, 49, 54, 82, 86, 89
Mars 13
Marsh 11
Marsh, Fred 166
Martes 37
Martin, Brian 120
Martin, Henry 10
Martin-JAP 10, 67
Marvin, Lee 161
Maserati 45
Masetti, Umberto 103
Matchless 10, 18, 19, 24, 27, 31, 35, 43, 49, 50, 56, 61, 71, 82, 82, 83, 91, 94, 120, 132
    350 Mercury 82
    G series 15, 37, 41, 119, 147
    Silver Arrow 15
    Silver Hawk 15
    see also AMC
Matchless engines 120
Matchless Motor Cycles Ltd 15
materials see construction materials
Matsumoto, Toshio 69
Maudes trophy 79
Mauser 23
Maxim, Hiram 11
Maybach, Wilhelm 7, 7, 13
Mazda 172
Mazzetti, Mario 24
MBA 105, 106
Medd 11
Meek, Rob 127
Meguro 41, 67, 68, 171
Meier, Georg 52, 96, 146
Mentasi, Guido 95
Merkel 11
Merkel, Fred 114, 115
Mertens, Stephane 115
Meshkovsky, A 75
Michaux, Ernest 16
micro-engines 64
Mikuni carburettors 151
Milan Shows 35, 44, 45, 88, 114, 160, 171, 175
Milano-Tranto road races 100-1, 101
Military Lightweights (MLs) 40
military machines 11, 12, 15, 231, 29, 31, 37-41, 37, 39-41, 51, 88
Miller, Sammy 121, 130
Miller-Balsamo Jupiter 44
Miller's Classic Motorcycles Price Guide 140
Millet, Felix Theordore 9, 9, 16
the Millet Rotary 9, 9
Minerelli 105, 106
Minerva 10, 13, 14
Mingels, Auguste 119
miniature bikes 79, 180-1, 181
Ministockers 111
Minter, Derek 104
mirrors 68, 72
Mishima 67
missile technology 99, 131
Mitchell 11
Miyata 63, 67
Mizuho 67
MM company 24, 44
MMC engines 15
MOC-Benelli 166
Mods and Rockers 76-7, 77, 80
Moko 174
Monark 119, 121
Mondial 100
Monet-Goyon 108
monoshock suspension systems 109, 175
Montesa 54, 55, 55
Monthléry circuit 53, 58, 59, 108
Monza track 15, 59, 72, 95
mopeds 15, 24, 64, 79
Morbidelli 105
Morini, Alfonso 24
Morri, Giuseppe 171
Morrison, Brian 109
Mossman, Pitt 67
Moto Cross des Nations 119, 119, 120, 120
Moto Guzzi 24, 29, 35, 44, 59, 93, 95, 96, 99, 101, 102, 166, 170, 179, 186
1000S 148, 149
Airone 137
Alce 37
California 178
Daytona 187
Falcone 57, 88
Motoleggera 44
Spada 179
Tippo Normale 24
Trialce 37
V7 88, 88, 165, 166
V8 102
V10 Centauro 151, 151
Moto Guzzi engines 88, 88, 175
Moto Martin 174
Moto Morini 24, 44, 100
Moto Reve 31
Motobécane 108, 166
Motobi Catria 71
motocarris 37, 39
motocross 15, 65, 119-21, 119-21, 132-5, 133, 135, 145, 145
Motodd-Laverdas 166
Motom 44, 45
Motor Cycle 29, 35
Motor Cycle News 148, 163, 186
Motor Cycling 56
Motor Cycling Club (MCC) 14
Motor Cyclist 169
motorcycle clubs 63
    see also clubman machines and races
motorcycle gangs 153, 154
Motorcycle Show, Olympia 28
Motorcycle Sport and Leisure 146
Motorcycling 'Grand National' 119
Motorfahrrad-Fabrik Hildebrand & Wolfmüller see Hildebrand & Wolfmüller
motorrad 8
Motorraderwerke Zschopau see MZ
Motosacohe 106
Mototrans 55
the Motorwagen 13
de Mouzilly St Mars, Marquis 91
mudguards 7, 9, 56, 72, 76
mufflers see silencers
Muller, H P 102
Multi Action System (HMAS) 176-7
multi-cylinder machines 68, 104, 115
Munch, Friedl 166, 174, 175
    Mammoth 166, 175
museums 7, 99, 142
Muth, Hans 166
Muzzy-Kawasakis 115
MV Agusta 44, 100, 102-3, 103, 104, 105, 137, 165, 175
    750 America 166
    850 Monza 166
MZ 46, 65, 75, 99, 102, 104, 122, 133
MZ racing 111

N

Nadin, Brian 145
National Cyc-Auto Club 35
National Sprint Association (NSA) 110
navigational problems 131
Neander 26
Neckarsulmer Strickwaren Union see NSU
Neveu, Cyril 131
New Era club 111
New Imperial 50
New Zealand 58, 115
nickel plating 29
Nicks, Freddie 32
Nicholson, Jack 161
Nielson, Hans 124
Nikasil 151

Nikoden, 17
Nillson, Bill 119
Nippon Gakki 65
Nixon, Gary 100, 112, 129
'Noddy Bikes' 57
Noll, Wilhelm 58
North London Garages (NLG) 19, 94
Northern International 138
Norton 15, 24, 27, 29, 31, 39, 43, 49, 59, 59, 82, 83, 93, 102, 112, 120, 121, 129, 145, 174
   16H 37, 39, 41
   500T 99
   Atlas 61
   Commando 132-3
   Dominator 60, 80, 137
   Domiracer 81
   Electra 71
   Energette 10
   F1 172
   International 60, 61, 108
   Jubilee 71
   Manx 119
   Model 7 60-1
   Model 77 61
   Model 88 60-1
   Model 99 61
   Navigator 71
   Norvin 76
   Scott 96
Norton, James Lansdowne 'Pa' 10, 10, 29
Norton brakes 81
Norton engines 83
Norton forks 81
Norton Villiers Triumph (NVT) 172
Norton Wankel:
   Classic Commander 172
   F1 172
   Interpol II 172
Noyce, Graham 120, 135
Nozue, Toshio 159
NSU 13, 13, 19, 26, 35, 37, 37, 49, 58, 59, 63, 71, 96, 102, 103, 172
NSU engines 175
Nürburgring circuit 95, 99, 105

O

Obruba, 17
O'Donovan, 94
OEC-Temple 32
oil cooling systems 109, 148, 151, 176
OK-Supreme 24
Oldani brakes 81
Olds, Ransom 112
Oliver, Eric 59, 96, 102, 116
Oliver's Mount circuit 146
Olympia shows 30
Olympus 67
On Any Sunday (film) 161
Opel 13, 26
Opel, Adam 13
Opel engines 13
Orioli, Edi 131
Orman, Des 143
Orman, Geoff 143
Osso 54
Otto, Nicholaus 7, 13
the 'Otto Cycle' 7, 16
Oulton Park races 100
overhead camshaft engines 24, 31, 45, 52, 72, 72, 74, 75, 79, 86, 102, 104, 119, 138, 148, 151, 158, 159, 162-3, 165, 166, 169, 169, 175, 178, 178, 181
overhead valve (ohv) engines 10, 15, 24, 29, 31, 32, 35, 37, 45, 52, 53, 60, 61, 71, 72, 76, 82, 89, 112, 119, 166, 178

P

Pagani, Alberto 53

Pagani, Nello 102
Page, Val 15, 27, 51
Panhard 9
the 'Panhead' 49
panniers 159, 178
Panther 24, 37, 50
parades 144, 144
paratroopers:
   motorbikes for 40-1, 40-1, 51, 71
   see also military machines
Parilla 44, 44, 49
Paris Salons 23, 52
Paris-Dakar Rally 131, 131
Paris-Vienna Race 17
Parodi, Giorgio 29
Patchett, George 24
Paul Record circuit 177
P & C 143
pedal cycles see bicycles
Permanyer, Pedro 55
Perris, Frank 104
Peterhansel, Stephane 131
Petrali, Joe 156
petrol engines 7, 11, 16, 64
petrol prices 46
petrol tanks see fuel tanks
the 'Petrol-Cycle'
   see Butler's Petrol-Cycle
Petrol-Cycle Syndicate Ltd 7
Petrolette 9
the 'Petroleum Reitwagen' 7, 7
Peugeot 9, 15, 94
Peugeot engines 15, 19, 29
Phelon & Moore see Panther
Phillis, Tom 102
Pickrell, Ray 100, 109
pillions see seats
Pinhard, Frederick 143
Pioneer Register 143
Pioneer Runs 143, 143
Pirbright Common events 119-20
piston engines 8, 24
pistons 83, 134
plastic body work 134, 151
platinum hot tubes see hot tube ignition
P & M see Panther
pneumatic tyres 7, 9, 12
'Pocket rockets' 180
Pointer 67, 68
Poland 75, 119
Polen, Doug 115
police machines 21, 29, 57, 57, 172
political influences 35, 37, 74, 95, 122
pollution see environmental issues
Pope, Albert 11
   Columbia motorcycle 11
Pope, Noel 29, 94, 110
Porsche 27
Potter, E J 110
Power Jet Control (PJC)
   carburettors 134
power units see engines
power valves 134
power-to-weight ratio 182, 183, 184
pressed steel frames 74
Prestwich, John Alfred 10
prices see production costs
   selling prices
Prinz engines 175
prize money 104
prizes see trophies and prizes
production costs 9, 10, 38, 39, 43
production lines 16, 21, 43, 43
production runs 8, 11, 12, 21, 24, 30, 40, 41, 43, 44-5, 46, 49, 64, 68, 82
   overproduction 46
Progress 63
Pro-Link rear suspension 176, 185
'Promenade Percys' 80
public order 76-7, 77

Puch 17, 37, 95, 132
Puch, Johann 17

Q

Quadrophenia (film) 77
quality control 43
Quandt, Herbert 46
Quasar 166

R

Rabbit 68
races and racing 7, 11, 15, 17, 24, 29, 31, 52, 53, 55, 63, 64, 65, 72, 75, 79, 83, 89, 95, 95, 100-17, 101-17
   see also specific races and circuits
racing licences 111
radial tyres 177, 178
radiators 134
Rahier, Gaston 131
Rainey, Wayne 106, 112, 114
Raleigh 10, 50
Rambler 11
Rapp 23
Rassmussen, Jorgan Skafte 30, 99
Ravelli, Giovanni 29
Rayborn, Cal 100, 112, 156
Raynal 35
Read, Phil 104, 105, 146, 147
rear brakes 13, 14, 45, 72, 81, 106, 109, 124, 134, 151, 163
rear engines 59, 59
rear suspension 15, 52, 56, 74, 109, 133, 134, 151, 157, 175, 177, 178
Redman, Jim 104, 146
Reeb, Hermann 24
Reed, Phil 93
reed valves 134
Reiman, Roger 112
reliability trials 15
   see also endurance racing
Reliant engines 166
Remor 32
replica machines 146, 166, 169
research and development 68, 71
restoration and conservation 142, 142
Resweber, Carroll 129
retros 148, 150-1, 149-51
   see also classic bikes
Rex Acme 93
Rheingold 26
Rhind-Tutt, Robin 133
Rickman 174, 175
Rickman, Derek 119, 120, 120, 174
Rickman, Don 119, 120, 120, 175
Rikuo 41, 67
road racing 80-1, 81, 91, 91, 100-17, 101-17
   see also Dutch TT races
   Isle of Man TT races
road taxes 46
Roadholder forks 60, 83
Robb, Tommy 104
Robbiano, Sergio 183
Robert, Joel 121, 130
Roberts, Kenny 100, 100, 106, 10-7, 112, 112, 116, 116, 129, 129
Robertson, Archie 99
Roche, Raymond 115
Rockers see Mods and Rockers
Rogers, Ralph B 49
Rolls, C S 17
Romero, Gene 113
rotary engines 9, 9, 72, 172, 172, 175
Rotax 15
Rowley, George 122
Royal 11
Royal Enfield 10, 24, 37, 40, 41, 49, 50, 51, 51, 61, 71, 80, 121

Bullet 61, 71, 129
Constellation 71, 80
Prince 51
RE 51
WDRE 41
Royal Enfield engines 174
Royal Mail machines 50
Rudge 24, 27, 31, 35
   Multis 37
   Ulster 35
Rudge engines 52
Ruffo, Bruno 102
Ruhmkorff ignition 7
Rumi 44, 109
Ruppe, Hugo 30
Russell, Scott 115
Russia 74-5, 75, 119, 126

S

S & W shock absorbers 159
Saarineen, Jarno 112
Sachs engines 172
safety and comfort 56, 57, 93, 106, 147, 178
   helmets 57, 81, 93, 111
Sagem fuel injection 187
St Germain circuit 106
sales 10, 14, 15, 19, 21, 24, 26, 43, 53, 56, 61, 63, 65, 67, 68, 72, 172, 173, 178
   see also dealer networks
sales declines 71, 72, 82-3
the Salzburg Incident 122
sand racing 133, 133
Sanglas 54
Sangster, Jack 15, 27, 79
Saroléa 14
Scheidegger, Fritz 52
Schnuerle, Ing 31
schoolboy sport 135, 135
Schulte, Mauritz 10
Schults, Jon 146
Schwantz, Kevin 65, 106, 112, 114
scooters 40, 44-5, 44-5, 46, 50, 53, 76, 77, 79, 82, 109
   see also lightweight machines
Scott 15, 24, 35
Scott, Alfred Angus 15
Scottish Trials 121
scrambles and scrambling
   see motocross
Seagrave, Henry 12
seats 37, 72, 76, 157, 163, 166, 178
Second World War
   see World War II
Sedgley, Ken 145
Seeley 146, 174
selling prices 9, 29, 35, 64, 150, 163, 165, 177, 181
   of classic bikes 137, 138, 140
Selpeds 64
Serafini, Dorino 97
series production 8, 11
   see also production runs
Sertum 24, 35
sewing machines 13, 19
shaft drive 14, 52, 56, 74, 178
Sheene, Barry 65, 100, 100, 106, 107, 116-17, 117, 146
Shelley, R T 29
Shepard, Alan 99
Shergold, Bill 81
Shimazu, Narazo 63
shock absorbers 159
shops see suppliers and shops
short circuit racing 80-1
Showa 67
shows 141, 141
   see also specific shows
Shrubland Park 119
side valve engines 15, 24, 112
Sidecar Cross races 132-3, 133
sidecar racing 52, 58, 59, 93, 94, 96, 96, 102, 106

sidecars 15, 21, 23, 24, 29, 31, 37, 38, 39, 50, 50, 56, 57, 143, 143
silencers 56, 72, 76, 80, 94, 148, 163, 177
Simmonds, Dave 105, 171
Simson 46
single cylinder machines 11, 12, 24, 29, 35, 37, 40, 46, 74, 99, 102, 124, 129, 131, 134, 137, 138
single shock suspension 134
single-purpose machines 132
Sirera, Jorge 55
six-cylinder machines 159, 159, 166
six-speed gearboxes 83, 104, 134, 148, 151, 177, 180
Slater, Roger 166
Slight, Arran 114, 115
Smart, Paul 100, 108
Smith, Bill 72
Smith, Dave 127
Smith, Don 121
Smith, Ernie 27
Smith, Gilbert 37
Smith, Jeff 119, 119, 120, 121, 130
Smiths Instruments 43
Snetterton race track 111
solid tyres 63
Sopwith 23
   ABC 400 23
Sotheby's 140
South Africa 124
Southern Scott Trials 119, 120, 121
Southwell, Doug 76
Soviet Union see Russia
Spain 54-5, 54-5, 119, 121
spare parts 138
spark plugs 176
specialist super bikes 174-5, 175
specials 80, 166, 166
spectators 93, 101, 108, 112, 124, 125, 127, 145, 153
speed limits 10, 57, 91, 153
   see also engine speed
speed records and trials 15, 17, 19, 21, 29, 30, 31, 32-3, 32-3, 52, 53, 56, 58-9, 58-9, 83, 83, 91, 94, 95, 112, 177
speedway racing 124, 124
Speedway Test Matches 124
Speedway World Championships 124, 124
Spencer, Freddie 106, 112, 114
sponsorship 100, 111, 115
Sport Scouts 21
Sports Marketing Company 115
Springsteen, Jay 129, 156
sprinting 110, 110
Sprints 53
Spryt engines 40
the Squariel see Aerial Sqare Four
Stafford classic bike shows 141
stands 9
Staner, H W 91
Stanley Cycle Show 7
starting systems 157
   crank handles 7
   electric 45, 68, 72, 134, 165, 166
   ignition systems 7
state ownership 46
stays see forks and stays
steam power 7, 63
steel frames 30, 76, 148, 178
steering systems 9, 178
Steib 50
Stevens brothers 27, 31
   see also AJS
Stock 26
Stolle, Martin 52
Stonebridge, Brian 119, 121
Straight, F 91
streamlining 102, 106, 176

Sturgis Rallies 160, 160
Sturmey Archer gearboxes 29
Suberbie, Louis 8-9
Sunbeam 15, 24, 27, 31, 50, 82, 96, 108, 143
Sunbeam Motor Cycle Club 143
super bikes 153, 165-89, 165-89
Super Sports machines 176-7, 176-7
superchargers 52, 58, 96, 172-3, 173
SuperTeens 111, 111, 135
suppliers and shops 76
surface carburettors 8
Surtees, John 93, 102, 103, 117, 117
suspension systems 56, 106, 169, 181, 185
  front 133
  rear 15, 52, 56, 74, 109, 133, 134, 151, 157, 175, 177, 178
Suzuki 63, 64, 68, 69, 72, 83, 83, 93, 99, 104, 105, 106, 107, 109, 121, 132, 146, 173, 174
  Colleda 64
  Diamond Free 64
  G series 65, 165
  GSF600 Bandit 148, 150, 150
  GSF1200 148, 150, 150
  GSX series 109, 129, 148, 150, 169, 180, 181
  GT750 165
  Katana 173
  Power Free 64
  RE5 172
  RG500 146, 180
  T10 72, 83
  T20 Super Six 65, 83, 83
  TL1000 186, 186
  XN85 173
  VZ800 Marauder 163, 163
Suzuki, Michio 64
Suzuki engines 148, 150
Swain, Beryl 93, 93
Swallow 50
Sweden 57, 110, 119, 120, 126
Switzerland 19, 119, 120, 122
SWM 121, 132

T
Tabia 166
Tada, Kenzo 63
Taglioni, Fabio 166
Tait, 109
Tama River circuit 64
Tamburini, Massimo 171, 183
Tandon 51
Tardozzi, Davide 114
Taruffi, Piero 33, 33
Taveri, Luigi 104
Taylor, Dow 76
Teflon coatings 134
telescopic forks 15, 49, 54, 56, 74, 157, 166
Temple, Claude 32

test drives 7
T-head engines 13
Thiern 11
Thomas, F 119
Thomsen, Robert William 7
Thor 11
Thorpe, Dave 135
three-cylinder machines 79
three-speed gearboxes 52, 74
three-wheelers and tricycles 7, 7 12, 15, 17, 41, 58
Thruxton 500-mile races 72, 89
Tibblin, Rolf 121, 122
Tiger Cub 76
TIZ-AM-600 (Soviet Union) 74
Todd, Phil 166
Tognon, Francesco 187
Tohatsu 67, 67, 68, 72
Tokyo Shows 150
toolboxes 56
Toricelli, 95
touring bikes 156, 178, 178-9
Tourist scooters 46
Tourist Trophy races 15
tracked vehicles 37, 37
Traction Control System (TCS) 178
training schools 11, 41
transverse engines 52
Trépardoux, 16
trials events 121
  see also endurance racing speed records and trials
Tribsas 145
Tribune 11
Triumph 10, 15, 24, 27, 37, 39, 41, 43, 43, 50, 57, 57, 63, 71, 94, 100, 106, 112, 113, 119, 121, 132, 133, 142, 143, 143, 145, 145, 146, 178
  550 37
  750 Bonneville 137
  Metisse 120, 145, 145, 175
  Speed Twin 60, 79, 96
  T120 Bonneville 60, 76, 79, 80
  T140E-S 140
  T509 186, 187
  T595 186-7
  Thunderbird 60, 79, 150-1
  Tiger 60, 72, 79
  Trident 89, 89, 108, 150-1
  Trophy 119, 178
Triumph engines 120, 133, 174
Triumph (Germany) see TWN
TRM Honda CR250 127
trophies and prizes 91
  prize money 104
Truffault forks 12
Tuman, Bill 48
turbochargers 173, 173
Turner, Edward 15, 27, 27, 43, 60, 71, 79, 89
twin/two cylinder machines 7, 8, 9, 15, 19, 23, 24, 37, 39, 46, 46, 49, 52, 53, 56, 56, 60, 69, 85-6, 96, 99, 102, 104, 146, 178, 180

TWN 35, 37, 40, 47
two-stroke engines 7, 15, 24, 30, 31, 46, 47, 51, 51, 53, 65, 67, 72, 74, 79, 99, 104, 105, 105, 106, 112, 121, 122, 134, 145, 180, 182, 182
tyres 39, 40, 106, 109, 163
  pneumatic 7, 9, 12
  radial 177, 178
  solid 63
  see also wheels

U
Ubbiali, Carlo 102
Uhl, Ignác 24
Ulster Grand Prix 95, 97
Ultra lightweight machines 103
  see also lightweight machines
Uncini, Franco 106
United States see America
Uni-Trak suspension 169
US National races 48
Utah Salt Flats 58, 110
Utrecht 'Old Timers' show 141

V
valve springs 86
valves 10, 134
Van Veen 172, 172, 174-5
Vandervell family 29
Vaujours circuit 106
the Velo-á-petrole 9
Velocette 24, 41, 53, 61, 61, 63, 80, 93, 96, 99, 108, 119
  K series 53, 102, 133, 138
  LE series 53, 57
  Roarer 96
  Scrambler 119
  Thruxton 53
  Valiant 53
  Venom 53, 61, 80
  Venom Clubman 53
  Victory scooter 53
  Viper 53, 61, 61
  Vogue 53
Venezuelan Grand Prix 107
Venturi, Remo 101, 101
Verralls Atlantic Motorcycles 140
Vespa scooters 44, 44, 49, 76
veteran machines 143
  see also classic bikes
vibration problems 9
  see also damping devices
Victoria 13, 23, 35, 52
  KR35WHS 37
Villa, Walter 53, 105
Villiers engines 24, 40, 51, 54
Vincent 24, 49, 52, 134, 138
  A series 52
  Black Lightning 52, 58
  Black Prince 52
  Black Shadow 52
  Comet 52, 61, 138
  Gray Flash 52
  Nero 52

  Rapide 52, 58
  Super Nero 52
Vincent, Philip C 52
Vincent suspension systems 52
Vincent-HRD 52, 58, 60, 61, 71, 76
  see also HRD
Vindec 94
Vink, Henk 110
Vintage Car Club (VCC) 143
Volkswagen 27, 39
Volugrafo Aeromoto 40
von Braun, Wernher 99
Vondrich, Vada 17
v-twin engines 12, 24, 29, 32, 32, 35, 41, 49, 52, 60-1, 61, 88, 88, 100, 112, 114, 115 132, 146, 166, 178, 179, 180

W
Wagner 11
Walker, Eugene 'Gene' 32
Walker, Mick 111
Walter, Jaroslav 17
Walter, Josef 17
Wanderer 13, 24, 26, 99
Wankel, Felix 172
Wankel Rotary engines 172, 175
war reparations 43
Ward, Geoff 119
Wasp sidecar chassis 133, 145
water cooling systems 7, 10, 15, 37, 102, 109, 114, 134, 159
water pumps 134
water tanks 7
Watford & Bushey Club 60
Watson, Peter 137
Watsonian 50
Webb, Ike 29
Weber-Marelli computer memory 186
Weber-Marelli fuel injection 178
weight see lightweight machine, machine weight
Welbike 40, 41
Werner 16, 17, 17, 122
Werner, Eugene 16, 17
Werner, Michel 16, 17
Werring, Eduardo 55
Weslake 110, 124
Weslake engines 133
West, Jock 15, 146
West Germany see Germany
Westmorland and Cumberland County Motor Cycle Club 122
Weston-Super-Mare beach races 127, 127
What Bike? 181
wheel hubs 56, 76
wheels 7, 9, 24, 56, 58, 63, 133, 163, 169, 177, 185
  see also tyres
White, Ralph 112
Wicks, Jack 89
Wickshead, Ivan 96
The Wild One (film) 80, 153, 161, 161

Wimshurst machines 7
Windhoff 26
Windjammer fairing 159
Winkler, Waldfried 30
Winton, Alexander 112
wire wheels 133
Withers, Gary 127
wooden frames 7
wooden wheels 7
  see also wheels
Woods, Ernie 110
Woods, Stanley 29, 93, 93, 99, 99
Wooler fours 166
workers co-operatives 79, 140
World Championships 29, 53, 65, 119
World SuperBike Series (WSB) 112, 114-15, 114-15
World War I, 1914-18 11, 12, 14, 15, 21, 23, 29, 31, 37, 39, 74, 156
World War II, 1939-4515, 19, 21, 29, 31, 35, 37-41, 37, 39-41, 44, 46, 49, 54, 63, 65, 67, 74, 75, 96, 99, 122, 156, 172
Wright, David K 154
Wright, Joe 32, 32, 33
Wright, Russell 58
WSK 75

Y
Yale 11
Yamaha 63, 65, 68, 72, 93, 96, 104, 105, 106, 109, 112, 113, 129, 131, 132, 162-3, 180
  FJ series 148
  FZ series 109, 169, 173, 181
  GTS1000 178
  LC series 65
  RD series 65
  Royal Star 163
  SRX600 137
  T series 65, 146, 180, 183
  Thundercat 181
  XJ650T 173
  XJR1200 148, 150
  XS series 133, 150, 165
  XT500 131
  XV535 162-3
  XVS650 Drag Star 163
  Y series 72, 73, 114
  YR3 165
Yamaha, Torakusa 65
Yamaha OWO engines 114, 169
Youth Motorcycle Sporting Association (YMSA) 135

Z
Zedel engines 13, 19
Zeller, Walter 52, 146
Zenith-JAP 32, 94
Zundapp 13, 23-4, 26-7, 35, 37, 38, 49, 121, 132
  KS600 39

PHOTOGRAPHIC ACKNOWLEDGMENTS

Garry Clarke 1, 106, 148, 149 bottom, 178 top, 181 top, 181 bottom, 184
David Hodges 2 top
Terry Howe 91, 110-111, 115, 132-133, 135, 140-141, 141, 144-145, 150 bottom, 159 bottom
Hulton Getty Picture Collection 1, 2 bottom, 16, 19 bottom, 21 top, 22-23, 28, 30-31, 35 right, 44, 76-77, 77 bottom, 90, 119 top
Kobal Collection /Columbia 161 top, 161 bottom
Andrew Morland 74, 93 right, 112, 113 top, 126, 129, 137, 138 bottom left, 139, 143 right, 146, 152, 153 top, 153 bottom, 154 right, 155, 156,

157, 160-161, 166, 168-169, 170-171
The National Motor Museum, Beaulieu 13 top
Pictorial Press /Polygram 77 top
TRH Pictures 37 left, 37 right, 39 right, 40, /US National Archives 41
Triumph 187Mick Walker 2-3, 4-5, 9, 11 top, 12, 13 top, 13 bottom, 15 left, 15 top right, 15 bottom left, 15 bottom right, 17 bottom, 19 top, 19 centre, 26, 29 top left, 29 bottom left, 29 bottom right, 30 top, 31 top right, 31 bottom right, 33, 34, 42, 43 left, 43 right, 45 left, 45 right, 46 top, 46 bottom, 47, 48 top, 48 bottom, 49,

50, 52-53, 52 top, 52 bottom, 53 top, 53 bottom, 55 top, 55 centre, 55 bottom, 57, 58, 60, 61 bottom, 63, 64 top, 64 bottom, 64-65, 65, 68 top, 68 centre, 69, 70, 71 left, 71 right, 72, 72-73, 73, 75 top, 78, 79 left, 79 top right, 79 centre right, 79 bottom right, 80, 81 top, 81 bottom, 82 left, 82 right, 83, 83-84, 84-85, 86, 87, 88 top, 88 bottom, 89 top, 89 bottom, 93 left, 99 top, 100, 101 top, 101 bottom, 102 right, 109 bottom, 114, 116, 117 top, 117 bottom, 121, 123, 124-125, 127, 132, 133, 134-135, 136, 138 top, 140, 147, 149 top, 151, 156 inset, 158, 162-163, 163,

164, 165 top, 165 bottom left, 165 bottom right, 167, 168 top, 168 bottom, 169, 171 top, 171 bottom, 172, 174, 175 top, 175 bottom, 176, 176-177, 177, 179, 180-181, 182 top, 182 bottom, 183, 185, /David Reygondeau 108
Mark Wernham jacket inset
The World's Motorcycles News Agency 8-9, 23 inset, 51, 54-55, 56 top, 56 bottom, 61 top, 62, 66-67, 67, 68 bottom, 75 bottom, 122, 131, 150 top, 162, 173 top, 178 bottom, 186 top, 186 bottom
Mick Woollett jacket background, endpapers, 2, 10 top, 10 bottom, 11

bottom, 14 top, 14 bottom, 17 top, 18, 20, 21 bottom, 26-27, 27, 29 top right, 30 bottom, 32, 32-33, 35 left, 36, 38-39, 39 left, 40-41, 50-51, 58-59, 59, 69 top, 92, 92 inset, 94 top, 94 bottom, 95, 96 left, 96 right, 97, 98, 99 bottom, 102 left, 103 top, 103 left, 103 right, 104, 104-105, 105, 107, 109 top, 110, 113 bottom, 118, 119 bottom, 120 top, 120 bottom, 122-123, 128-129, 130, 138 bottom right, 142, 143 top, 144, 146-147, 154 left, 159 top, 173 bottom